IMAGES
of America

LA PALMA

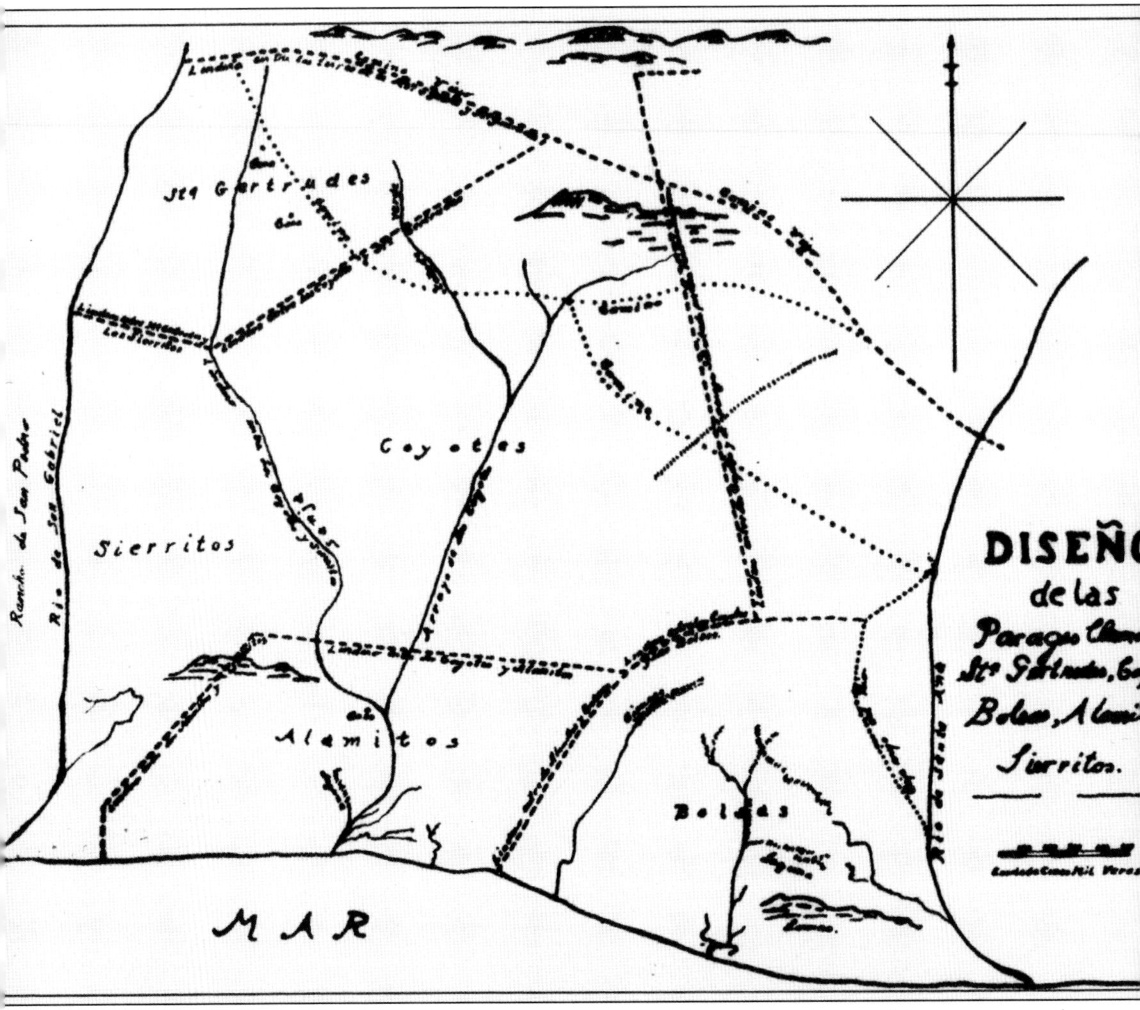

This diseño of the 1834 Nieto land grant map, housed in the Huntington Library, was used in Robert Glass Cleland's second edition of *The Cattle on a Thousand Hills*. The original land grant of 300,000 acres was given to José Manuel Nieto in 1784 for his service to the king of Spain in California with the Gaspar de Portolá expedition in 1769. When Nieto died in 1804, a rich man in terms of land holdings, the grant was divided into six ranchos for his heirs. This area was part of the Los Coyotes Rancho given to his eldest son, Juan José Nieto. (Courtesy Buena Park Historical Society.)

On the Cover: Drum major Jeff Lenning leads the Kennedy Band in the La Palma International Days Parade of 1987. (Courtesy of City of La Palma Archives with permission granted by Jeff Lenning.)

IMAGES
of America

LA PALMA

Ron and Elfriede Mac Iver

ARCADIA
PUBLISHING

ISBN 978-0-7385-5957-5

Published by Arcadia Publishing
Charleston SC, Chicago IL, Portsmouth NH, San Francisco CA

Printed in the United States of America

Library of Congress Catalog Card Number: 2008928798

For all general information contact Arcadia Publishing at:
Telephone 843-853-2070
Fax 843-853-0044
E-mail sales@arcadiapublishing.com
For customer service and orders:
Toll-Free 1-888-313-2665

Visit us on the Internet at www.arcadiapublishing.com

To Janet Cates, the community services supervisor at Central Park, for her friendship, trust, help, and encouragement over these many years.

Contents

ACKNOWLEDGMENTS

Our community is unique and generous. We begin with Phil Brigandi and Chris Jepsen, the archivists at the Old Courthouse in Santa Ana, and John Olson, Cypress archivist. They nurtured our interest in history from our first meeting, treated us as colleagues, and shared time, their archives, and expertise over many years.

We would like to acknowledge our La Palma Library branch manager, Julia Reardon, and her talented staff; Carol Schroeter, research librarian, and staff at the Cypress library; and librarians from the past—Charlotte Flower, Jesse Thompson, Joe Bearse, Alice Mizu, and Kit Winters to name only a few—who took an interest in our five children. They encouraged them and were especially loved by our daughter Cathe, who worked for them.

Our Central Park staff is amazing, hardworking, and always obliging. Director Jan Hobson keeps everything on an even keel; Janet Cates encouraged our writing; and Mike Belknap, Nancy Brewer, and the "crew" are always there when needed, especially for La Palma Days. Cindy Robinson and Tony Kim shared photographs that were barely out of their cameras. Jim Dynda, Mike Yasuda, and June and Don Plapp generously shared their photographs. Dominic Lazzaretto, our city manager, and Laurie Murray, administrative services manager, gave us access to the city archives. We would like to thank: Chet Corbin, Kimberly Kenney, David Morgan, Michelle Rusu, Renée Allard, and all the wonderful secretaries on both sides of the aisle, who greet us and help us with a smile; Chief Ed Ethell and the police department; fire authority; city council, past and present; Ismile Noorbaksh, Paul Pitts, and the public works department; Centralia and Cypress School Districts; Kennedy, Walker, Luther, Los Coyotes, and George B. Miller Schools; and everyone named and unnamed, who keep our city beautiful, safe, and ranked as the 16th best place to live in the United States.

We have had invaluable help from our "kids," Cathe Kreitz, Mike, and Alex, and our team of "contributors, researchers, and picture-namers," which include the following: Hoppy Fikse, Lisa and Paul Walker, Alta Duke, Ulla and Larry Herman, Mary Collins, Cathy Wesenberg, Ismile Noorbaksh, Linda and Mark Waldman, Diana and Ralph Rodriguez, Marilyn and Ed Byrne, Christine and Keith Nelson, Christine and John Piper, Tom Sibley, Sharon Gutjahr, Carl Eriksen, Shirley Giacomi, Ric Maurice, Richard Polis, Claude and Marynell Coker, Rosemary Scichilone, Juan Mesta, Linnea and Tom Wright, Cathy Standiford, Karen and Ken Blake, Nancy and Bryan Westra, Linda Houston, Henry Shah, Esther De Leon Hernandez, Brian O'Neal, Tim George, Linda Hinman Guglielmana, Loreen Berlin, Laura Smilkstein, Herb Sutherland, Jeff Lenning, Anna Palminteri, Mary Stone, Susan Sassone, Antonette Ferguson, Jack de Vries, Fawn Hammond, Joan and Richard Lutz, Hilda and Hugh Braly, Laverne Moody, Joe Tye, Linda and Hank Frese, Joy and John Berton, Carol and Tom McCarty, Sherrie and Jay Goldberg, Sharon and Dan Nix, Nellie Trautman, Tymen's daughter, Henry Charoen, Raul Alvarez, Bob Jordan, Gail and Bert Poan, and the Kennedy Band Boosters. We sincerely apologize to anyone inadvertently not mentioned and give a very special thank you to our editors, Jerry Roberts, Devon Weston, and Ryan Easterling, for their kindness and patience throughout this sometimes painful process!

INTRODUCTION

This is a success story. The story of the creation of a city, from its first land grant to its appointment as 16th best small city in the entire country and California's second best small city to live in, according to *Money* magazine. The dairy farmers, who settled in the area, first tried to save their lifestyle by incorporating into Dairyland in 1955. Many cities across the country copied that trendsetting idea. However, when these farmers realized that their urban way of life would not be saved by incorporating, they set about to develop the best city possible.

They gathered the best minds as advisors and rejected easy solutions, such as using money provided by gambling interests. Jack de Vries, one of the founding fathers, gave credit to Rodger Howell, Michael S. Bernard, and Coldwell Banker for their guidance, but he knew that they had been successful businessmen when they began their venture. They developed a master plan, which included flood control, underground utilities, and a modern sewer system. They planned for industry, small business, families, parks, and churches.

Jack de Vries, as one of the founders, looked back in his later years—long after he had built a city and given up dairy farming—and smiled at the naysayers who thought a group of dairymen and egg farmers were not smart enough to succeed in building a city. These men were thrifty, but you will see the generosity and kindness that created the unique city of La Palma.

The early residents liked the hometown feel of their new city; La Palma is 1.8 square miles. Due to its slow development, there is no "downtown." Activities center around the parks, library, and schools. There are solemn Memorial Day observances, and everyone gathers on the Fourth of July for the La Palma Fitness Run for Fun (a 5 and 10 kilometer walk/run) on the streets of the city. The Kiwanis Club serves breakfast and neighbors meet at the park to run and walk, or eat and chat. There are concerts in the park from July to August on Saturday evenings. October celebrations are held in the park, a safe "Trick or Treat" carnival for the little ones. La Palma Days is celebrated in the park, after the official Veteran's Day Parade for Orange County, a day of entertainment from various groups with booths set up for displays and vendors. In December, schoolchildren and residents gather in the park for Christmas caroling and the tree-lighting ceremony. The library and chamber of commerce also hold events throughout the year. The Relay for Life, on behalf of the American Cancer Society, collaborates with the City of Buena Park for an annual two-day event. The chamber holds events with Cypress College and Los Alamitos Training Base as well as ribbon cuttings for new businesses in the city and mixers. The number and quality of our city events rival larger cities.

Our new mayor enjoys a first—the first person of Thai descent to hold elected public office in the United States. La Palma always awaits the next challenge as a "City of Vision."

One

THE EARLY YEARS

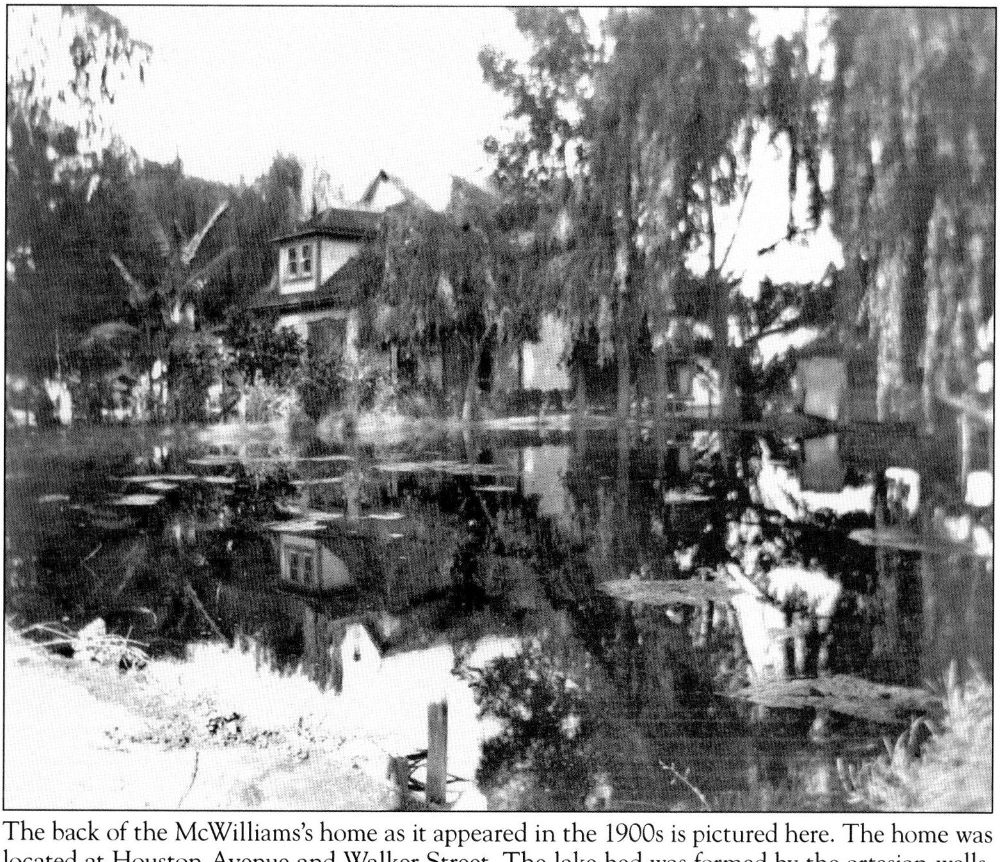

The back of the McWilliams's home as it appeared in the 1900s is pictured here. The home was located at Houston Avenue and Walker Street. The lake bed was formed by the artesian wells, which were abundant in the Waterville area. Waterville's name was in use until the advent of the Red Car in 1905, when the station was renamed Cypress after the local school district. (Courtesy of Orange County Archives.)

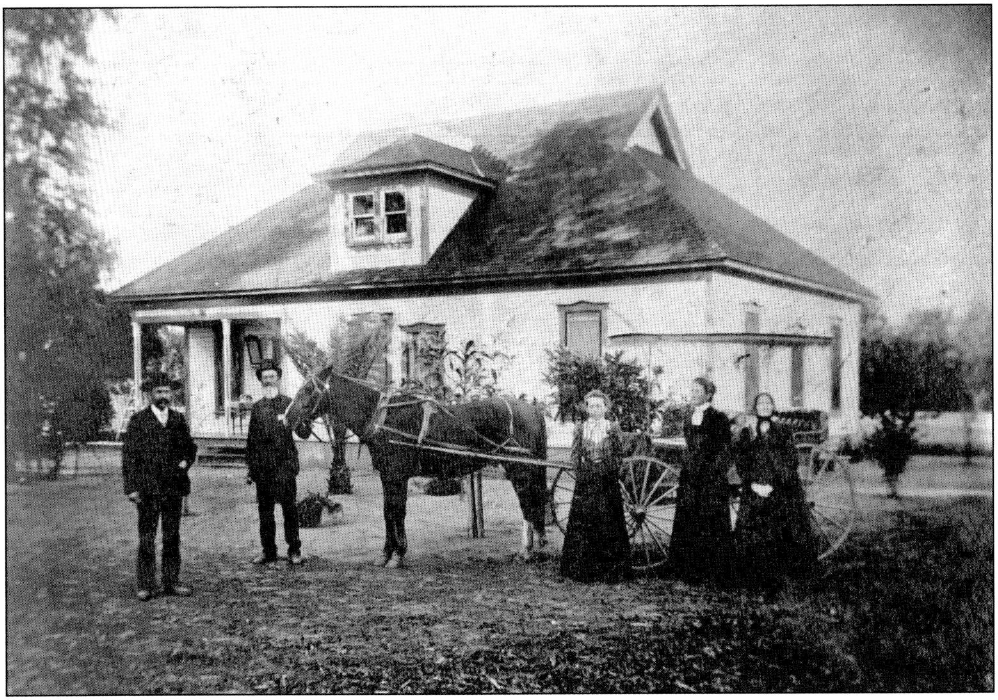

The McWilliams family gathered in front of the family home around 1910. George Lacey McWilliams arrived from Texas in the late 1890s. He established a successful sorghum mill on his property, with the local farmers growing the sugar beets. The mill soon outgrew its home-based operation, and McWilliams moved the mill to the 5500 block of Lincoln Avenue. (Courtesy of Chris Jepsen, Old Courthouse Archives, Santa Ana.)

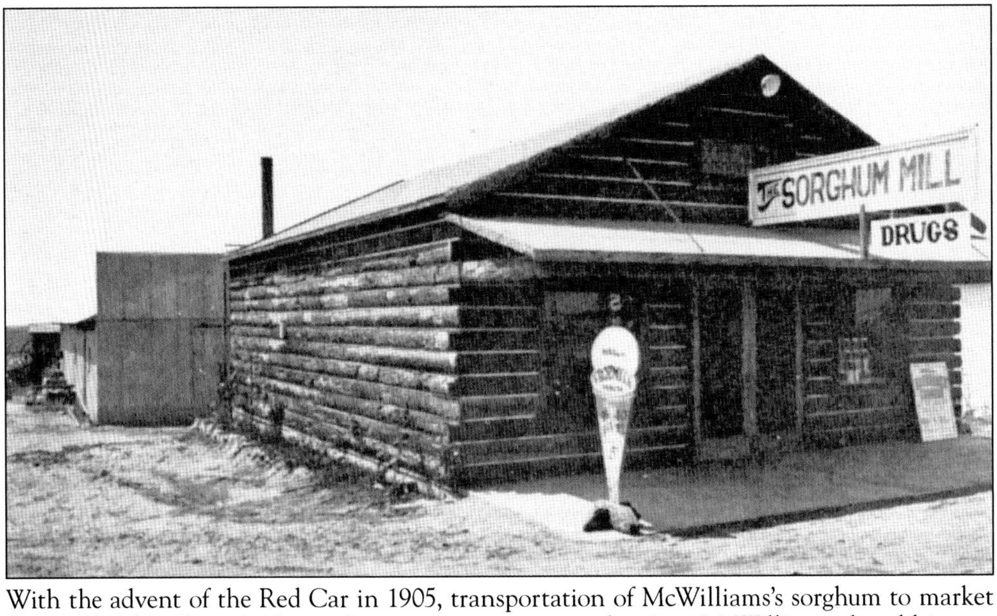

With the advent of the Red Car in 1905, transportation of McWilliams's sorghum to market became quicker than the horse-drawn wagons in use at the time. McWilliams placed his new sorghum mill near the Cypress Red Car Station. (Courtesy of Chris Jepsen, Old Courthouse Archives, Santa Ana.)

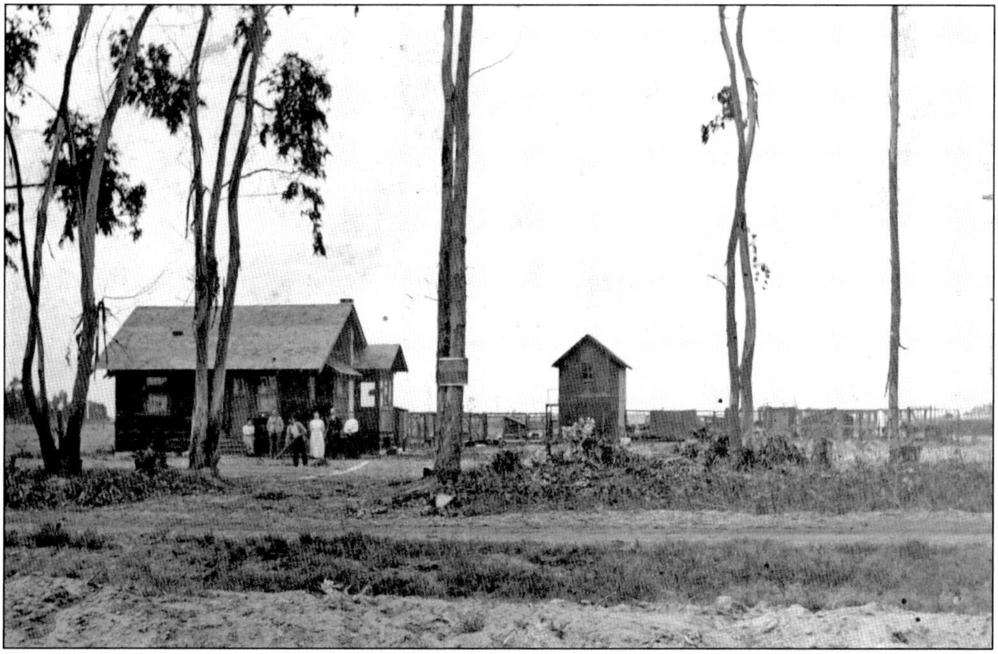

The Valentine properties were located on the east side of Walker Street and Houston Avenue. There were still family members living in the area in 1955, but little is known of these early residents. (Courtesy of Valentine Collection, Orange County Archives.)

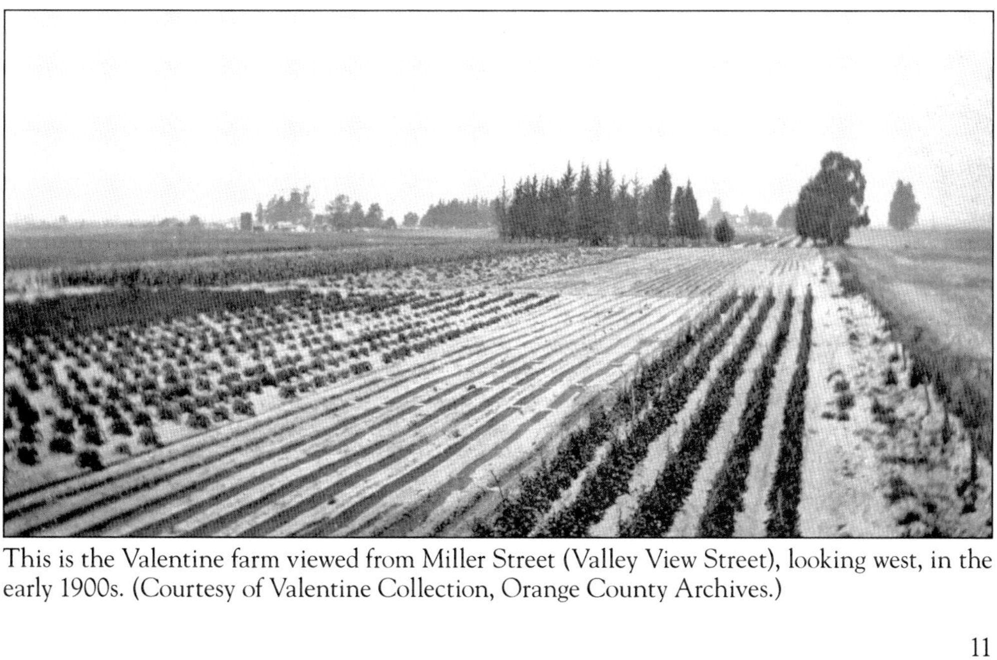

This is the Valentine farm viewed from Miller Street (Valley View Street), looking west, in the early 1900s. (Courtesy of Valentine Collection, Orange County Archives.)

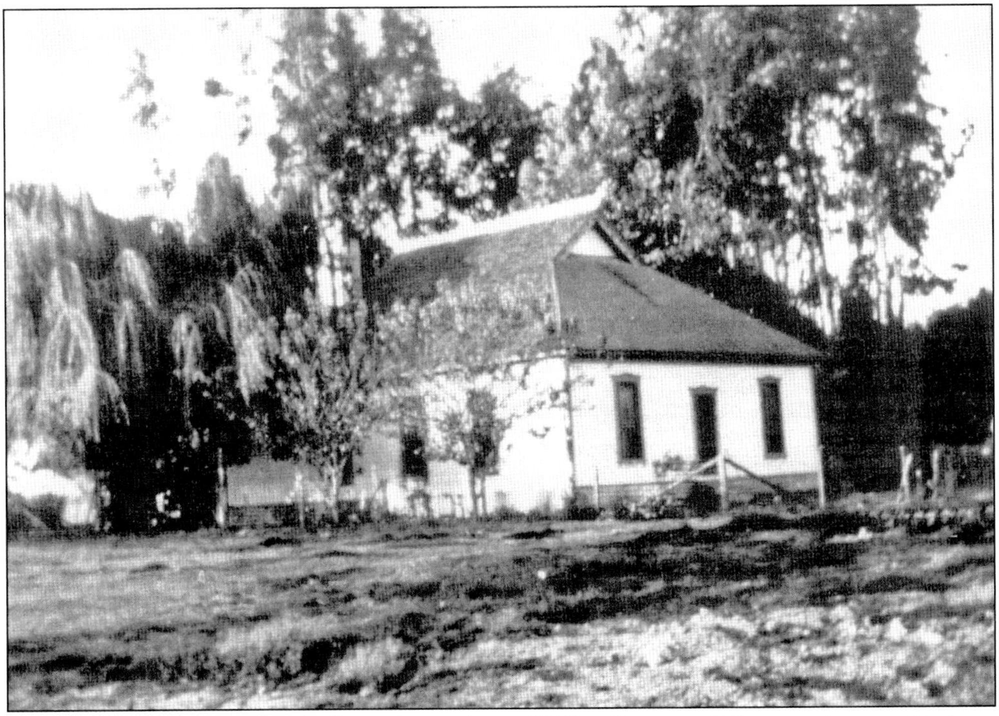

The Cole house, pictured in 1955, was located near Walker Street and Houston Avenue. Carlotta Cole arrived in the area from Texas in 1888 at the age of four. In an interview, Carlotta remembered good fishing in Coyote Creek and snow-white fields of alkali soil after a rain in the winter. Later, after cultivation, the ground yielded corn, sweet potatoes, and prize watermelons, which attracted customers from as far away as Norwalk. (Courtesy of City of La Palma Archives.)

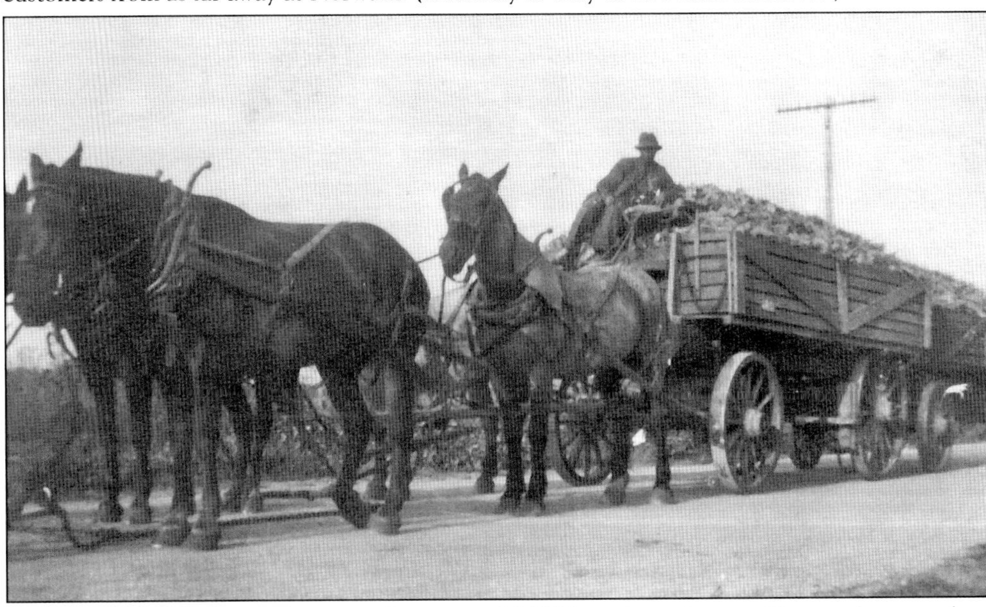

This wagon is full of sugar beets on the way to McWilliams's sorghum mill or to the sugar beet factory in Los Alamitos in the early 1900s. Local farmers grew the sugar beets and used wagons to transport their product for processing. (Courtesy of John Olson, Cypress Archives.)

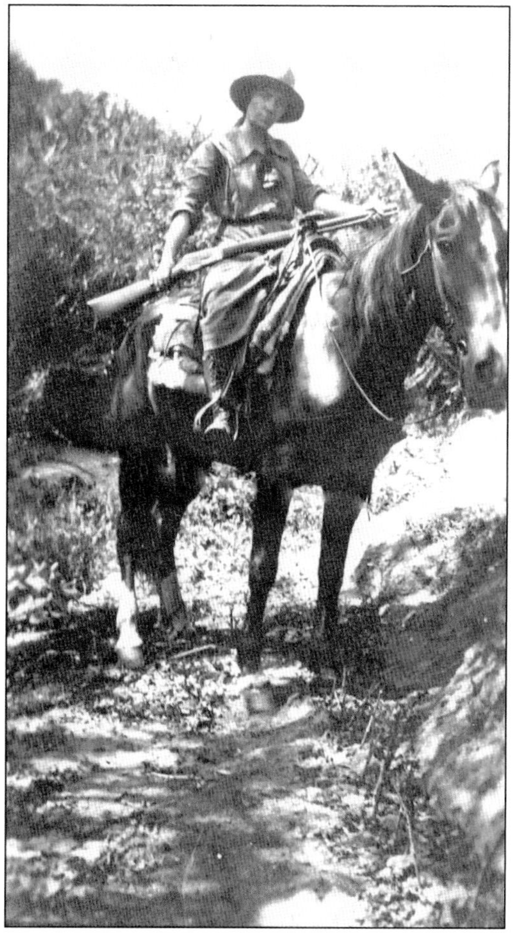

These pictures depict deer hunting in Coyote Creek. Smaller game was also available and fishing was popular. The car on the right below is parked by a farm building. (Both, courtesy of Luther School, Cypress.)

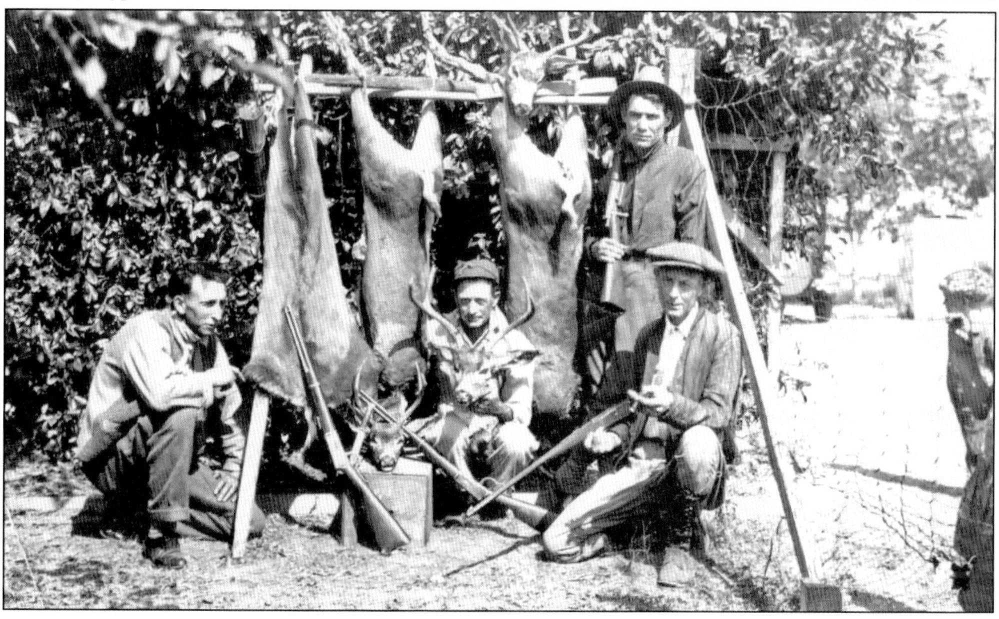

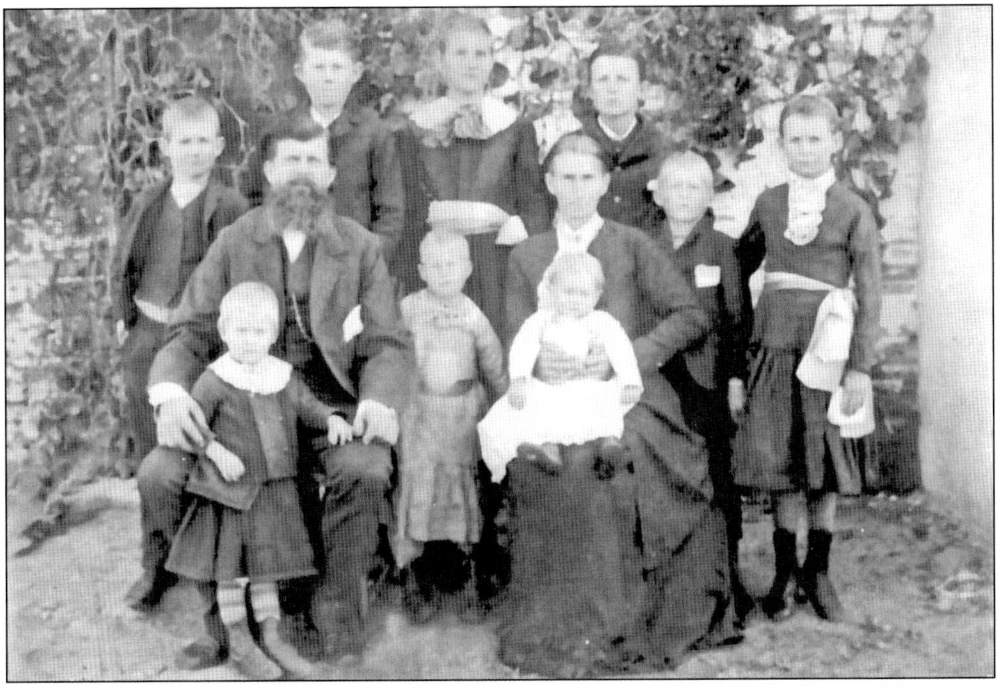

The Joseph Porter Moody family is pictured in 1887. From left to right are (first row) Joseph P., Earl (in front of J. P.), Grace, and Martha holding Harriet Nancy; (second row) Arthur, Charles, Lottie, William, Joseph E., and Mary. Joseph P. Moody, at age four, traveled with his mother and sister Harriet to meet William Henry Moody, a forty-niner, in 1852. His mother died while aboard the ship from blood poisoning, the result of a rat bite, and was buried at sea. His father remarried, and when Joseph P. grew up and married, he moved his family south in 1891. (Courtesy of Laverne Moody family.)

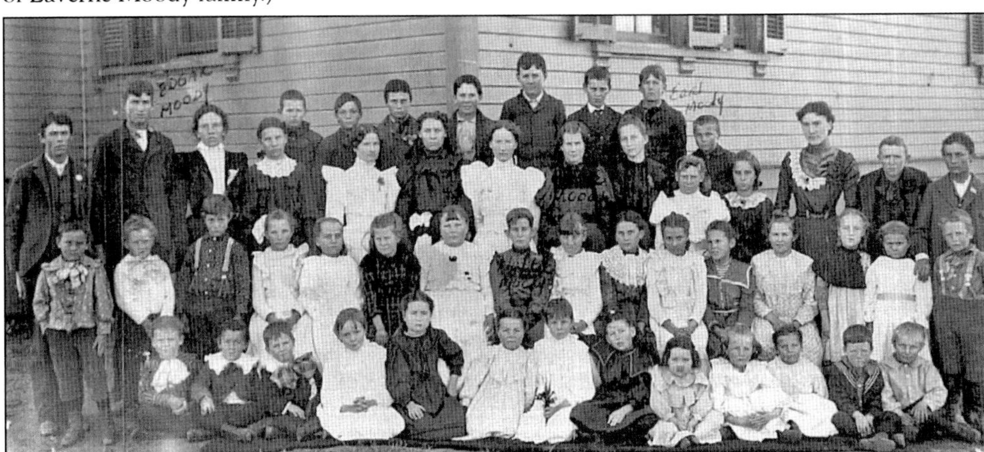

The Moody children lived at Crescent Avenue and Moody Street in 1898. They are pictured in the Cypress School in 1898. They are Harriet Nancy (second row, eighth from the left, in the black dress), Edgar Moody (third row, second from the left), Grace (third row, eighth from the left), and Earl Moody (fourth row, far right). In 1898, Joseph P. was appointed to the board of trustees of the Cypress School District. In 1899, he was elected to the board and served until 1905. He served again from 1910 to 1913. (Courtesy of Laverne Moody family.)

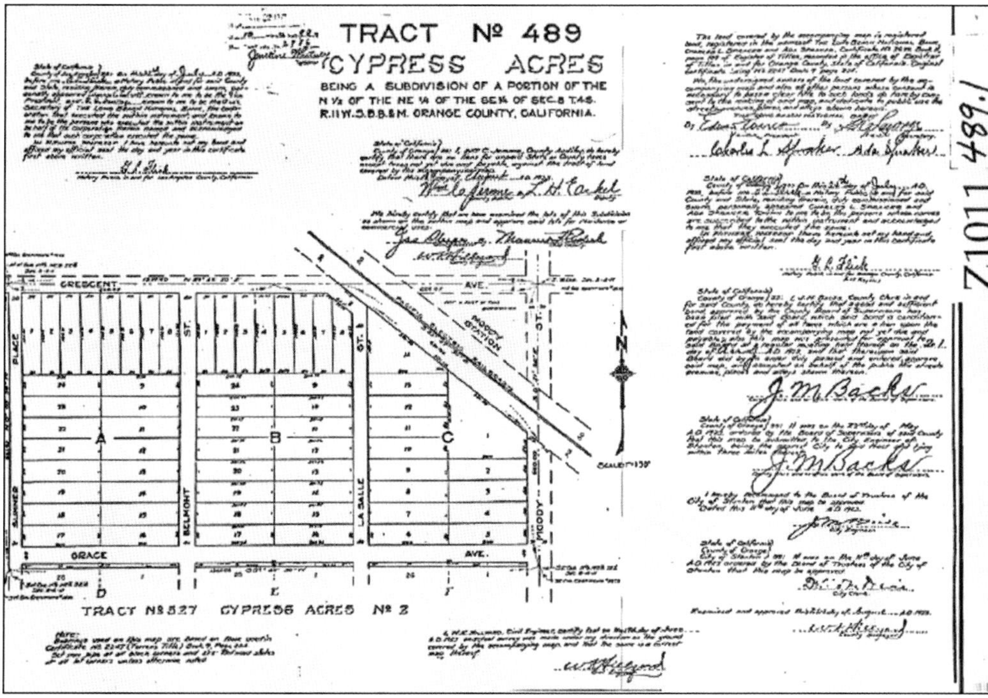

Tract Map No. 489, from 1923, shows Moody Street (vertical street to the right), Crescent Avenue (horizontal street at the top), and the Red Car line forming a triangle. The Moody station was located within the triangle. The Moody home was located in the area northwest of Crescent Avenue (not shown on the map). (Courtesy of John Olson, Cypress Archives.)

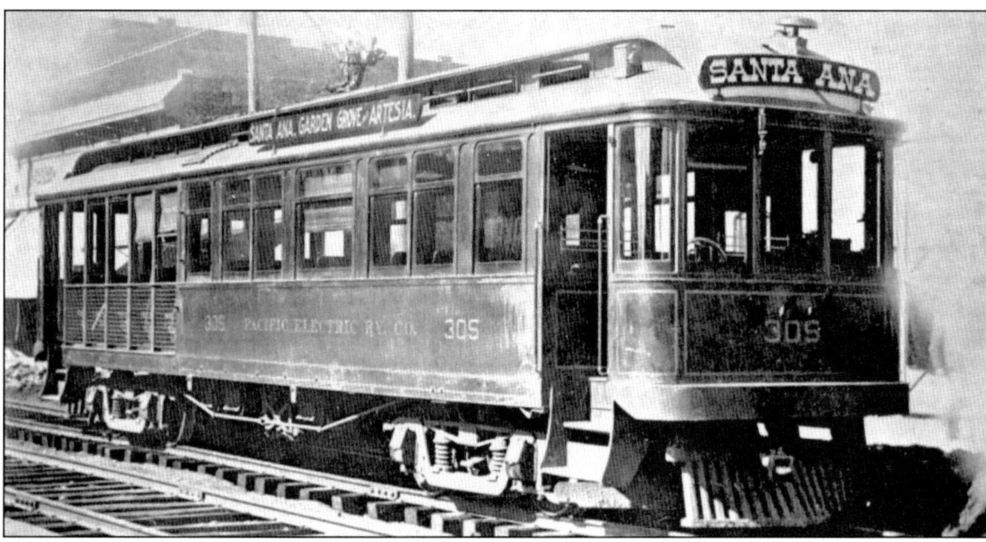

The Red Car made its maiden trip in 1905 between Watts in Los Angeles and Santa Ana in Orange County. It made travel quicker and easier for residents going to places farther away, to shop or visit friends and family in comfort. Farmers could transport their produce more quickly with less spoilage, and students could attend high school in Santa Ana until local high schools were built. The Red line was converted to a railroad line in 1950. (Courtesy of American Title Insurance Collection.)

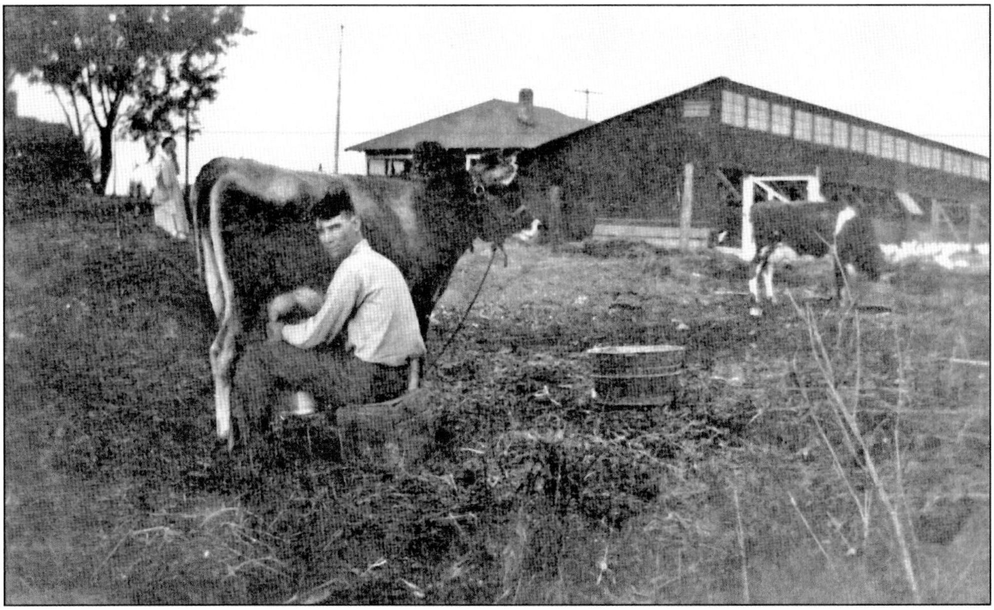

Here a local resident milks a cow in the early 1900s. Milking was a time-consuming operation before the invention of an affordable milking machine. (Courtesy of Luther School, Cypress.)

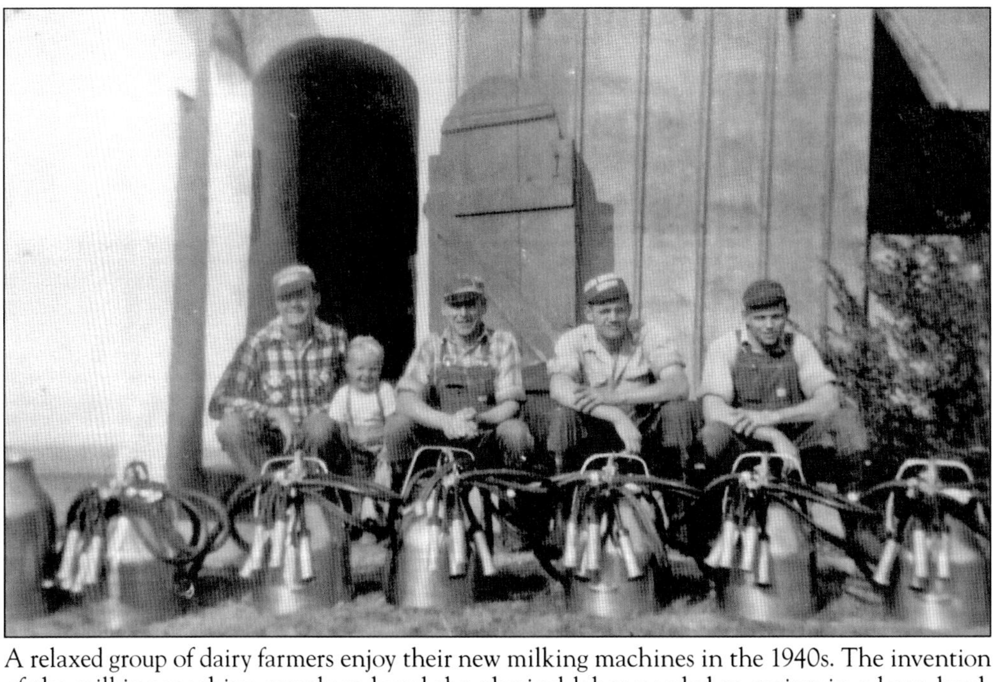

A relaxed group of dairy farmers enjoy their new milking machines in the 1940s. The invention of the milking machine greatly reduced the physical labor needed to maintain a large herd. (Courtesy of Bryan Westra family.)

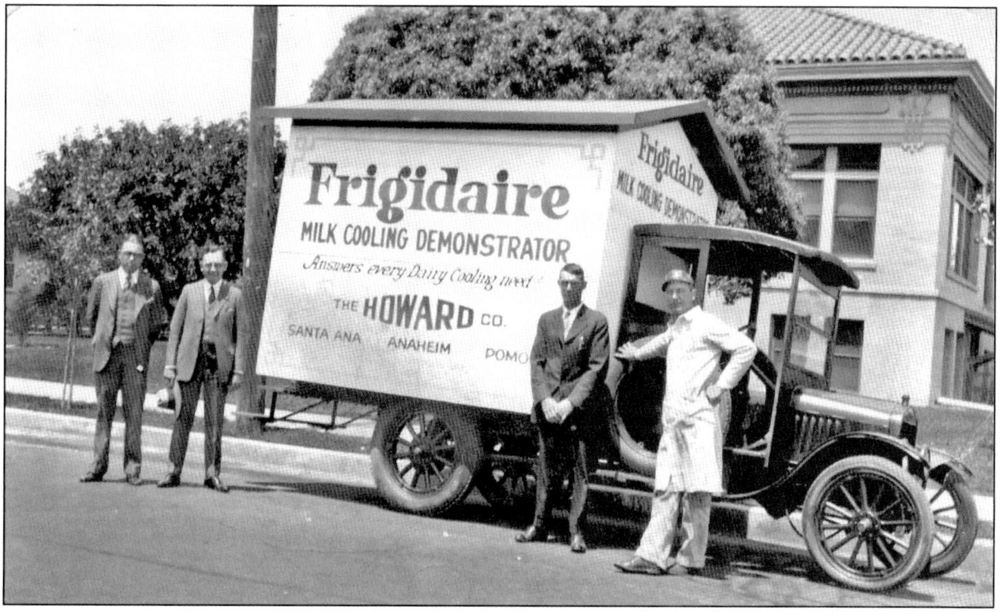

A milk-cooling demonstrator would travel to various dairies to demonstrate the latest technology. This truck appears to be a Ford Model T, which was manufactured from 1915 to 1927. It had a special door built in the back for customers to enter and watch the demonstration. Cream separators and refrigeration were available in the 1880s; however, it took several decades before the technology advanced enough to be cost effective for smaller dairy farms. (Both, courtesy of Luther School, Cypress.)

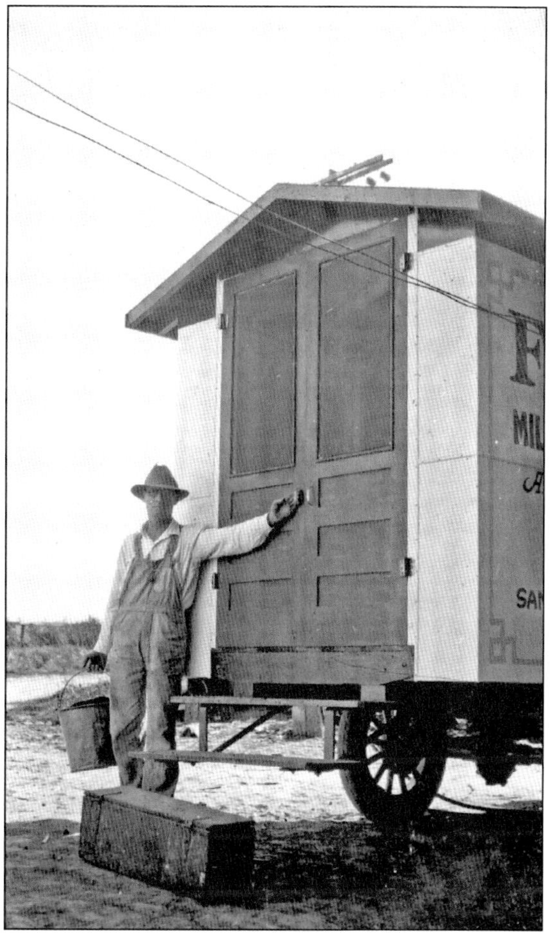

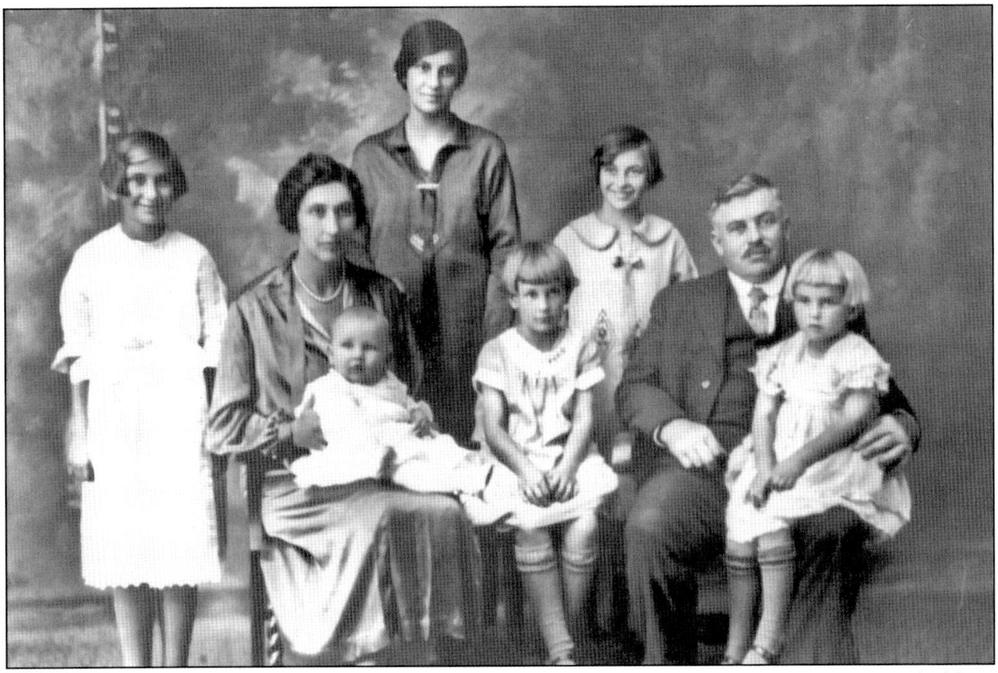

This *c.* 1927 Jobe Denni family portrait includes, from left to right, (first row) Lucy Denni holding Jobe Joseph Jr. at eight months of age, Josephine E. at six years, and Jobe Denni (1878–1964) holding four-year-old Catherine L.; (second row) Mary M. at 12 years of age, Juanita J. at 15 years of age, and Margaret T., 10 years old. Jobe Denni was a major landholder in Cypress and La Palma, and very influential in the transition of the community from rural to urban. Denni Street is named in his honor. (Courtesy of Cypress Library.)

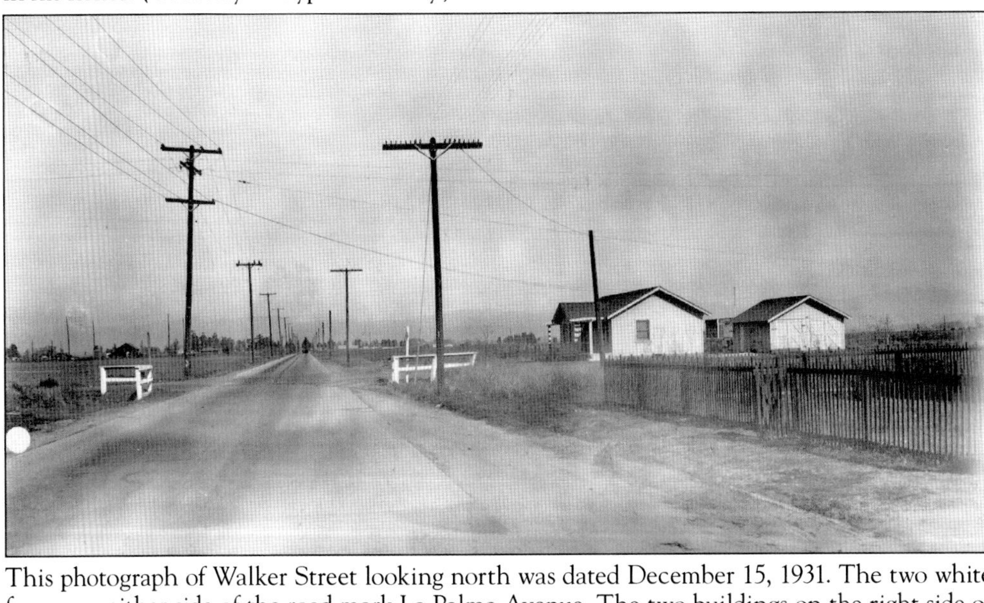

This photograph of Walker Street looking north was dated December 15, 1931. The two white fences on either side of the road mark La Palma Avenue. The two buildings on the right side of the picture are at the approximate location of the current Bank of America building. Moody Creek is located in front of the white fence on the left-hand side of the road. (Courtesy of Phil Brigandi, Old Courthouse Archives, Santa Ana.)

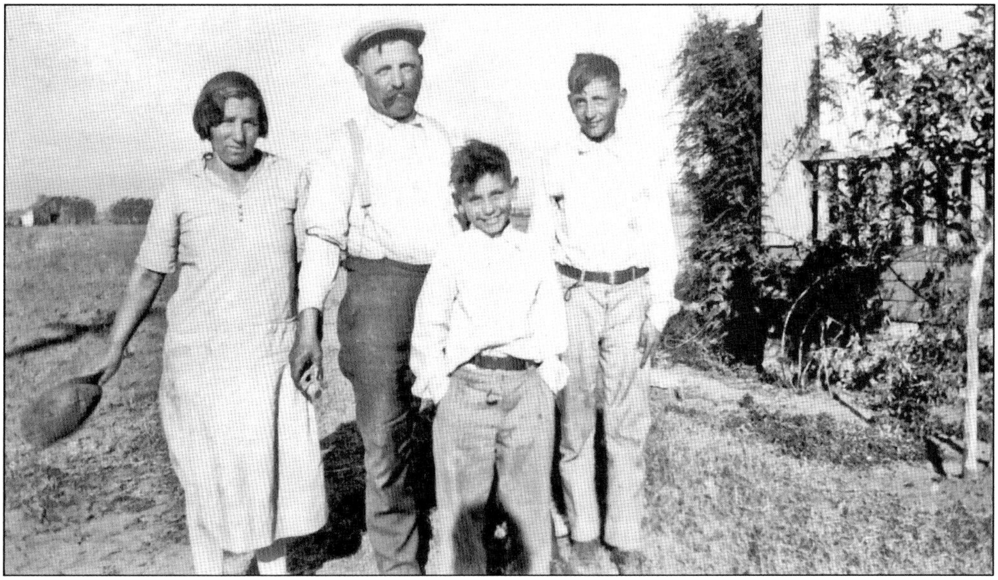

The Guglielmana family were very early residents of the area. They lived at the southwest corner of Walker Street and Orangethorpe Avenue. They were a hardworking, closely knit group, who also knew how to enjoy life. Pictured in 1929 are Lucia and Ortencio Guglielmana, who married on October 1, 1914, and moved in shortly thereafter. Morris, their younger son, is standing next to his dad and Ely is on the right. They farmed, raised cows, and owned a famous landmark gas station. (Courtesy of Linda Guglielmana Hinman family.)

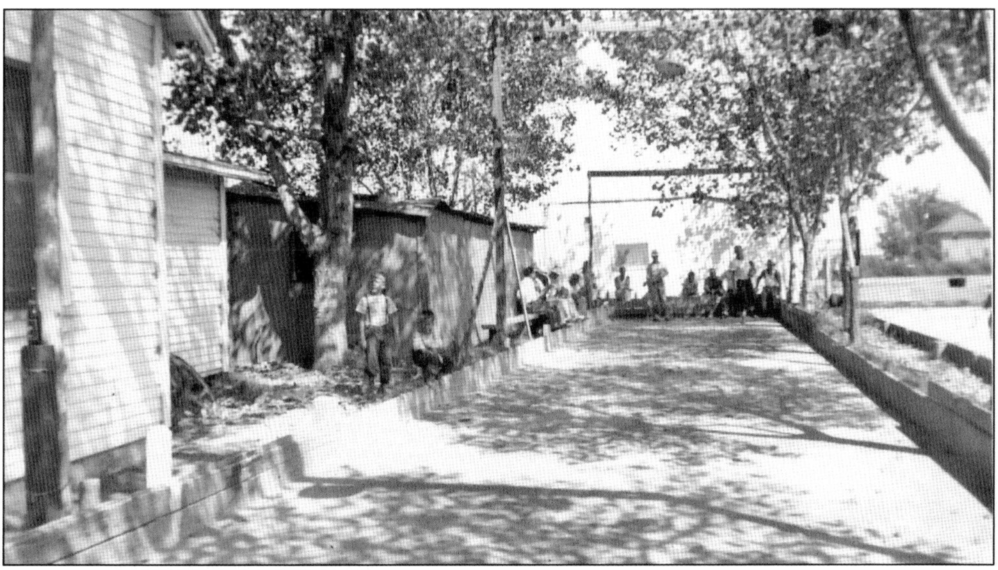

The bocce court was a well-established gathering place. The men enjoyed relaxing and playing a game, the women enjoyed socializing, and the children were free to play together with friends and cousins. This court was built on the side of the house, and everyone was free to drop in. (Courtesy of Linda Guglielmana Hinman family.)

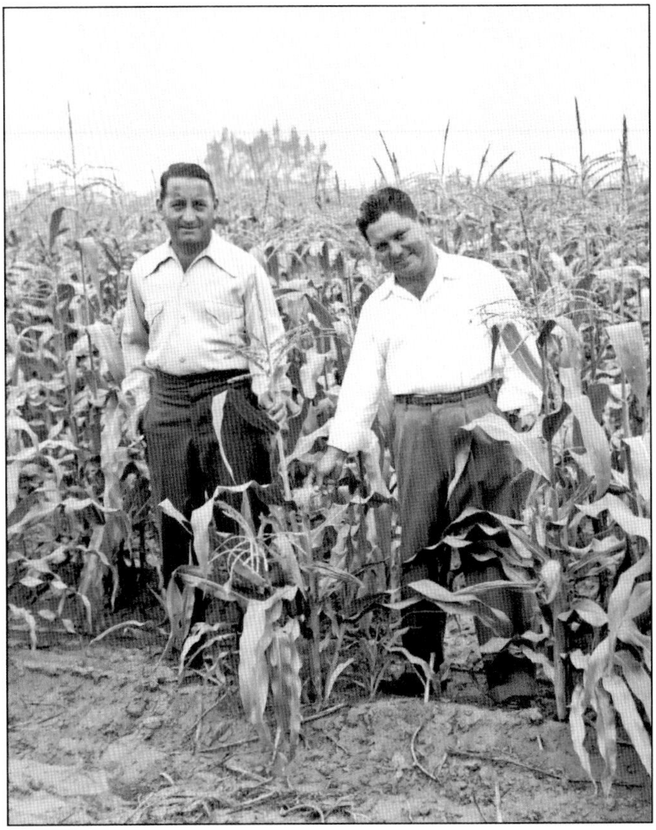

Ely and Morris Guglielmana worked together. Morris was a farmer and Ely ran the dairy. As they added wives and children, their growing families also joined in. A field across the street on Orangethorpe Avenue was rented to grow the corn. It was harvested by a mule-drawn wagon, sorted in a shed, and the largest ears were sold at market. When the crates were packed, they were soaked in water to preserve freshness for the trip to market. Smaller ears were sold at a roadside stand. (Courtesy of Linda Guglielmana Hinman family.)

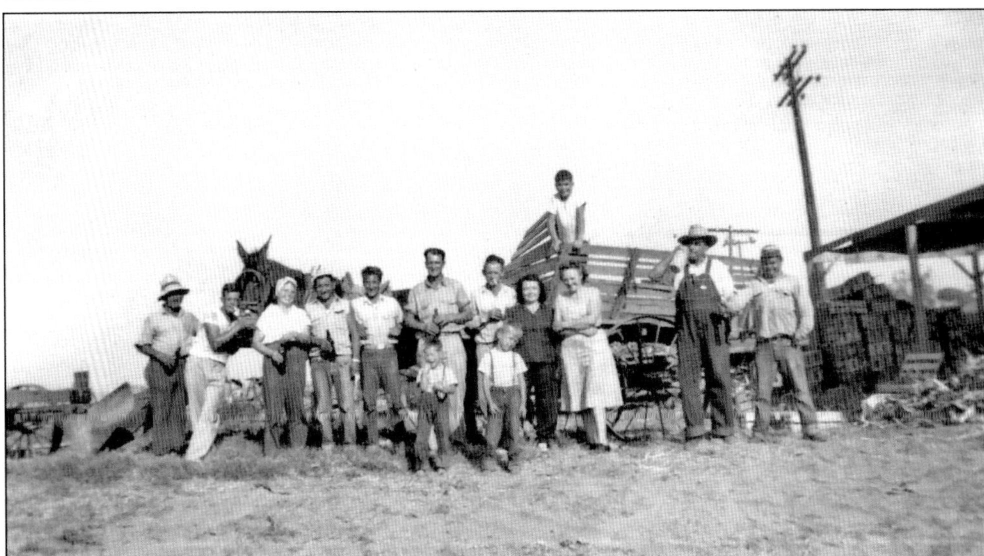

The family posed for this photograph around 1946. It includes Ely and Morris with their wives and children as well as a hired hand named "Fugista," who was remembered and accepted as "always being there." There is corn on the ground and the wagon is empty, but the rails are being put in place and the mule is harnessed, ready to pick up another load. (Courtesy of Linda Guglielmana Hinman family.)

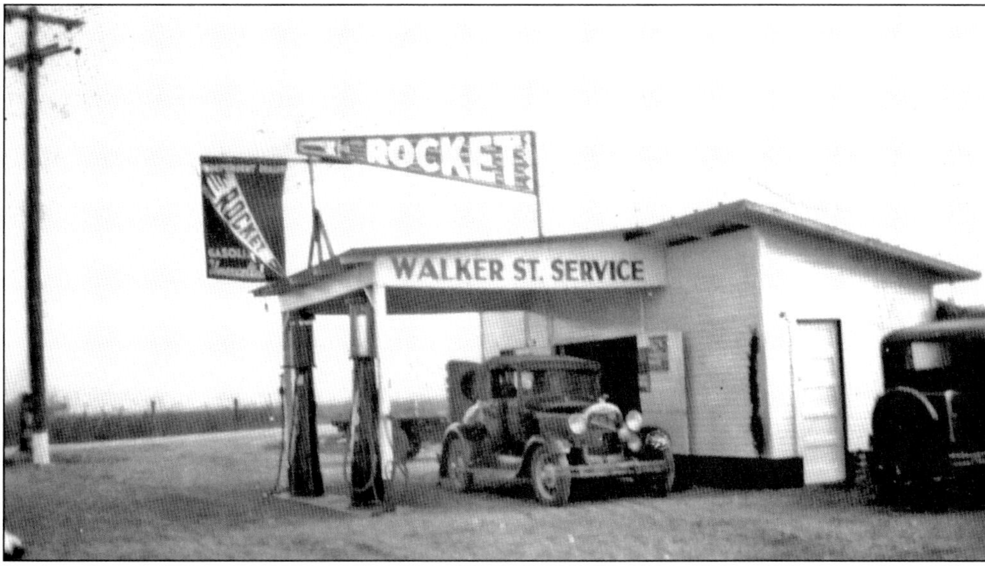

This Rocket gas station is the second gas station on the corner of Walker Street and Orangethorpe Avenue built before the 1930s. The next station to appear was Spelzini Service. It is currently an Arco station. (Courtesy of Linda Guglielmana Hinman family.)

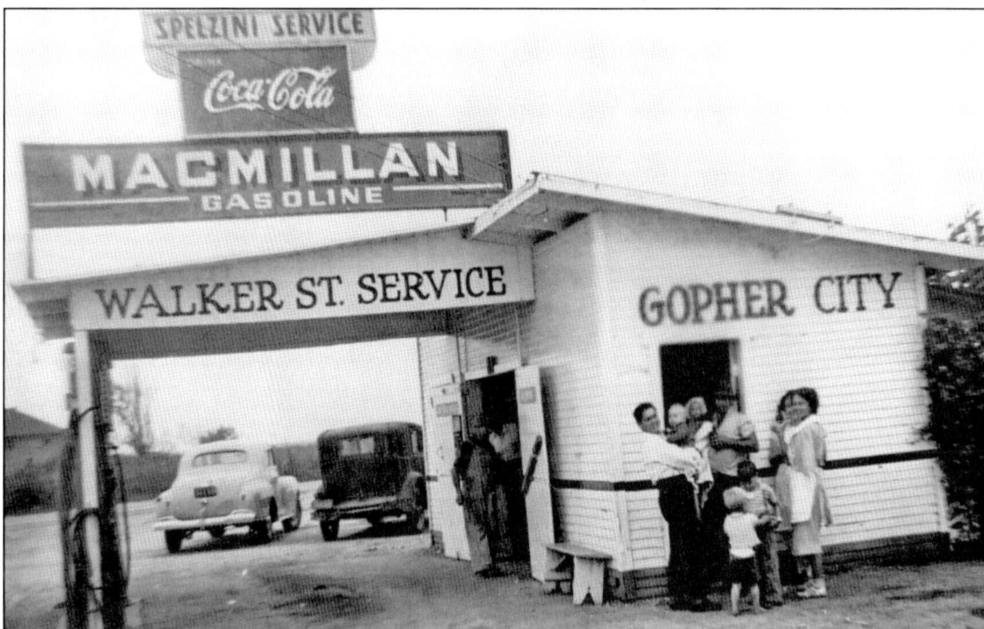

Spelzini Service had an additional sign painted on the side of the building, which over time made it a landmark. Everyone in the area knew where "Gopher City" was located. Many have seen this picture because it hangs in the Guglielmana home and in the La Palma City Hall. The people shown in this picture, taken in the summer of 1941, are, from left to right, Morris carrying his son Gary; Ely carrying Linda; Gary's mom, Pauline,; young Richard's mom, Ersilia; and Linda and Robert's mom, Elizabeth. Robert is the boy facing forward, and Richard is the smaller boy. Richard Sr. is in the doorway wearing a white shirt. The other man in the doorway is unidentified. (Courtesy of Linda Guglielmana Hinman family.)

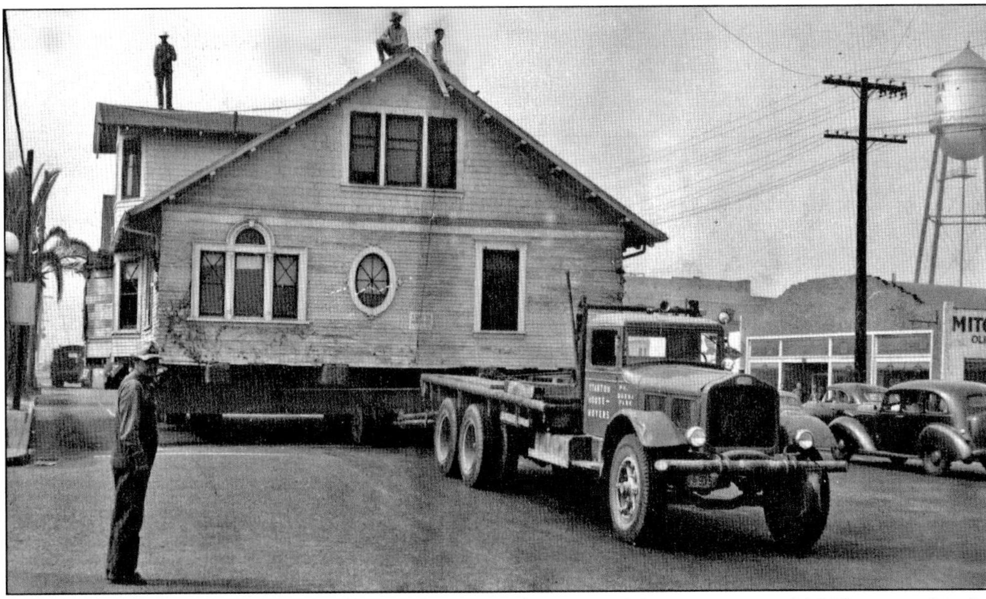

The Weatherly house, built in Fullerton between the turn of the century and 1903, arrived in La Palma sometime in 1943. Dairymen who moved to the area were in the market for these ready-built homes. Carl Eriksen shared this picture, city councilman Ralph Rodriquez shared his computer expertise, Lea Anderson added many details to the story, which was written by Ron and Elfriede Mac Iver for the *Source*, August 2006 (issue 6). (Courtesy of La Palma Police Department.)

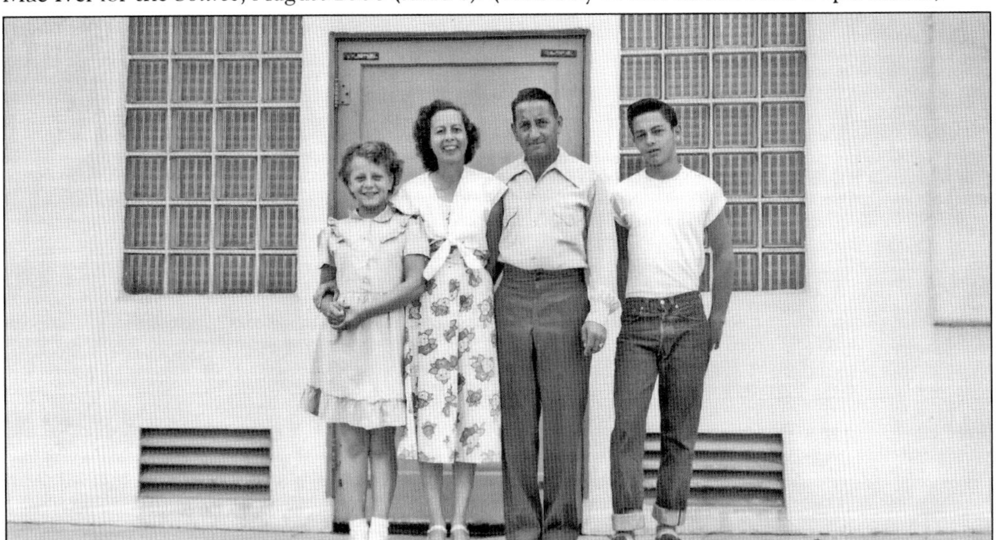

This picture of the Guglielmana Dairy in 1952 includes, from left to right, Linda, Elizabeth, Ely, and Robert. It was typical of the progress that had been made from milking by hand to milking machines. At the time of the incorporation on October 26, 1955, per the October 9, 1955, *Times* article found in the La Palma City Archives, there were "30 dairies, six poultry ranches, three commercial truck farms, and a collection of small country plots." It seemed an idyllic life that would not change; however, with the end of World War II and the Korean Conflict, much as had happened at the end of the Civil War, people were on the move. (Courtesy of Linda Guglielmana Hinman family.)

Two

A City is Born

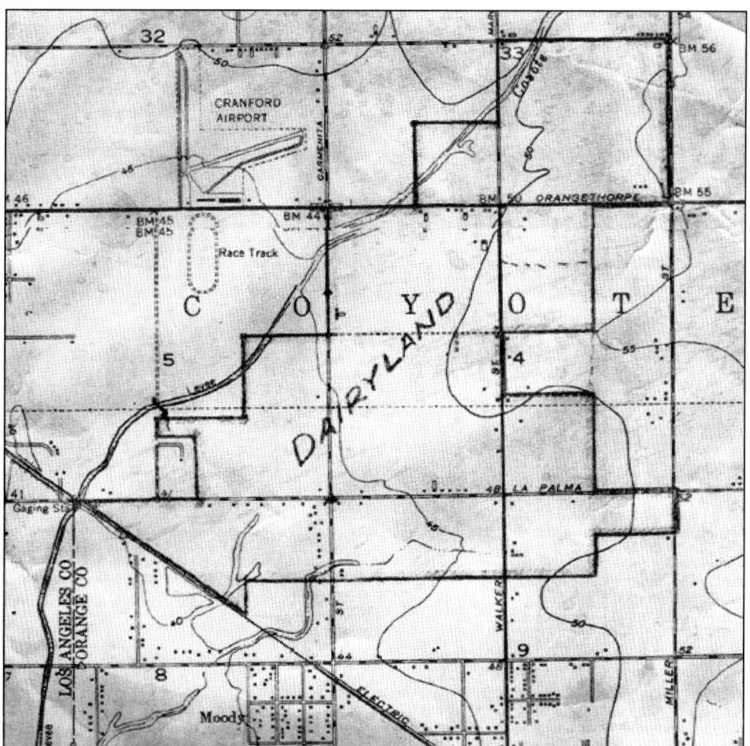

This is a map of the city of Dairyland at the time of incorporation in 1955. The incorporation was undertaken to save the lifestyle of this dairy and agricultural community. (Courtesy of Johnny and Christine Piper.)

PLEASE KEEP THIS CARD

(It tells you where to vote)

Your Voting Precinct for the

SPECIAL INCORPORATION OF CITY OF DAIRYLAND ELECTION OCTOBER 11, 1955 is

PRECINCT NO. 1

(Shall include all of the area within the boundaries of the proposed City of Dairyland.)

POLLING PLACE

FOSS GARAGE

4932 La Palma Ave., Buena Park

LOOK FOR THE AMERICAN FLAG

If a question should arise regarding your registration as a voter or your polling place, contact Registration of Voters Department, County Clerks Office.

B. J. SMITH, County Clerk

This card was given to the 92 registered voters in Dairyland to notify them of the incorporation of the city of Dairyland special election on October 11, 1955. The vote was to take place in Chester and Charlotte Foss's garage at 4932 La Palma Avenue. Precinct No. 1 would be open from 7:00 a.m. to 7:00 p.m. (Courtesy of Phil Brigandi, Old Courthouse Archives, Santa Ana.)

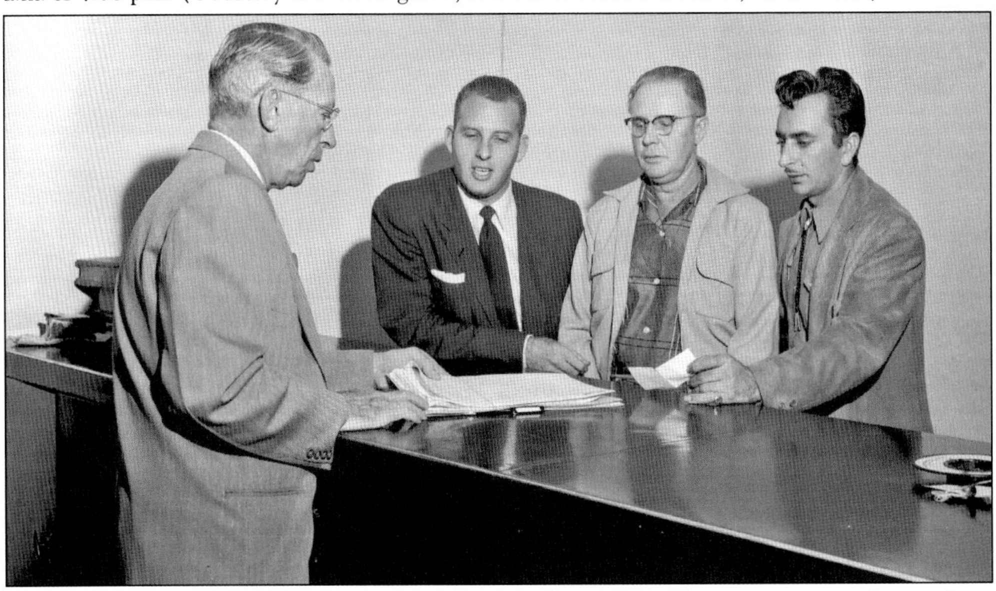

On the left, Orange County clerk B. J. Smith accepts the results of the incorporation election from city attorney Mike S. Bernard and two precinct workers. The results included five absentee ballots from Peter G. Bouma and his wife, Alice; Jack de Vries and his wife, Gertrude; and Howard Van Boven. The final count was Jack de Vries, 59; Paul Furman, 51; William De Jager, 50; Peter G. Bouma, 43; Peter De Groot, 41; and Peter D. Bouma, 39. Of the votes cast for incorporation, 50 were in favor and 19 were against the incorporation. (Courtesy of City of La Palma Archives.)

The Certificate of Election was processed through Sacramento and had to wait for the return of the newly elected mayor, Jack de Vries, from Holland. The papers were signed on November 2, 1955. The incorporation was dated October 26, 1955. (Courtesy of Ron and Elfriede Mac Iver.)

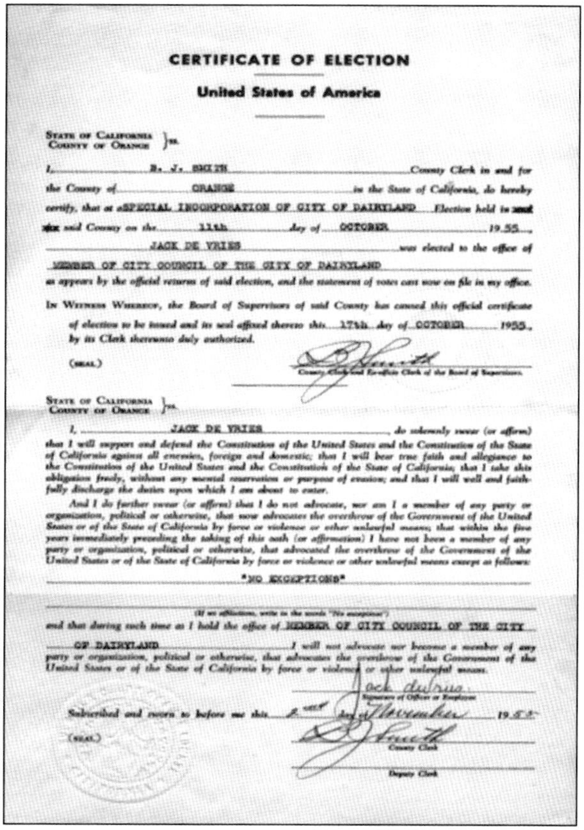

CERTIFICATE OF ELECTION

United States of America

State of California }ss.
County of Orange

I, B. J. SMITH County Clerk in and for the County of ORANGE in the State of California, do hereby certify, that at a SPECIAL INCORPORATION OF CITY OF DAIRYLAND Election held in said County on the 11th day of OCTOBER 1955, JACK DE VRIES was elected to the office of MEMBER OF CITY COUNCIL OF THE CITY OF DAIRYLAND as appears by the official returns of said election, and the statement of votes cast now on file in my office.

In Witness Whereof, the Board of Supervisors of said County has caused this official certificate of election to be issued and its seal affixed thereto this 17th day of OCTOBER 1955, by its Clerk thereunto duly authorized.

(SEAL.)

County Clerk and Ex-officio Clerk of the Board of Supervisors.

State of California }ss.
County of Orange

I, JACK DE VRIES, do solemnly swear (or affirm) that I will support and defend the Constitution of the United States and the Constitution of the State of California against all enemies, foreign and domestic; that I will bear true faith and allegiance to the Constitution of the United States and the Constitution of the State of California; that I take this obligation freely, without any mental reservation or purpose of evasion; and that I will well and faithfully discharge the duties upon which I am about to enter.

And I do further swear (or affirm) that I do not advocate, nor am I a member of any party or organization, political or otherwise, that now advocates the overthrow of the Government of the United States or of the State of California by force or violence or other unlawful means; that within the five years immediately preceding the taking of this oath (or affirmation) I have not been a member of any party or organization, political or otherwise, that advocated the overthrow of the Government of the United States or of the State of California by force or violence or other unlawful means except as follows:

"NO EXCEPTIONS"

(If no affiliations, write in the words "No exceptions")

and that during such time as I hold the office of MEMBER OF CITY COUNCIL OF THE CITY OF DAIRYLAND I will not advocate nor become a member of any party or organization, political or otherwise, that advocates the overthrow of the Government of the United States or of the State of California by force or violence or other unlawful means.

Jack deVries
Signature of Officer or Employee

Subscribed and sworn to before me this 2nd day of November 1955

(SEAL.)

County Clerk

Deputy Clerk

A new sign for the city of Dairyland was erected at the corner of Miller Street (Valley View Street) and La Palma Avenue. The population at the time was 550 people. (Courtesy of City of La Palma Archives.)

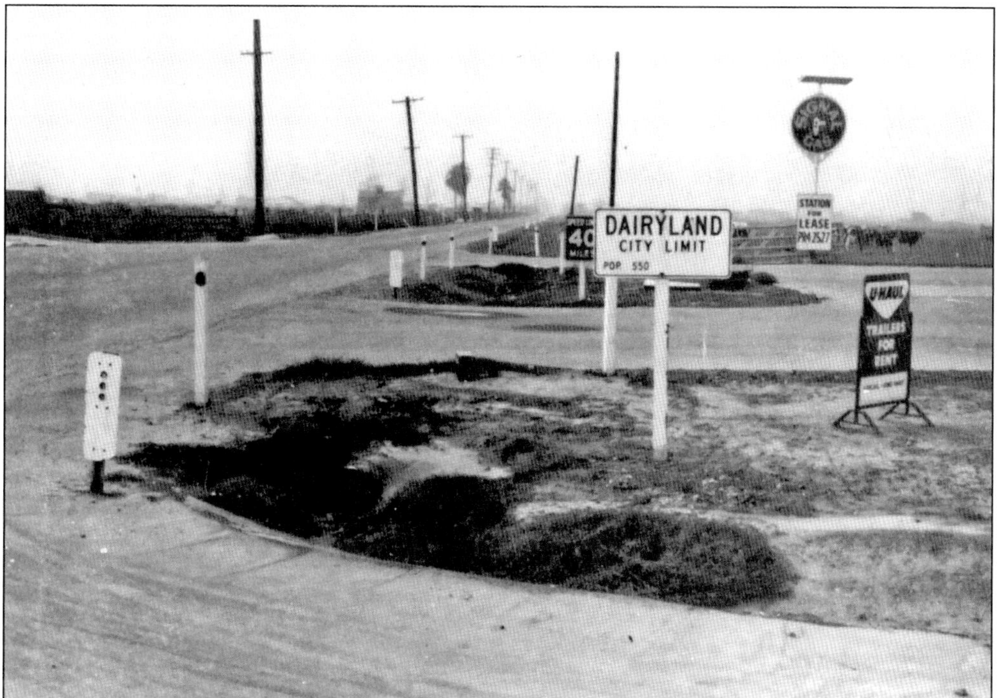

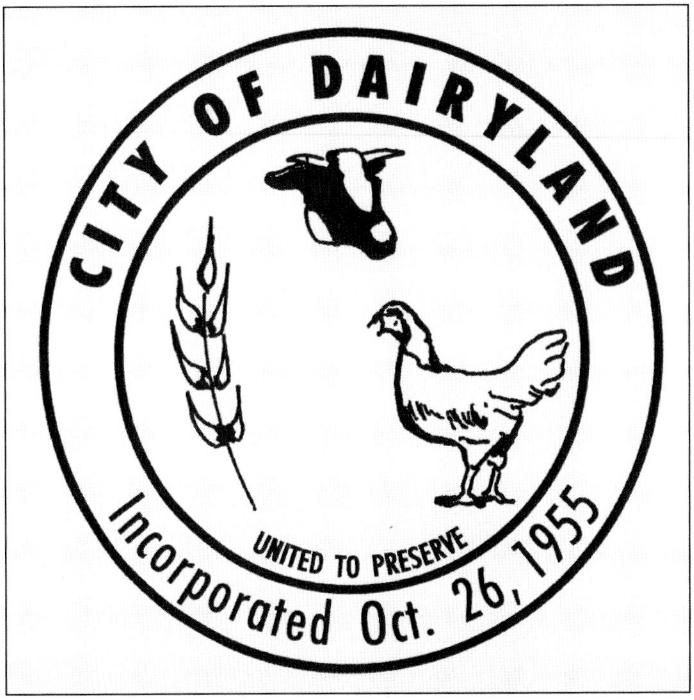

The 1955 city seal of Dairyland depicted the three major industries of the city: dairy, poultry, and agriculture. At the top, the city slogan stated, "United to Preserve." This innovative incorporation to preserve a lifestyle was imitated by several cities across the nation, and locally, the cities of Dairy Valley (Cerritos), Dairy City (Cypress), and Los Alamitos followed La Palma's lead. The area once known as Moo Valley filed petitions to incorporate. (Courtesy of City of La Palma Archives.)

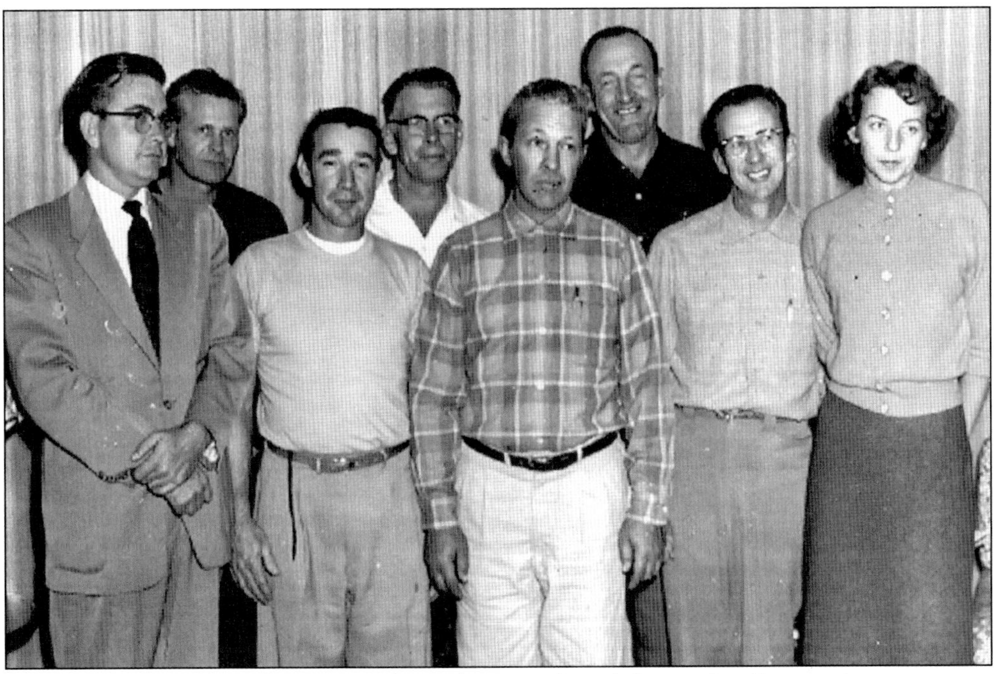

Dairyland's newly elected city council members are, from left to right, (first row) city attorney Rodger Howell, councilman Paul Furman, Vice Mayor Peter G. Bouma, Mayor Jack de Vries, and deputy city clerk Susan Guertin; (second row) city clerk and treasurer Peter D. Bouma, councilman William De Jager, and councilman Peter De Groot. Councilman De Groot owned dairies and poultry farms. Councilman Paul Furman and city clerk Peter D. Bouma were poultry farmers. The majority of the city council members were dairymen. (Courtesy of City of La Palma Archives.)

Jack de Vries, born in Holland, was a second-generation dairyman. In an interview by photographer Loreen Berlin for the *News Enterprise* on November 5, 2003, just prior to his 93rd birthday, Jack proudly remembered how he and his fellow dairymen created the city of La Palma, his service to the community as its first mayor, and the advice that he received. He knew "people didn't believe that dairymen could be smart enough to do what we did," but they surrounded themselves with smart people and, as he reminded, "we were all businessmen." Among his advisors, he listed his attorneys Mike S. Bernard and Rodger Howell as well as Coldwell Banker. The first city staff included Burton Wesenberg, city manager; Nat Neff, city engineer; Ray Meader, chief of police; and Susan Guertin, city clerk. (Courtesy of City of La Palma Archives.)

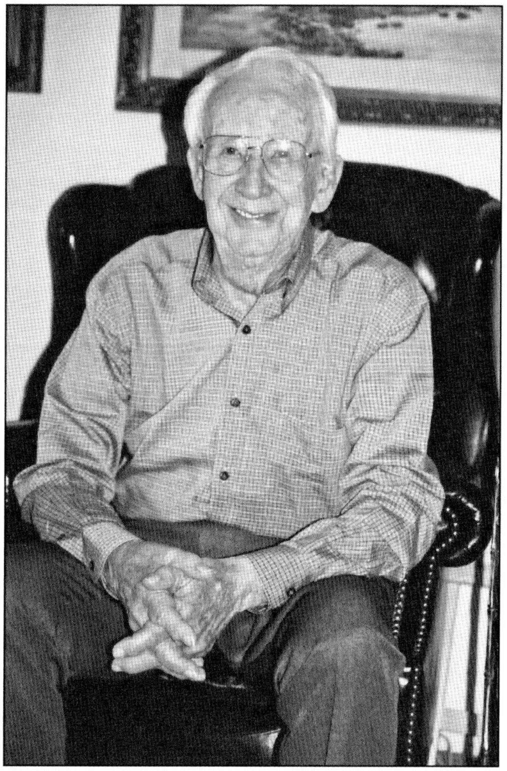

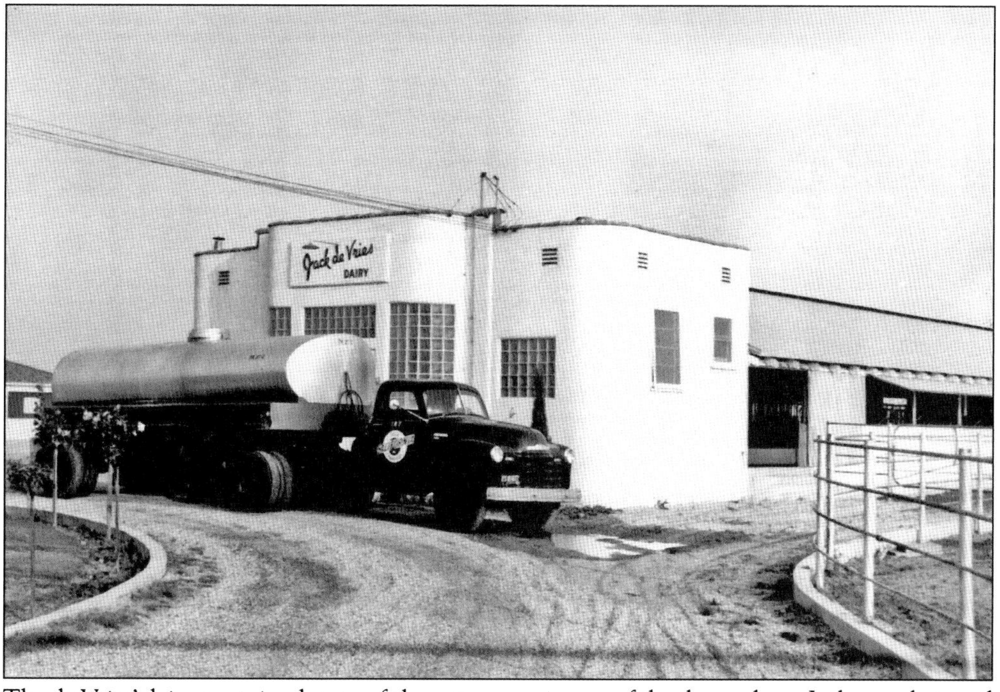

The de Vries' dairy contained state-of-the-art conveniences of the day and, per Jack, was designed in the streamline moderne architectural style. (Courtesy of Dale Kroesen and John Olson, Cypress Archives.)

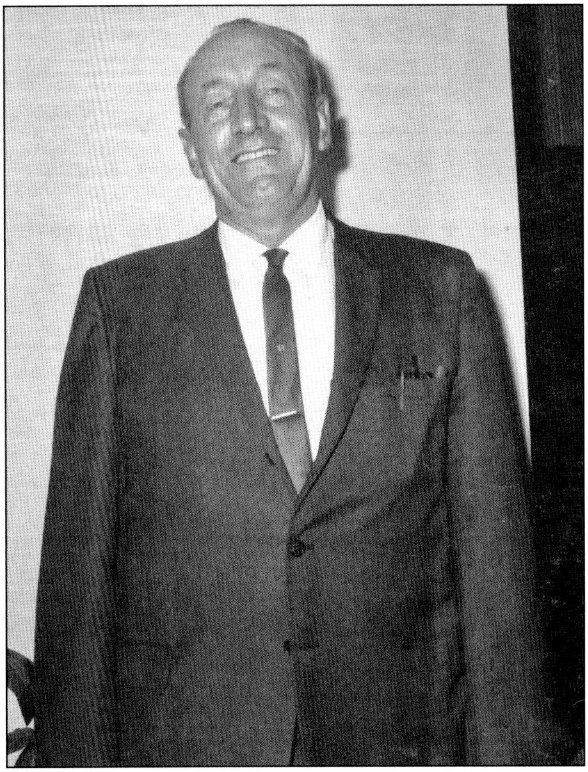

Peter De Groot was born in Holland and came to the United States in 1930. He worked as a hired hand for five years, living a very frugal life before he had saved enough money to buy his first dairy (per the *La Palma Review* in September 1967). He arrived in the La Palma area in the early 1950s and his business prospered. He bought Rockview Dairies in 1965. The business is still family owned. (Courtesy of June and Don Plapp.)

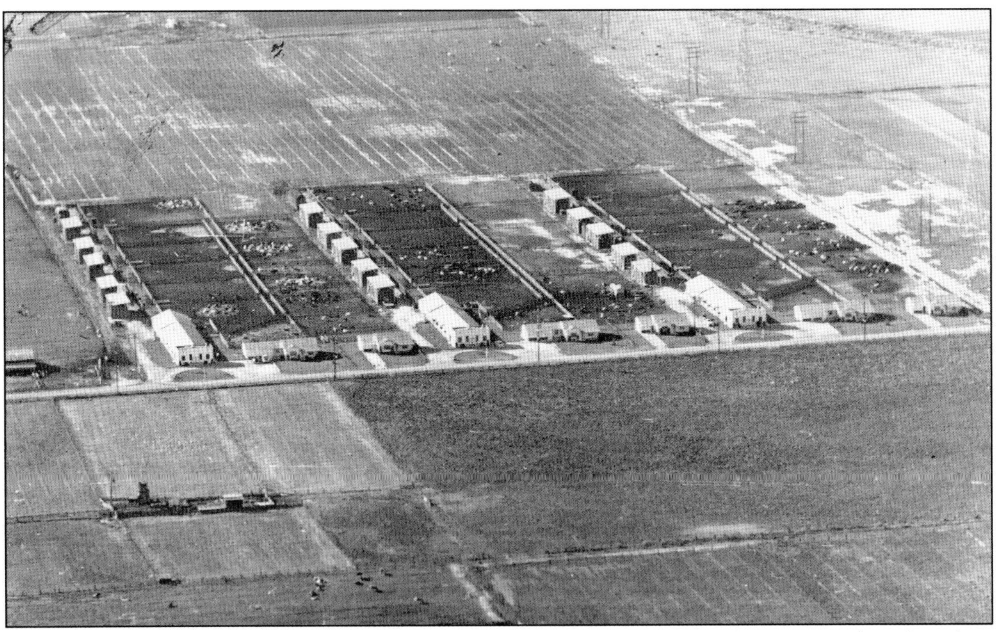

This is an aerial view of the De Groot dairies along Moody Street in the 1950s. The white line to the right of the last building marks the Edison right-of-way. The De Groot house was located between the first two dairies in the picture. A child's playhouse behind the house was the first city hall. Mayor Jack de Vries used to refer to it as a "unique city hall." The address was 7961 Moody Street. (Courtesy of June and Don Plapp.)

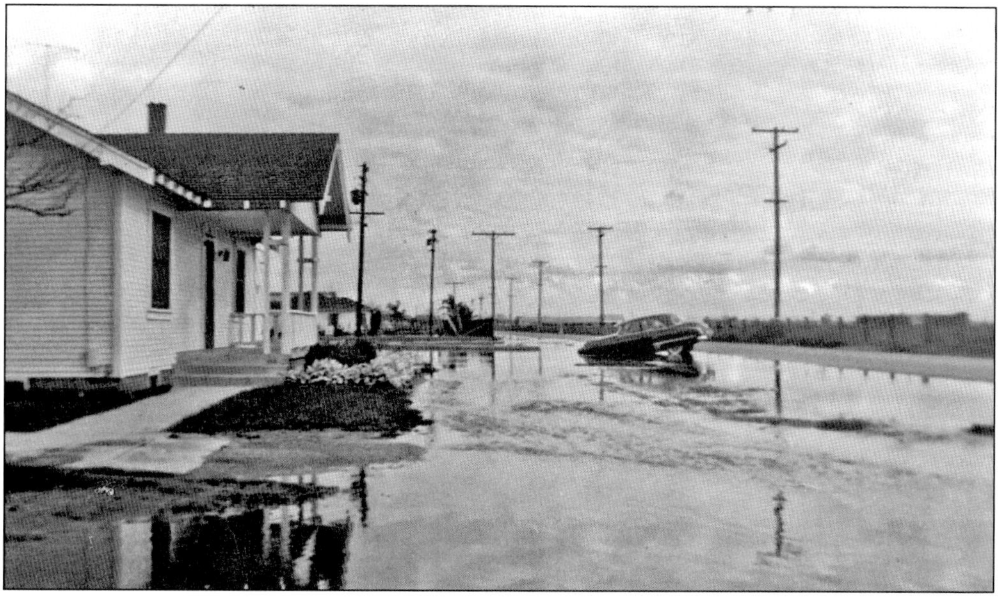

Peter De Groot also owned a poultry ranch at 4752 La Palma Avenue. The pictures above and below show the ranch in the 1952 flood, which was more devastating than the year before. The 1951 flood killed a large number of animals in the area and caused an extensive amount of property damage. Large financial losses forced the local residents to plan improvements to flood and storm drain systems for Coyote Creek. The only "bright side" of these floods, per the residents tongue-in-cheek comments, was the excellent fishing on La Palma Avenue. (Both, courtesy of June and Don Plapp.)

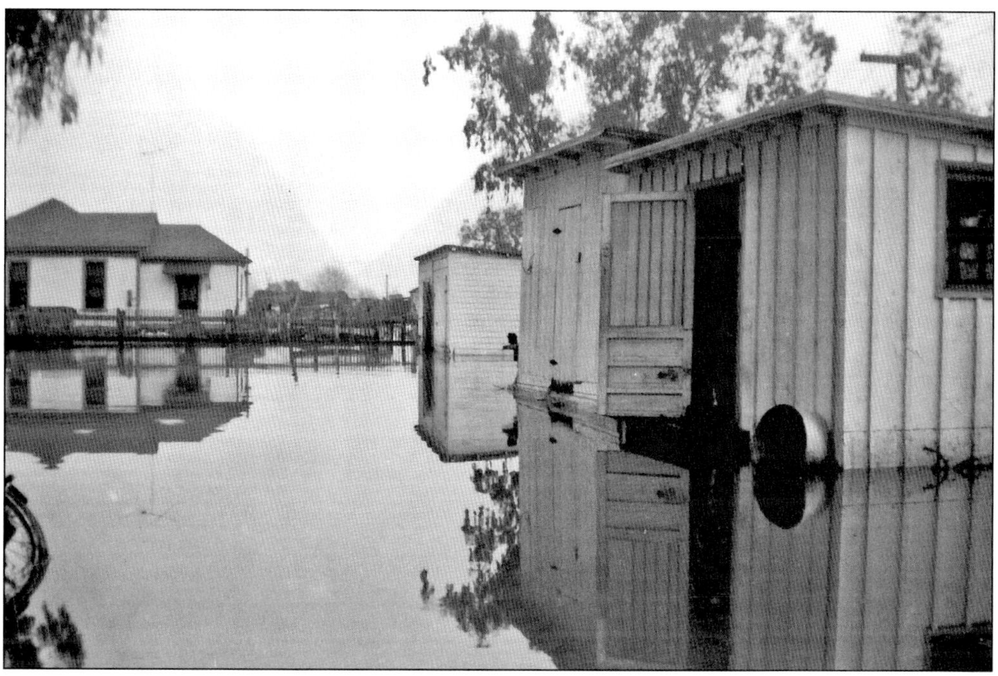

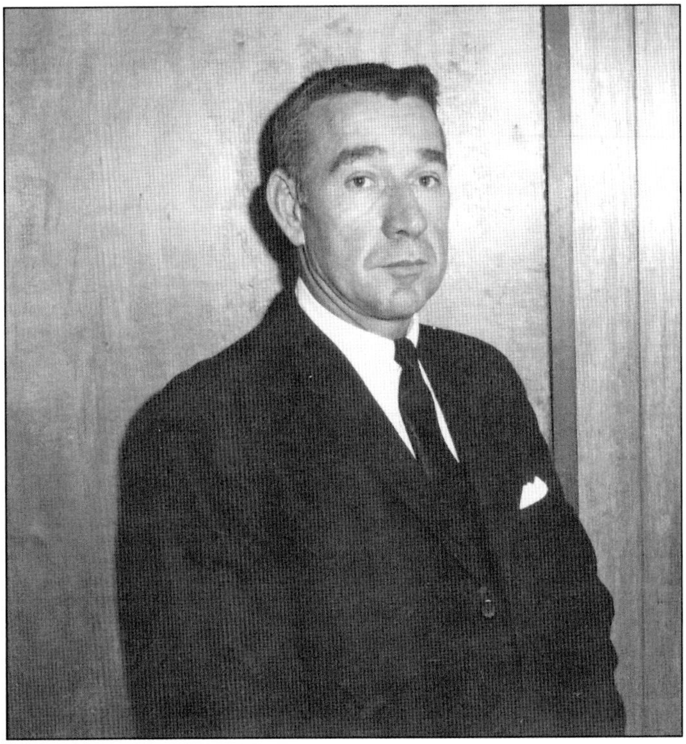

Paul Furman and his wife, Mary Jane, moved to La Palma in 1948. Paul was born and raised in Pennsylvania. He served five years in the U.S. Air Force as a radioman and was at Hickham Field in Pearl Harbor on December 7, 1941. Per the *La Palma Review* in May 1967, Paul took his job as a councilman very seriously and missed only three meetings in his first 12 years. He was also very generous in donating eggs to city causes such as Easter egg hunts. (Courtesy of June and Don Plapp.)

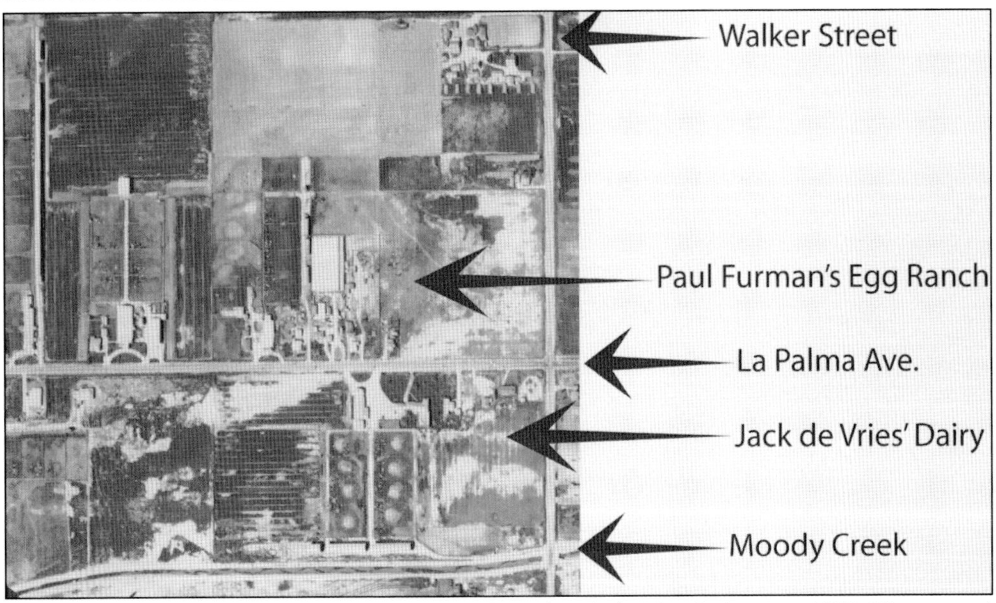

This aerial map shows Paul Furman's egg ranch and Jack de Vries's dairy in 1959. The curved line across the bottom of the map is Moody Creek. North of Moody Creek, the de Vries' dairy is marked on the lower right side of the map. From left to right at the dairy, starting with a rectangle, there appears to be a field, followed by two rows of eight circles, and another rectangle bordered on the right by white vertical line (Walker Street). North of the horizontal line, which is La Palma Avenue, on right side, the white rectangle is the Furman egg ranch. (Courtesy of Orange County Archives.)

Peter G. Bouma, per the *La Palma Review* in April 1967, was one of the founding fathers and vice mayor on the first city council. He was a very successful dairy farmer, active in the dairy industry and in the civic affairs of Dairyland-La Palma. He served as chairman and director of the Orange County Farm Bureau, Dairy Department. He was also a director of the Los Angeles Mutual Dairyman's Association. Pete Bouma was the major force behind the city's fireworks displays for the Fourth of July City of Vision Day. (Courtesy of June and Don Plapp.)

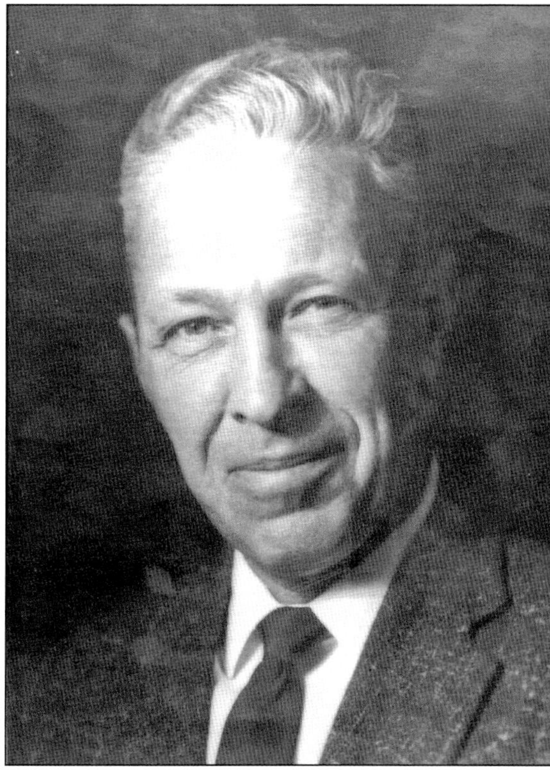

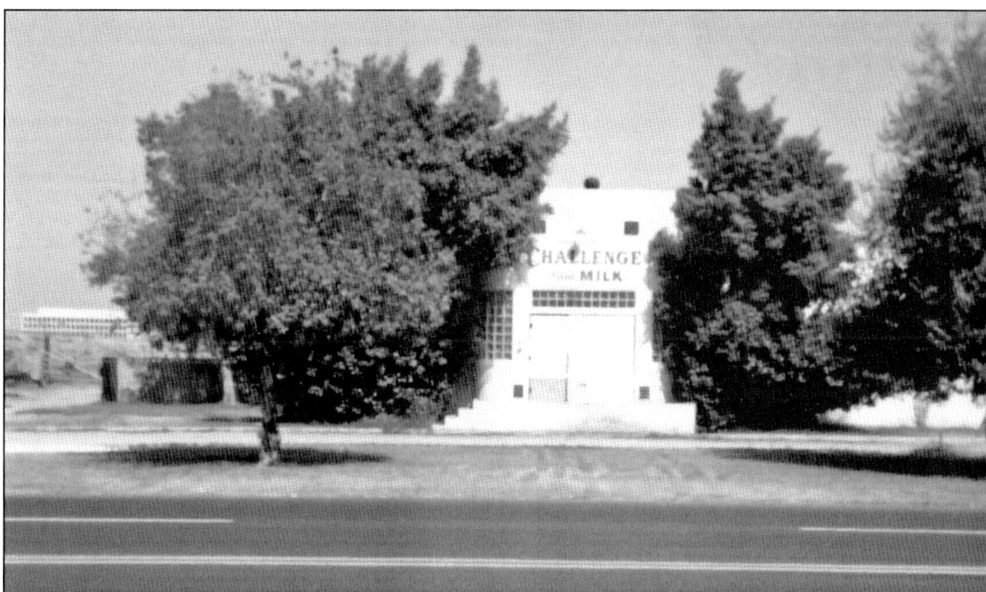

The Bouma dairy was located on the east side of Walker Street, south of Orangethorpe. It was built with the latest innovations of the dairy industry and was well maintained throughout its service in La Palma. The original dairy home is still in use. The building visible in the back of the picture was once a huge hog farm located in Buena Park. The Guglielmana family lived on the west side of Walker Street. (Courtesy of Linda Guglielmana Hinman family.)

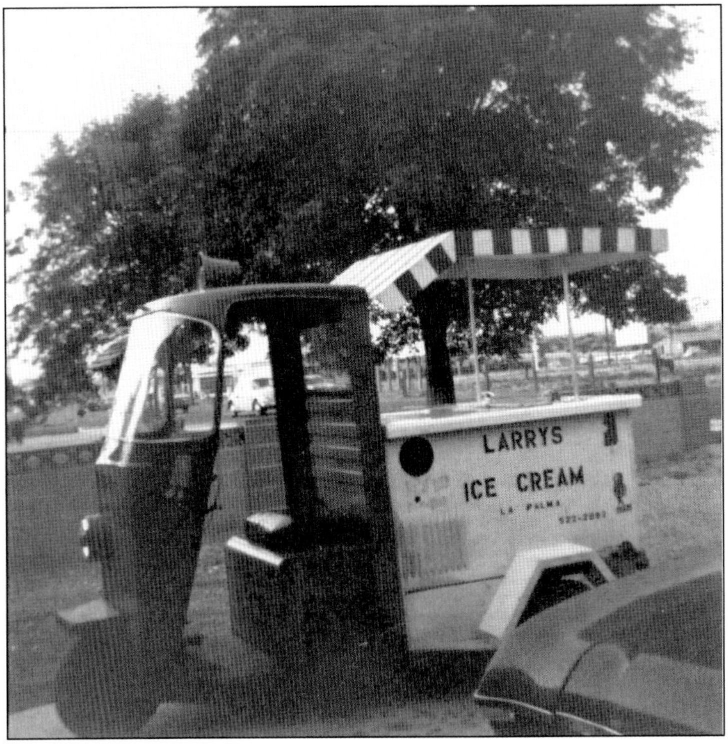

Larrys Ice Cream was an enterprise started by Larry Guglielmana. This picture was taken between 1964 and 1965. It might have been the source of some of the broken ice cream cones, which the dairy cows enjoyed in their feed. The hog farm, in Buena Park, yielded many trinkets to the younger Guglielmana who enjoyed visiting there after school. (Courtesy of Linda Guglielmana Hinman family.)

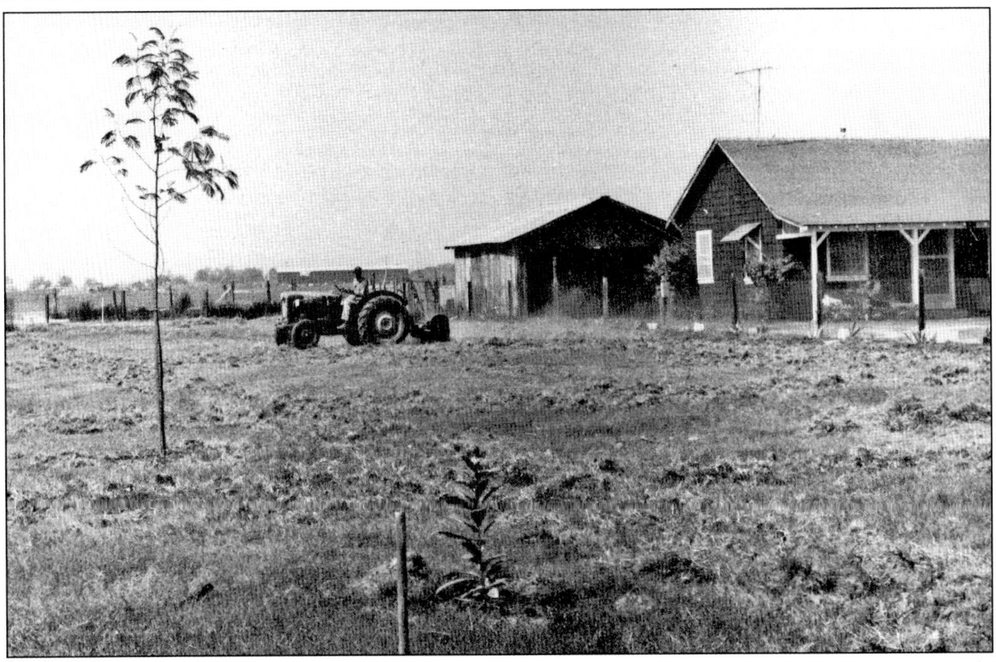

The Wells family farmed in the 1960s. They also had a small nursery business at 8235 Moody Street (Gay Nod Gardens) with attractive displays, nursery stock, and supplies. They would even lend spreaders and rollers to their customers, the new homeowners. The farming portion of this picture is in sharp contrast to the surroundings in the background of Larry's ice cream route, which shows cars and parklike surroundings. (Courtesy of City of La Palma Archives.)

Burton Wesenberg was born in Long Beach, where he received an associate in arts degree from Long Beach City College. He earned a bachelor's degree in public administration from the University of Southern California. Fresh out of college in 1955, he accepted a part-time, unpaid position as city manager of the city of Dairyland because the city had no money to pay him that first year. This evolved into a 25-year career. In 1956, he became the start-up city manager for Dairy City, which was soon renamed Cypress. His dual career ended in 1960. He retired in 1980 as the longest-running city manager in the state. (Courtesy of Catherine Wesenberg.)

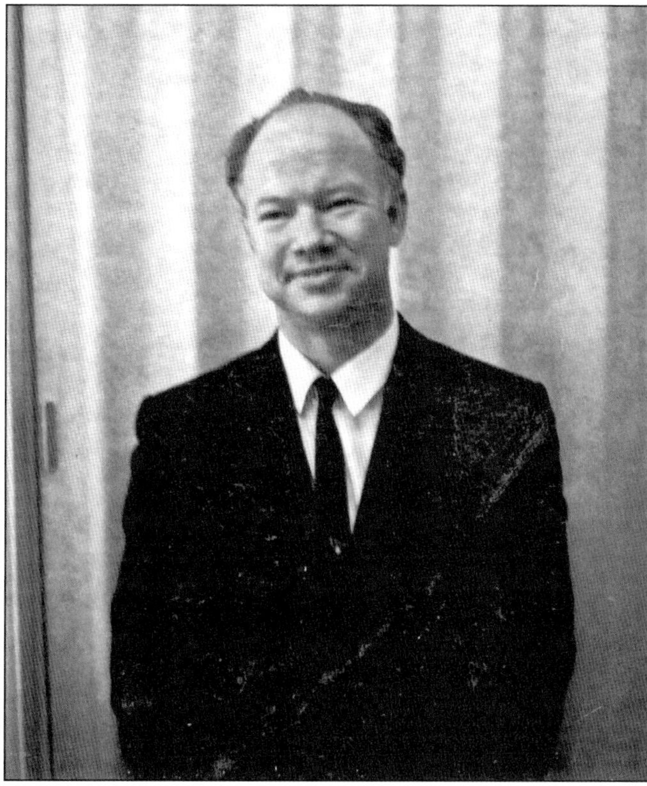

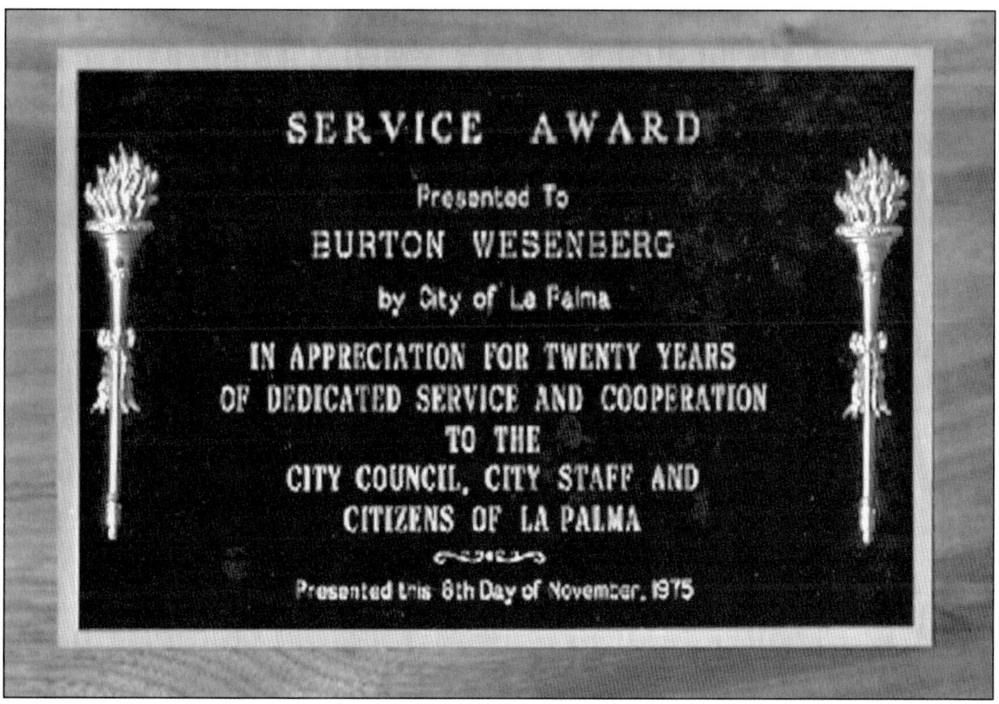

Here is Burt Wesenberg's service award for his 20 years of service to La Palma. (Courtesy of Catherine Wesenberg.)

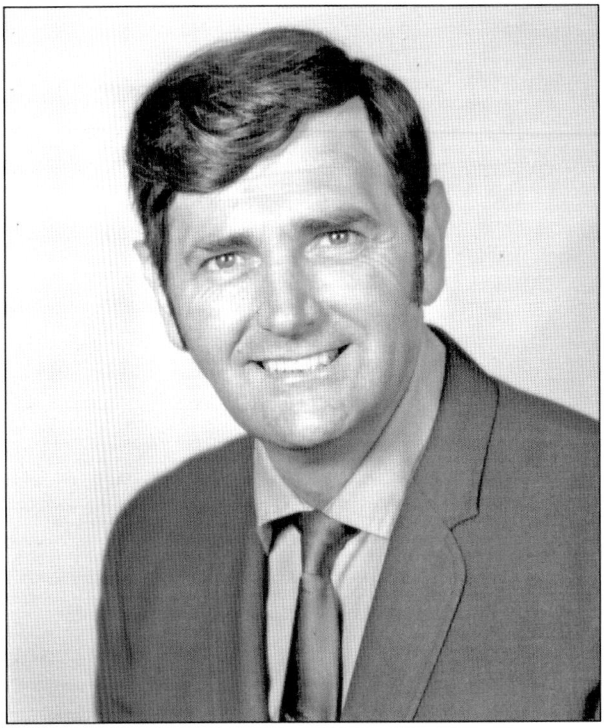

Cor Vander Dussen, per the *La Palma Review* in April 1970, was born in neighboring Artesia and became a resident of La Palma in the mid-1950s. His dairy was located on the north side of Houston and Moody Streets. He eventually moved his dairy to Chino, and by 1970, he was working in subdivision real estate. He was active in the La Palma Chamber of Commerce and the creation of the La Palma Park and Recreation Department and the civic center authority. (Courtesy of June and Don Plapp.)

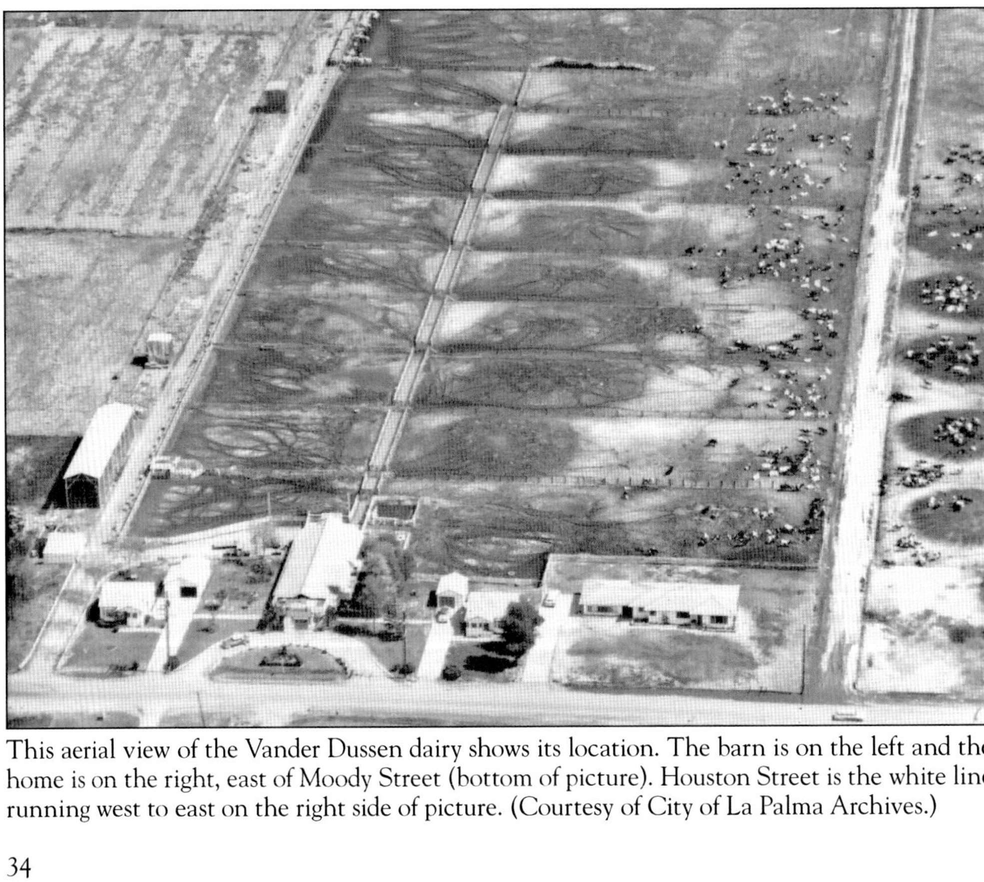

This aerial view of the Vander Dussen dairy shows its location. The barn is on the left and the home is on the right, east of Moody Street (bottom of picture). Houston Street is the white line running west to east on the right side of picture. (Courtesy of City of La Palma Archives.)

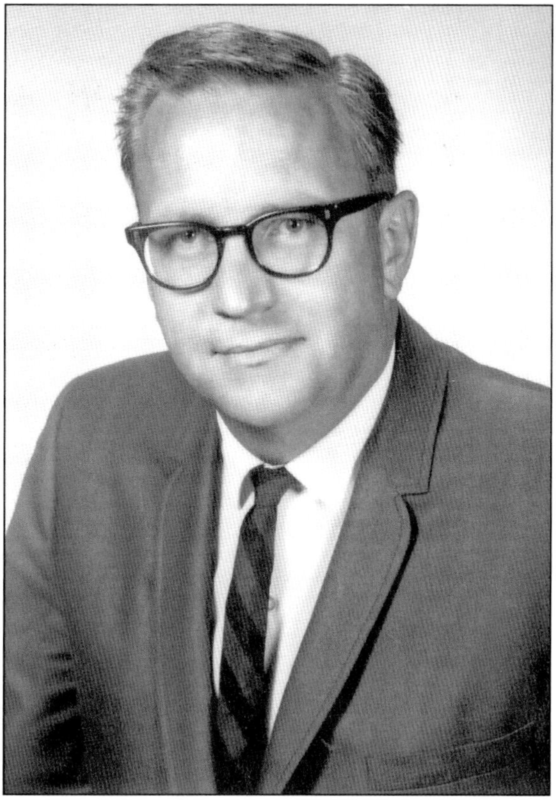

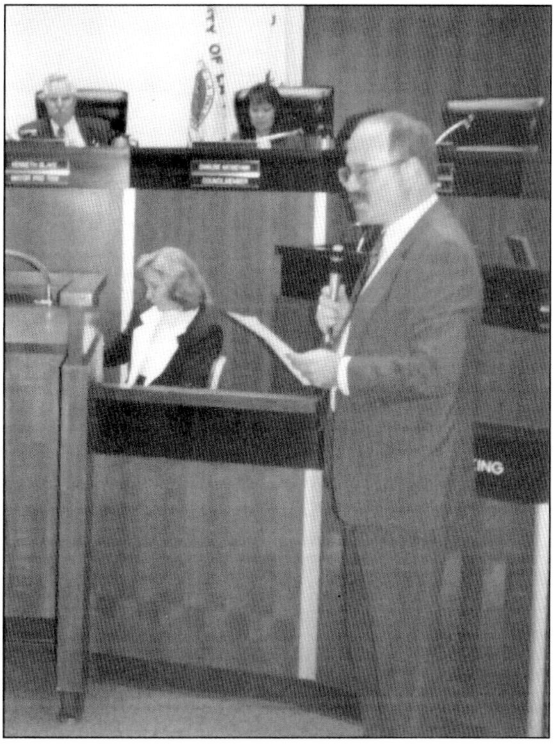

Rodger Howell (above right), per the *La Palma Review* in February 1968, was a native of Santa Ana. He started the firm Rutan and Tucker with five fellow attorneys. In 1968, it was one of the largest law firms in the western United States. His specialty was city government problems. He became involved with La Palma when a neighboring city attempted to annex the area that became Dairyland. Howell, with co-council Mike S. Bernard, became the guiding force in defending and creating this unique city. They were also instrumental in the incorporation of Cypress. Howell was a historian and a popular speaker. Bernard appeared in the publicity pictures for the city. Howell went on to play a role in the creation of the city of Irvine. Rutan and Tucker continue to represent La Palma in legal matters. Below right, city attorney Joel D. Kuperberg (far right) swears in newly elected council members in 1994. Pictured with him are Tami Pescotty, city clerk (center); Mayor Pro Tem Ken Blake (top left); and council member Charlene Hatakeyama (top right). (Both, courtesy of City of La Palma Archives.)

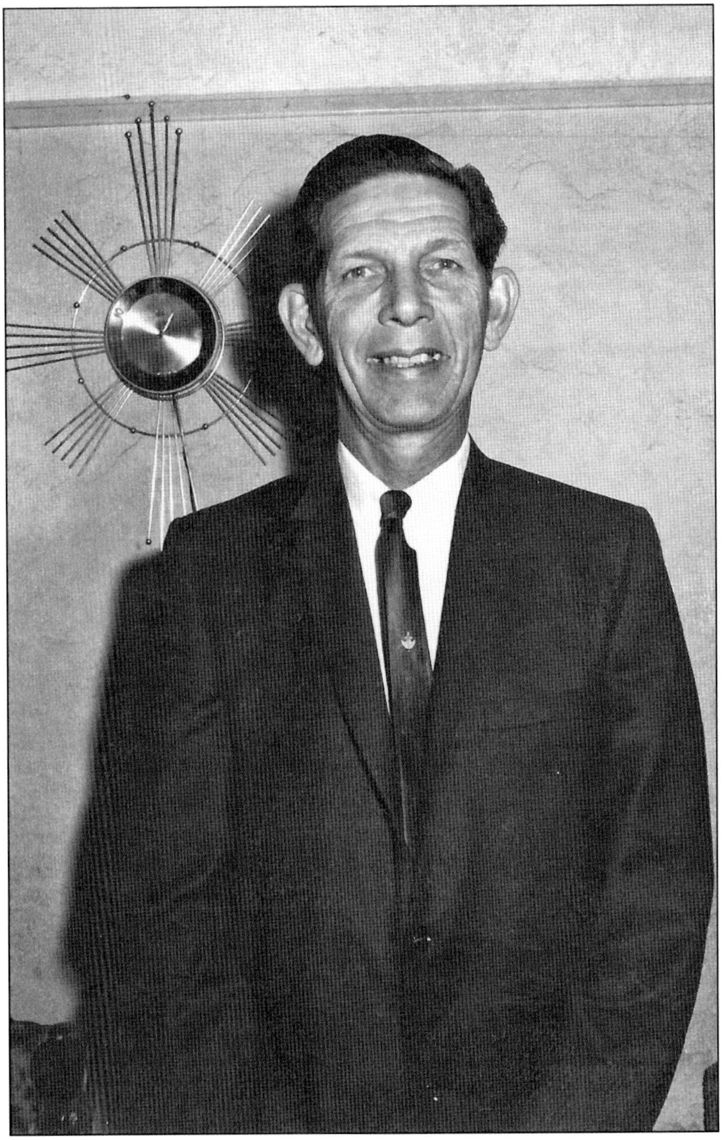

Armond Yost and family, per the *La Palma Review* in March 1967, moved to the La Palma area in 1941. He had a full-time job, but he started raising chickens as a side job. He began with 25 birds, which blossomed into a poultry ranch. At its peak, he was providing 2,000 chickens a week to restaurants and markets. Armond was more farsighted than most. He could see that urbanization was coming, so he slowly began downsizing. He created Yost Ranch Market in its place, located at 4821 Crescent Avenue. Armond and his wife, Eleanor, were active members of the community. They joined the homeowner's association, the La Palma Chamber of Commerce, and served on many city committees. (Courtesy of June and Don Plapp.)

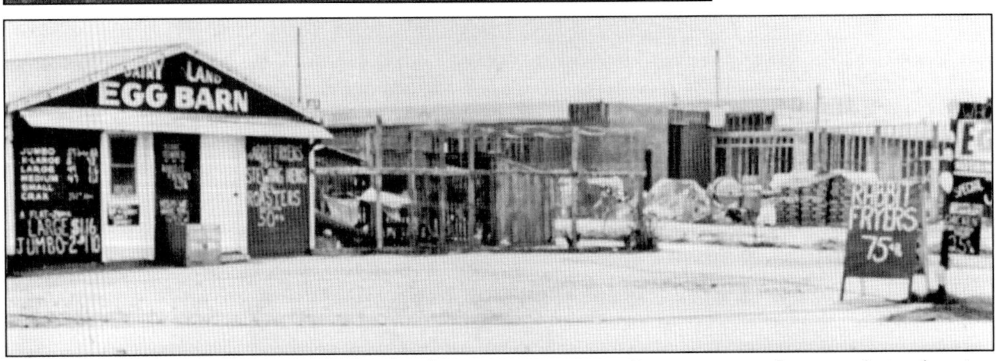

This c. 1960 egg barn, located at 7762 Walker Street, was another active poultry ranch in the city. (Courtesy of City of La Palma Archives.)

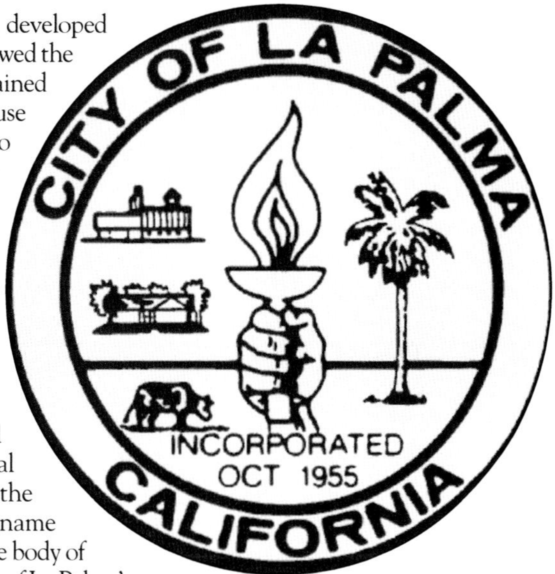

The *50th Anniversary Commemorative Book*, developed and edited by Ron and Elfriede Mac Iver, reviewed the city's history for La Palma's residents and explained how La Palma's new name came about because a group of 95 citizens signing a petition to rename Dairyland after the main street, La Palma Avenue. "The seal is dominated by a hand holding a torch, signifying freedom, which is set on a field of green grass and blue sky. Beneath the hand is the date of incorporation, October 1955. To the right of the torch is a palm tree denoting the change of the name of the city to 'City of La Palma,' which means 'the palm.' To the left of the torch is a factory representing potential industrial growth; a house depicting residential growth; and a cow representing the reason the city was originally incorporated under the name Dairyland. In the outer circle surrounding the body of the seal is the name of the city and state, 'City of La Palma' and 'California.'" (Courtesy of City of La Palma Archives.)

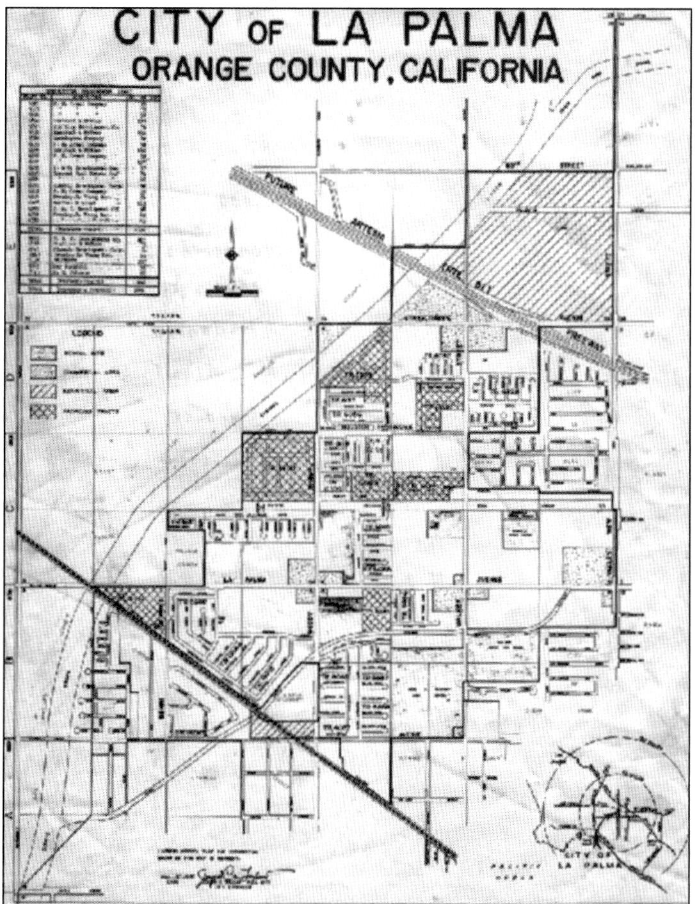

This is a map of La Palma in 1965. (Courtesy of City of La Palma Archives.)

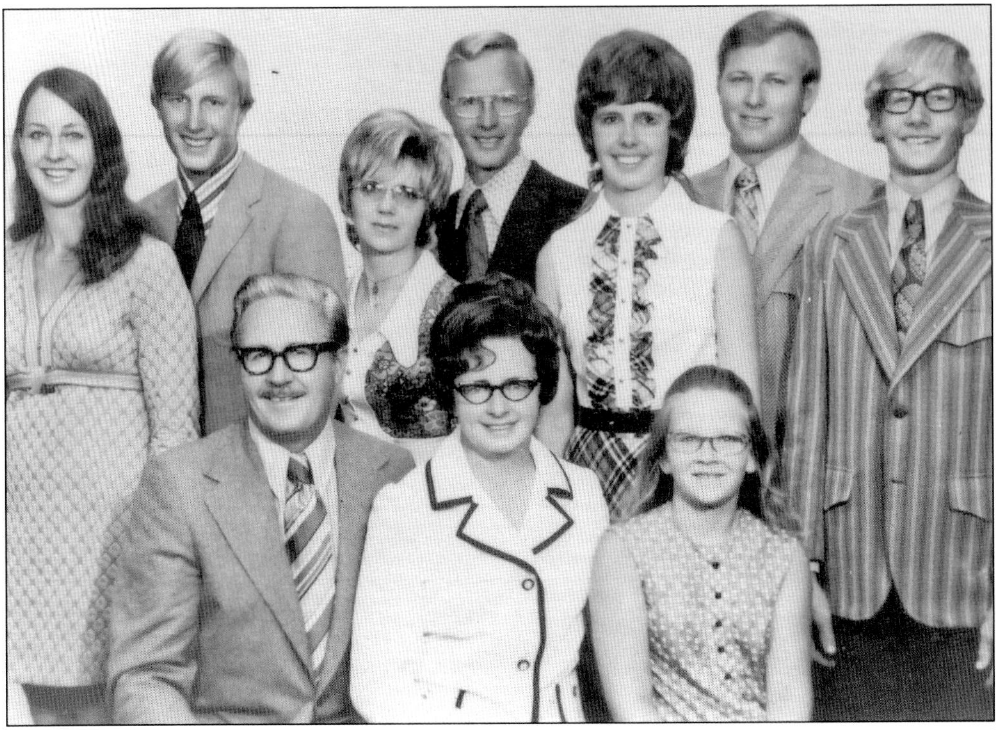

The Westra family is pictured, from left to right, as follows: (first row) Jake Westra, Alice, and Brenda (daughter); (second row) Tracy W., Sherwin (son), Eloise W., John (son), Pat Van Dyk (daughter), Pete Van Dyk, and Calvin (son). Jake served as a councilman and mayor and was a great supporter of the city. (Courtesy of Bryan Westra family.)

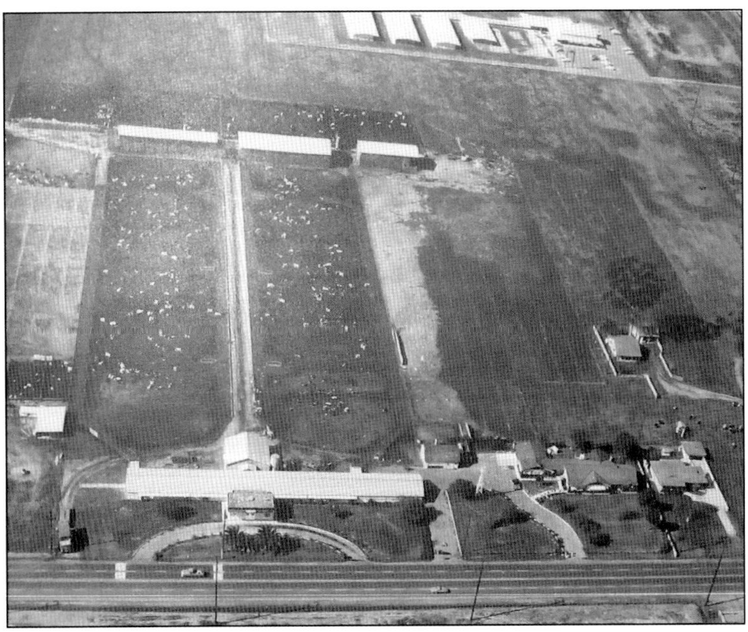

This aerial view of the Westra dairy shows Valley View Street running north and south at the bottom of picture. Not visible at the left of the picture is La Palma Avenue, which runs east and west. The George B. Miller School land, located at the top right of the picture, was taken from the Westra Dairy property by eminent domain. (Courtesy of Bryan Westra family.)

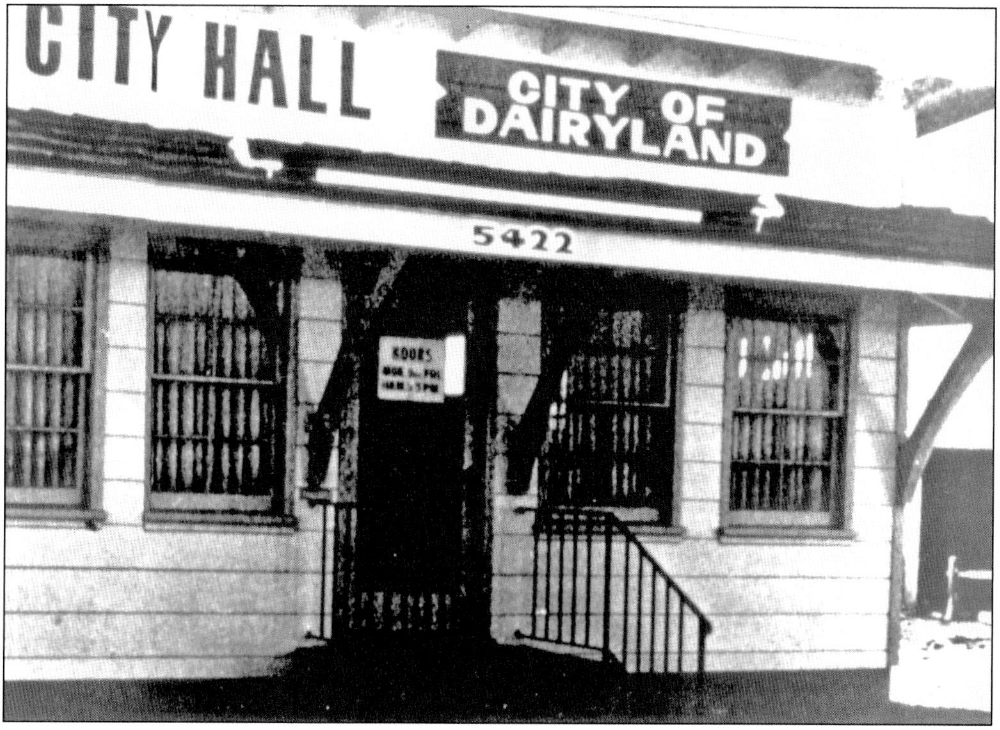

The first real city hall for Dairyland was originally a real estate office located on Lincoln Avenue (Carson Street) in Hawaiian Gardens. Jack and Gertrude de Vries were driving in the area and noticed the property for sale. With the approval of the city council, the property was purchased and moved to the corner of La Palma Avenue and Walker Street at 5422 La Palma Avenue around 1957. (Courtesy of City of La Palma Archives.)

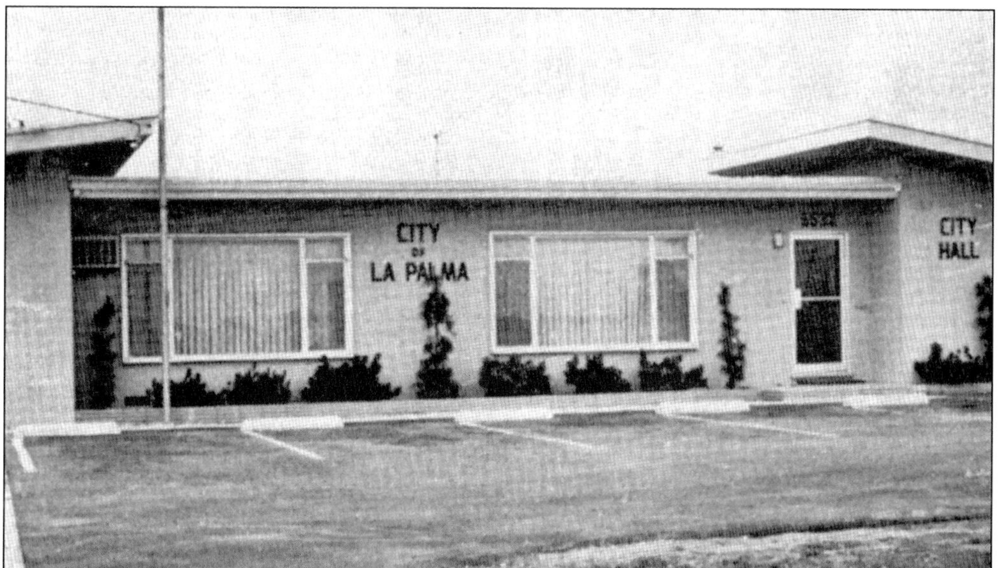

A new city hall complex was built for La Palma around 1965 at 5532 La Palma Avenue. The first city hall remained in place but was converted to serve the needs of the police department by changing the sign to identify the new tenants. (Courtesy of City of La Palma Archives.)

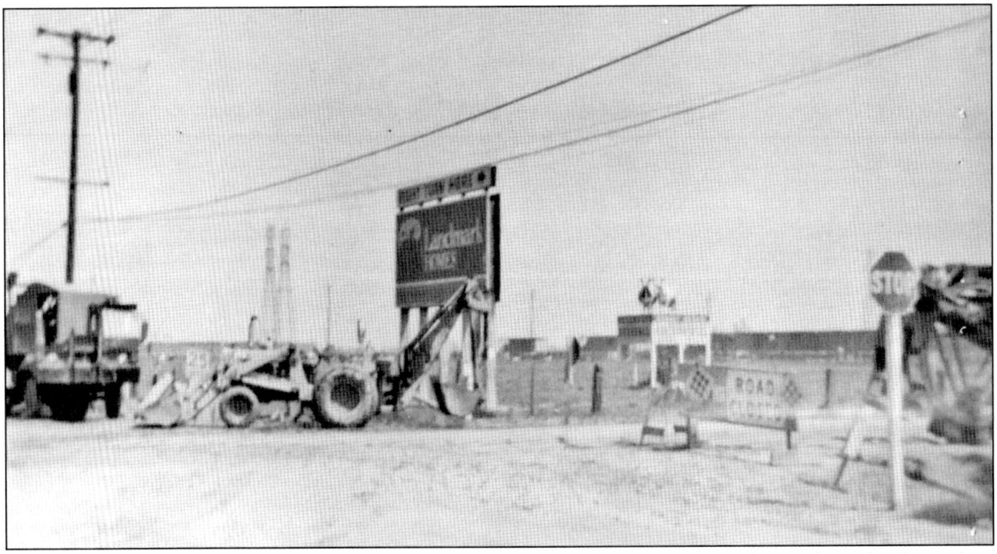

Landmark homes were under construction in 1965. (Courtesy of City of La Palma Archives.)

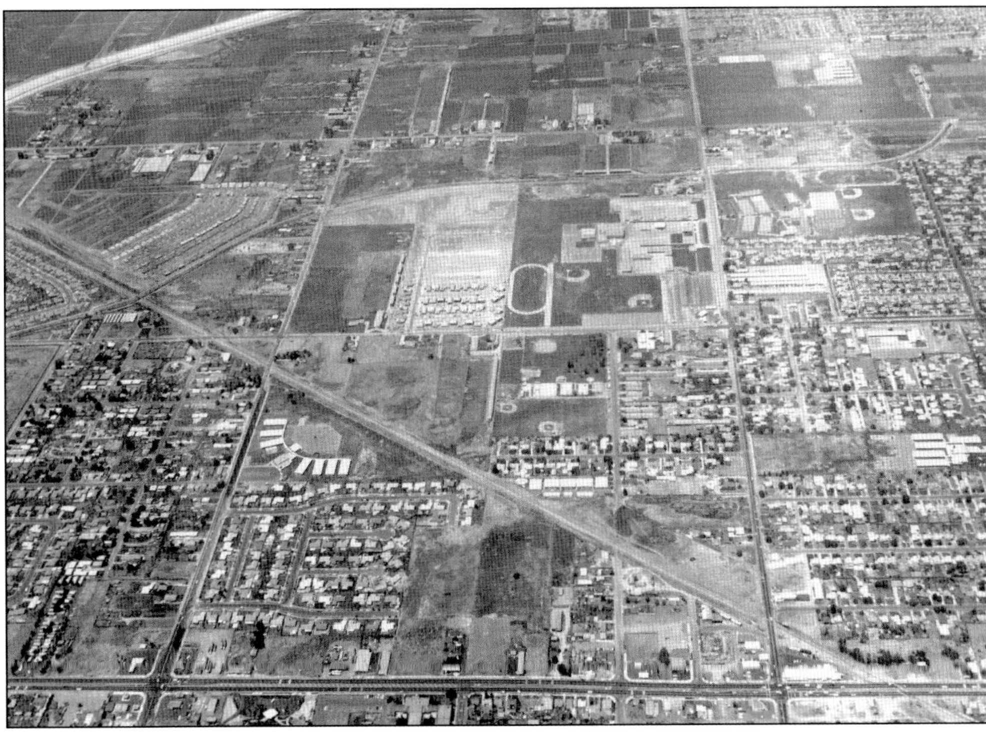

This aerial view of La Palma and Cypress shows Lincoln Avenue running east to west across the bottom of the picture. The diagonal line cutting across, from bottom right to top left, is the railroad line. On the right, going from north to south, is Walker Street, and on the left, going from north to south, is Moody Street. The next east to west street is Crescent Avenue. The John F. Kennedy track and surrounding school is visible north of Crescent Avenue. Just to the left of the white oval (the track), there is a tract of homes. These were the first Stardust homes being built at approximately the same time as the Landmark homes that are visible to the left of Moody Street, just north of the diagonal. (Courtesy of John Olson, Cypress Archives.)

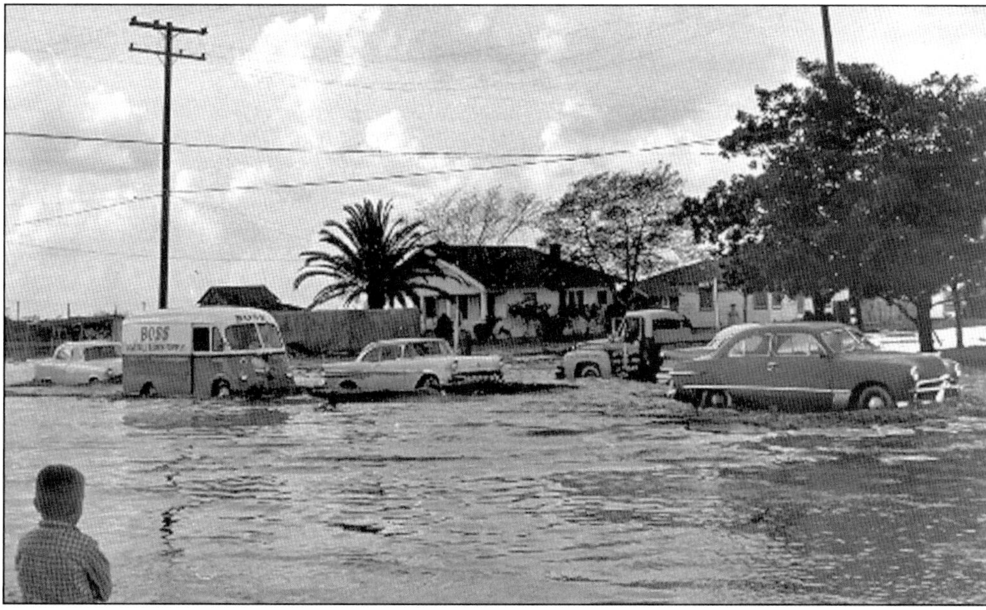

The floods of 1965 were a reminder of the heavy floods of the 1950s and the need to work faster on the development of a flood-control system. (Courtesy of City of La Palma Archives.)

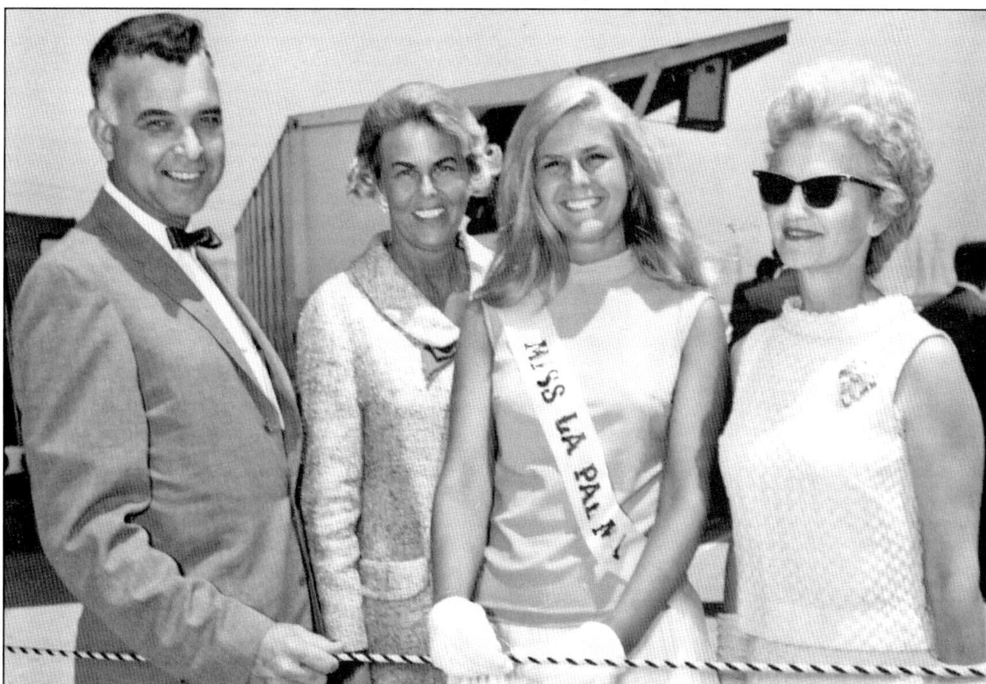

The ribbon-cutting ceremonies for the opening of the San Gabriel Freeway (605) are pictured above from a July 1966 issue of the *La Palma Review*. From left to right are Pink McKay, president of the La Palma Chamber of Commerce, Mrs. E. File, mother of Miss La Palma; Jan File, Miss La Palma; and Bea Sorrells, secretary of the La Palma Chamber of Commerce. The July *Independent Press-Telegram* correctly predicted that La Palma would benefit greatly from this freeway. (Courtesy of June and Don Plapp.)

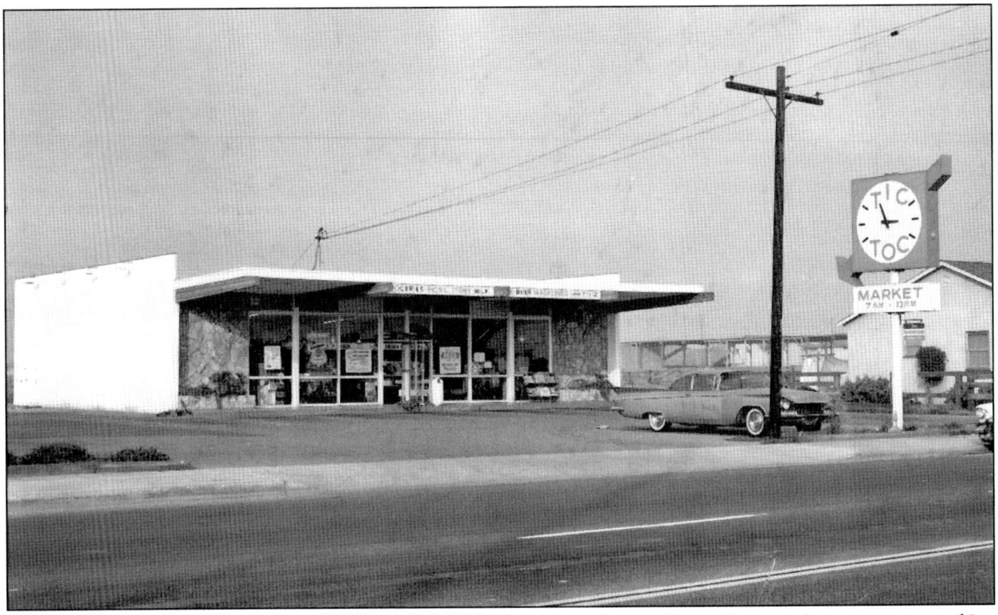

According to the *La Palma Review*, the Tic-Toc Market, located on the northeast corner of La Palma Avenue and Moody Street, opened its doors in October 1966. When larger markets moved to La Palma, it was converted to a real estate office. (Courtesy of June and Don Plapp.)

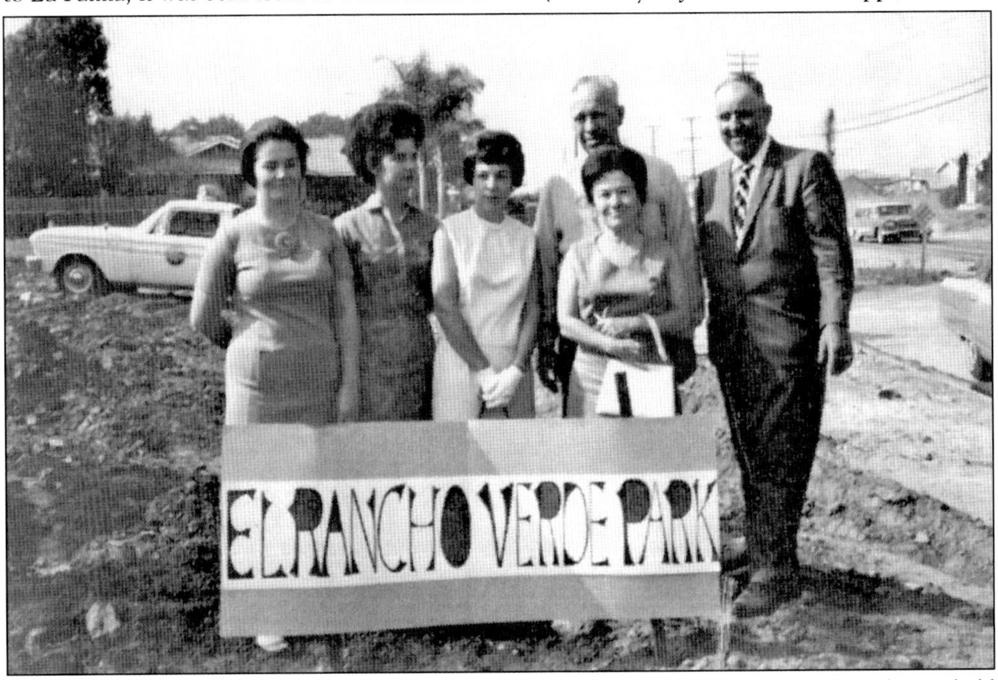

According to the *La Palma Review*, the ground-breaking ceremonies for El Rancho Verde Park were held in June 1967. This was La Palma's first park, built to accommodate the needs of a growing community and its younger citizens, the preschool children. They would join with mothers in the community as the La Palma Tot Lot. Pictured from left to right are Mary Thrasher, Tot Lot president; June Plapp; Mavis Crick and Virginia Bonar, cultural and education committee; Mayor Pete Bouma; and A. E. "Pat" Arnold, Cypress Park and Recreation District. (Courtesy of June and Don Plapp.)

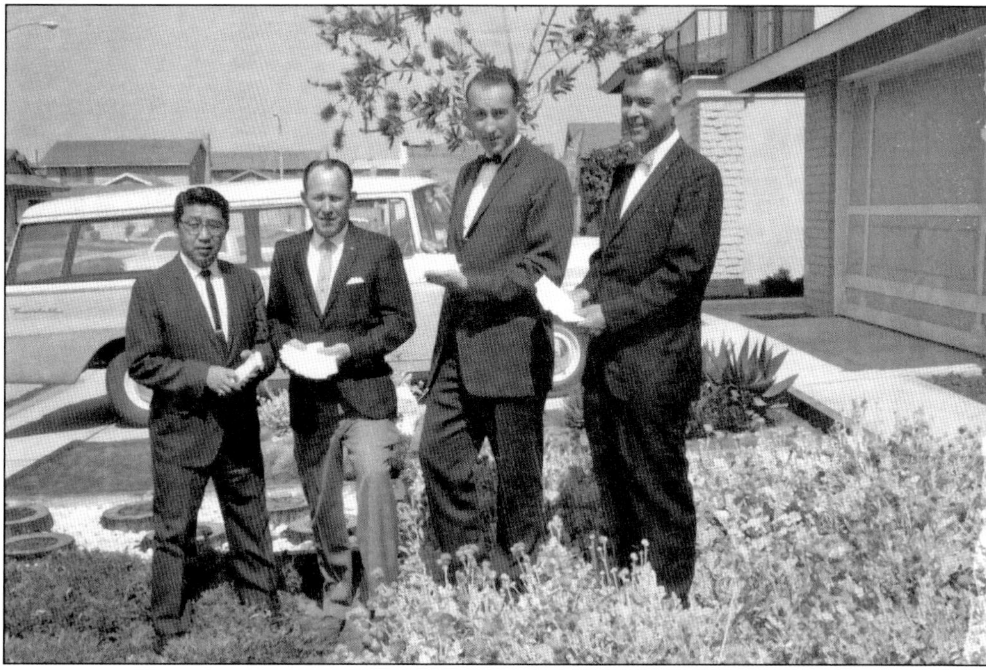

City of Vision Day raffle tickets were advertised for the grand prize of a 1967 Chevrolet Camaro. This was the first major citywide, joint undertaking by the La Palma City Council and Chamber of Commerce, per the July 1967 *La Palma Review*. From left to right are some of the chamber officers: Nappy Sekiguchi, publicity chairman; Joe Tye, treasurer and chairman of the parade and ticket committee; Jerry Patterson, chairman of City of Vision Day; and Pink McKay, president of the chamber. (Courtesy of June and Don Plapp.)

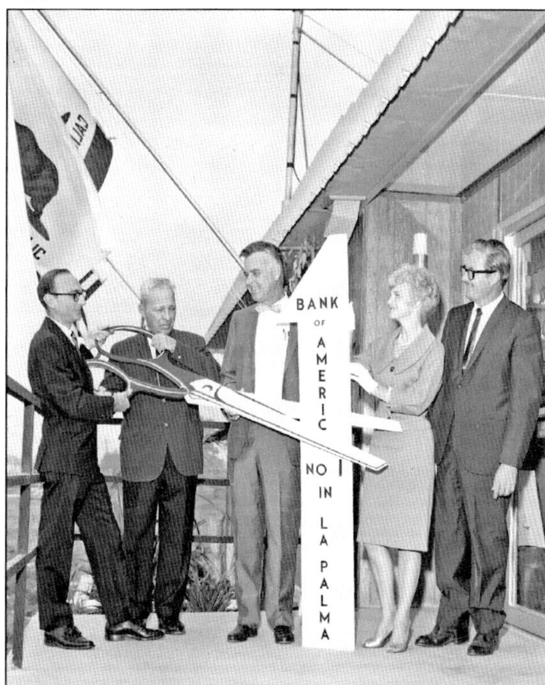

The ribbon-cutting ceremony for the temporary quarters of the Bank of America was held in September 1967, according to the *La Palma Review*. From left to right are Larry D. Freedman, bank manager; Mayor Pete Bouma; Pink McKay, president of the chamber of commerce; Bea Sorrells, chamber secretary; and councilman Jake Westra. (Courtesy of June and Don Plapp.)

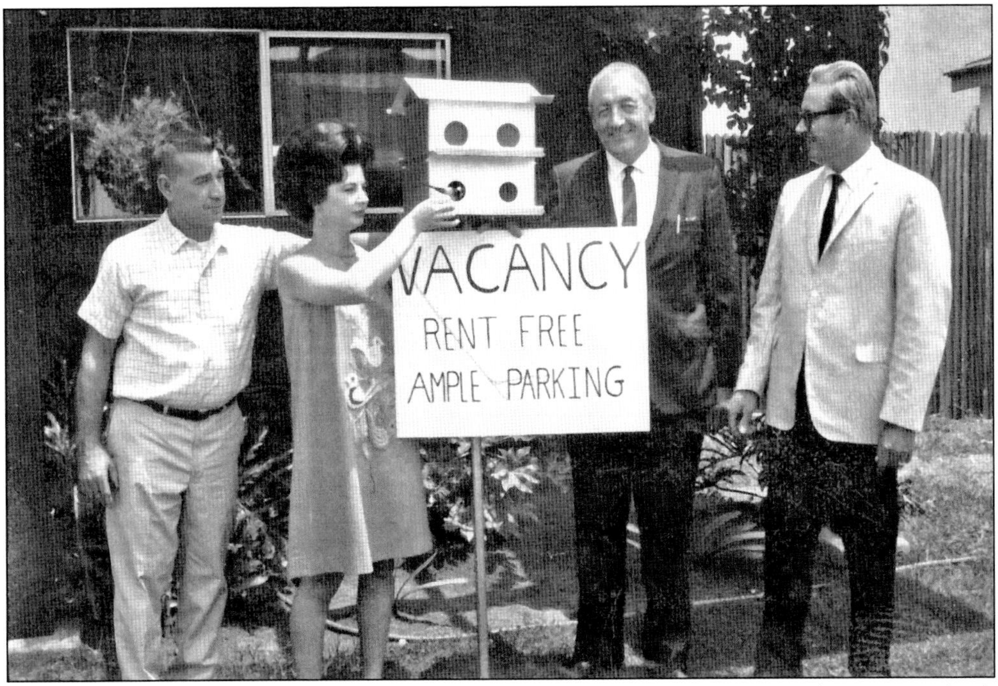

The purple martin is the largest of the swallows. It was once both a serious and tongue-in-cheek solution to the fly "problem" that accompanied the close proximity of the dairy farms to the new housing developments. Per the *La Palma Review* in October 1967, the martins might have solved the problem because of their diet of flying insects, but La Palma was not on their migration route to Mexico. Convincing the flock to stay did not seem a viable solution. The flock sent scouts to see if there was adequate food and places to colonize, but finding none, moved on. The cultural and education committee sensing that man had not provided these proud birds with proper housing attempted to remedy the situation, enlisting the help of the city council for their noble project. The council joined in the fun. Pictured from left to right are councilman Paul Furman; June Plapp, assistant editor of the *La Palma Review*; councilmen Pete De Groot; and Jake Westra. (Above, courtesy of June and Don Plapp; below, courtesy John Olson, City of Cypress Archives.)

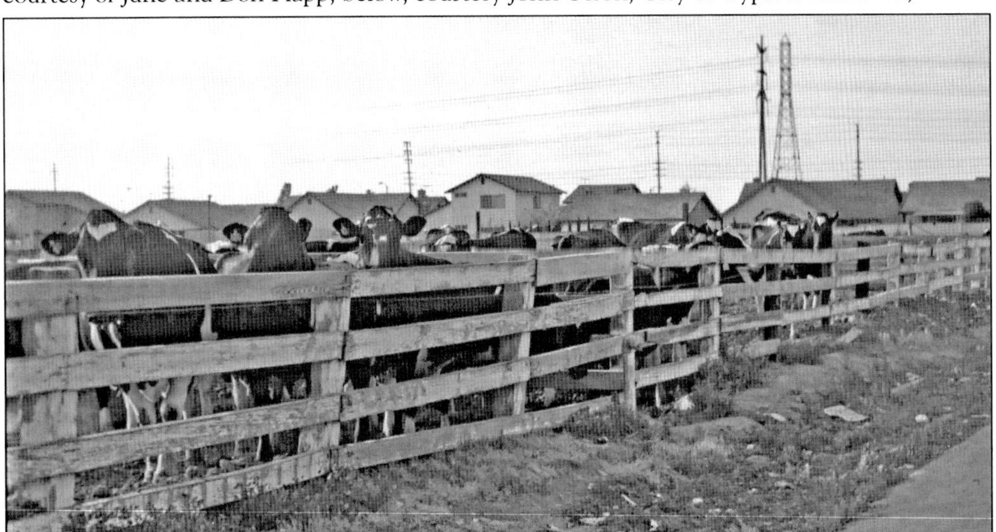

The city held a contest in early 1967 to design the first city sign. The sign was first erected at the corner of Valley View Street and La Palma Avenue, on councilman Jake Westra's dairy. From left to right are Ron Mac Iver, the winner of the design contest; Nappy Sekiguchi, chamber of commerce vice president; and Mayor Pete Bouma. (Courtesy of City of La Palma Archives.)

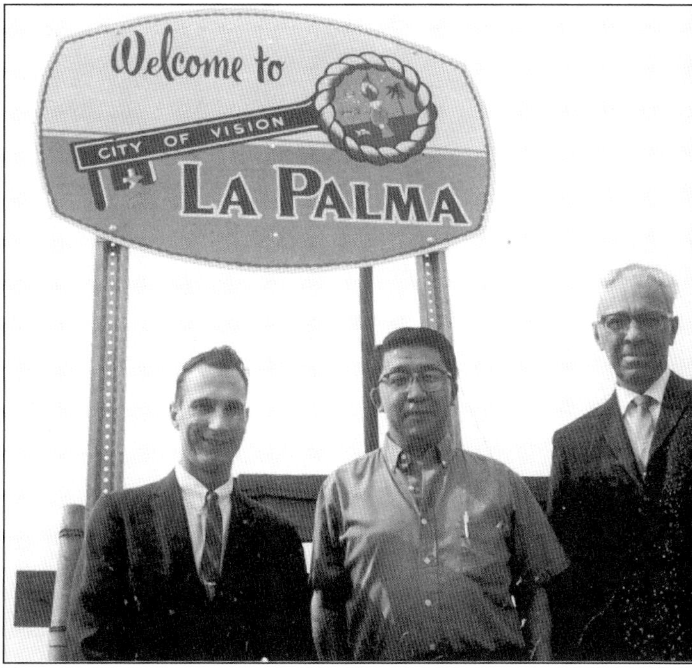

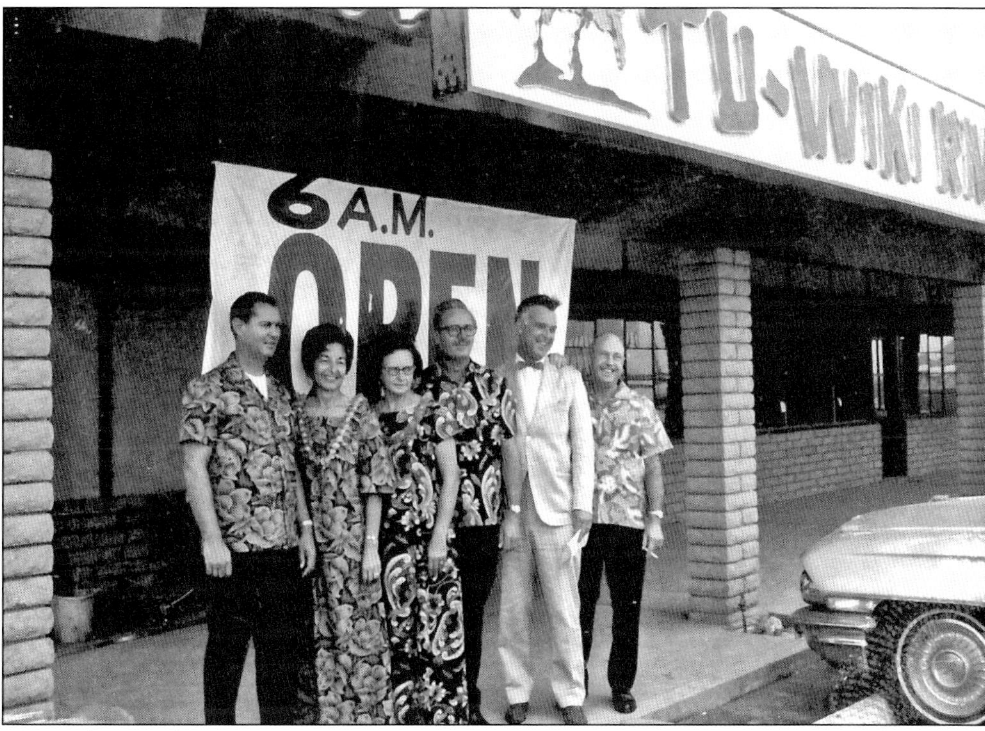

This is the grand opening of the new Tu-Wiki Room, October 27–28, 1967. Pictured from left to right are John McNutt with his wife, Florine; Alice Westra and her husband, councilman Jake Westra; Pink McKay, chamber of commerce president; and owner Mac McPherson. All profits from the grand opening venison barbecue were donated to the chamber. (Courtesy of June and Don Plapp.)

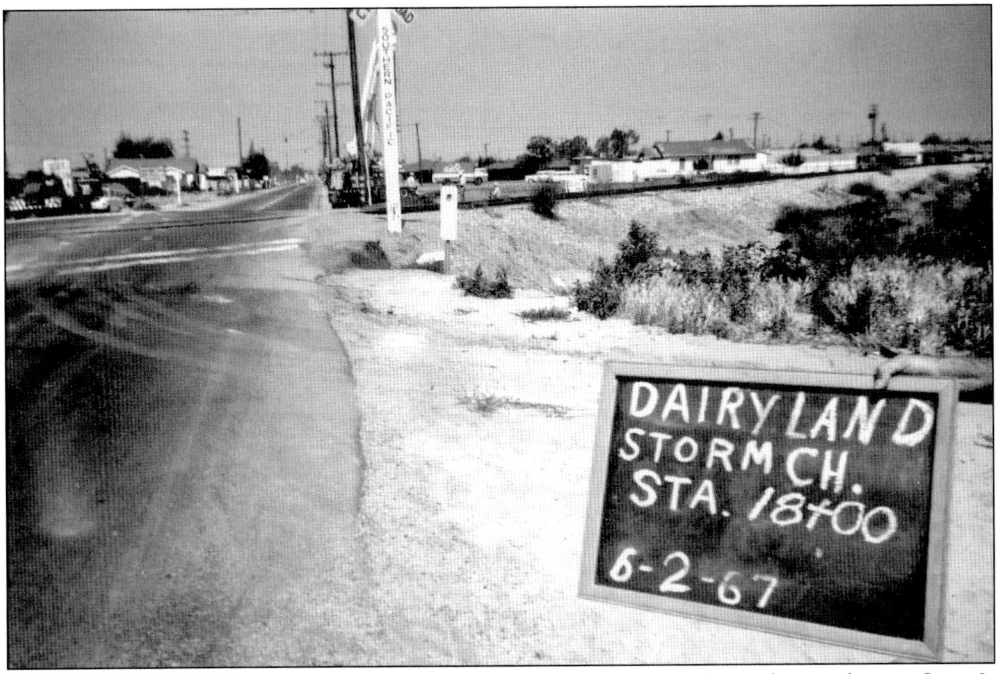

A photograph of the progress of the Dairyland (La Palma) Storm Channel was taken on June 2, 1967, from east to west along Crescent Avenue. Yost Market, with two cars parked at the entrance, appears on the right of the picture, across the tracks. Monies were appropriated during the time that the city's name was Dairyland. (Courtesy of City of La Palma Archives.)

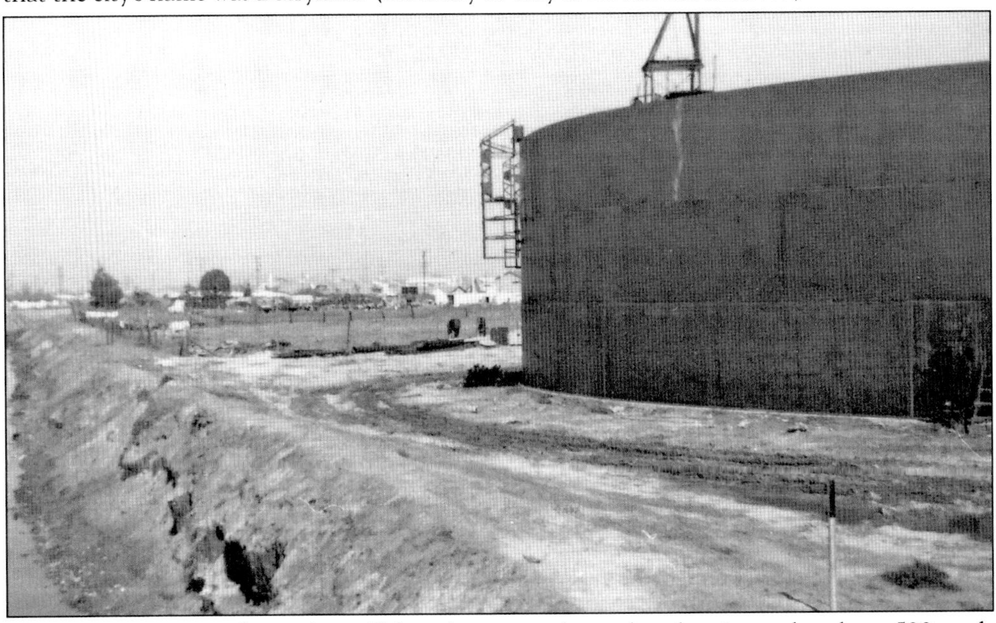

The water reservoir is located parallel to the storm channel and train tracks, about 500 yards beyond the earlier 1967 picture of the Dairyland Storm Channel. The reservoir is designed to hold 2.5 million gallons of water. It is 24 feet high and 130 feet in diameter. The project, according to the *La Palma Review* in June 1967, was begun in November 1966 and was completed in June 1967. (Courtesy of June and Don Plapp.)

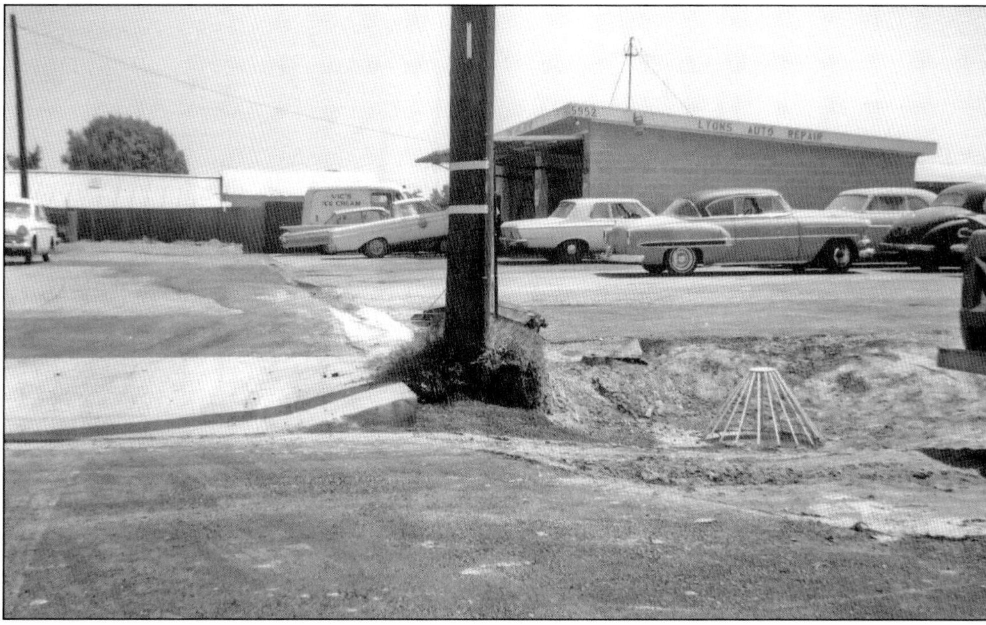

Frank Lyons Auto Repair was the neighborhood auto shop for many years in La Palma. His shop was located on Moody Street, north of Lincoln Avenue. Frank was talented and friendly, and his service was affordable. He was also very civic-minded and active in the chamber of commerce. (Courtesy of City of La Palma Archives.)

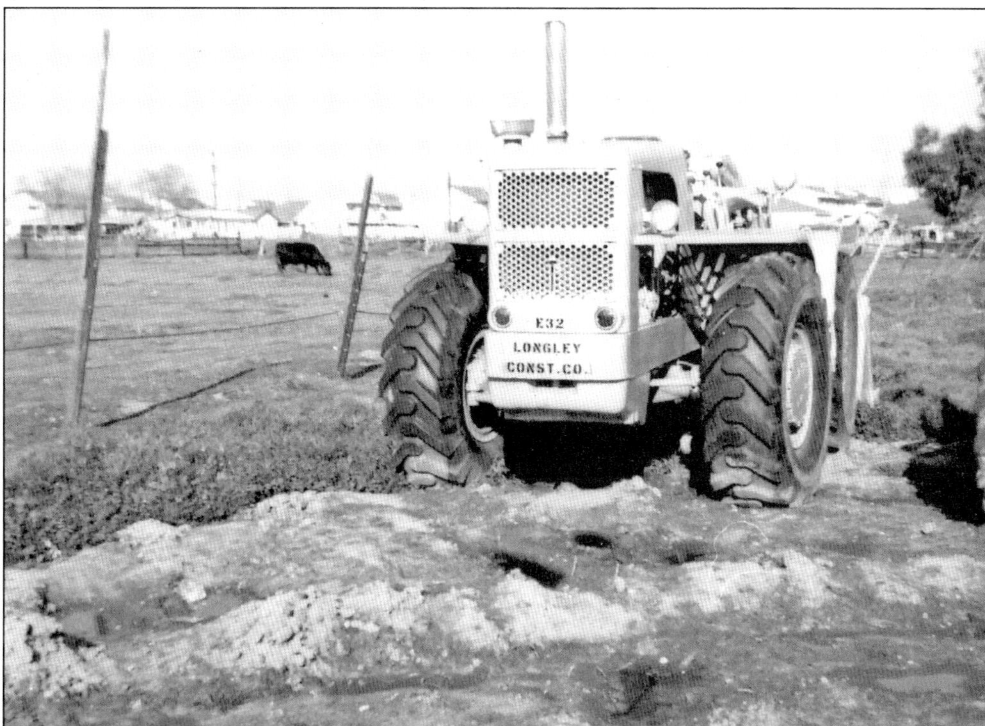

The local cows in the pasture had a first row seat as construction of new homes changed the landscape and their placid way of life. (Courtesy of City of La Palma Archives.)

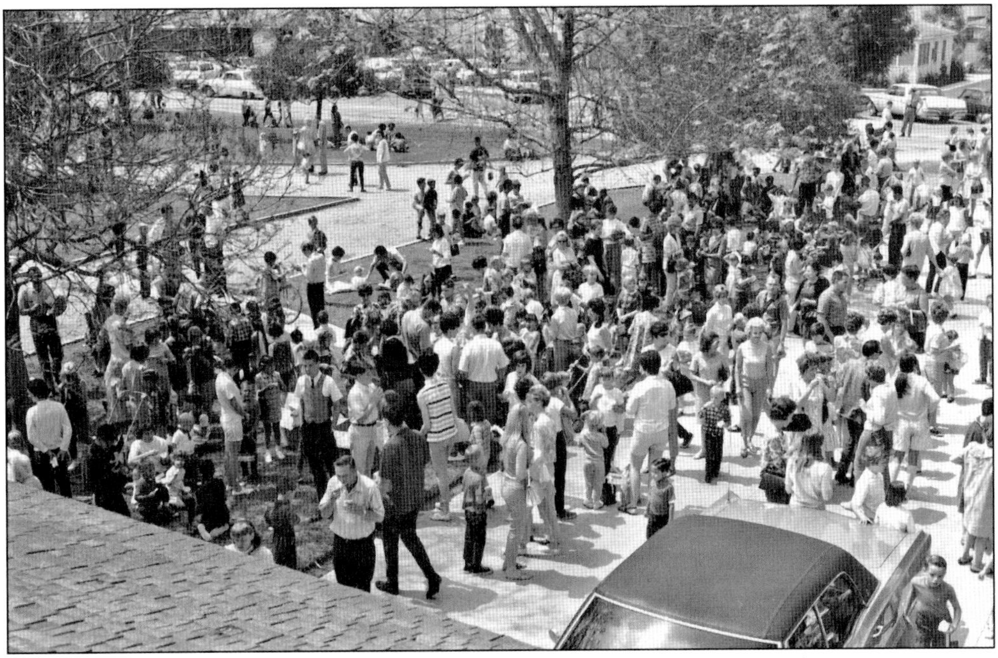

New residents of the city enthusiastically participated in the mayor's Easter egg hunt. Parents came with their children, in awe of the generosity of their mayor. There were helping hands from the chamber and all the other local organizations. Children, including the youngest toddlers, were able to find the eggs, thanks to the egg farmers' donations and the many volunteers who spent the night before hard-boiling and dyeing eggs. (Courtesy of June and Don Plapp.)

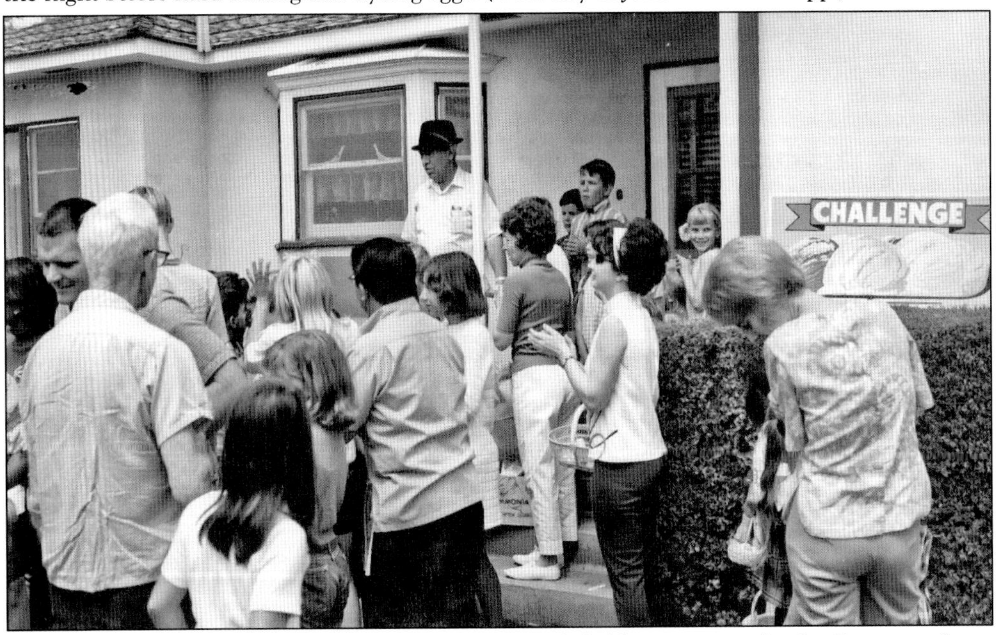

Mayor Bouma, in a black fedora, greets grown-ups and children arriving for the Easter egg hunt on his front lawn. All eyes seem to be looking to the left of picture. It might be Bea Sorrells arriving in her Easter bunny outfit. She thoroughly enjoyed hopping through the grass, hunting for eggs with the children. (Courtesy of June and Don Plapp.)

Bea Sorrells came dressed for her part of the festivities as an Easter bunny. All were willing participants and their enthusiasm, combined with the children's, made the day memorable. The grown-ups understood that this was a very special occasion and that it would not be repeated for very long. (Courtesy of Thomas and Carol Sorrells McCarty family.)

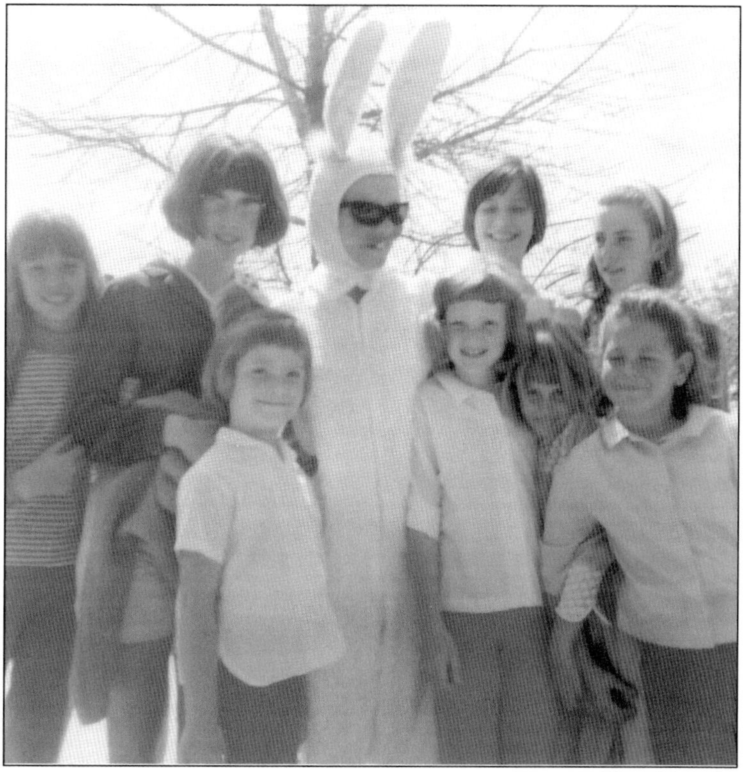

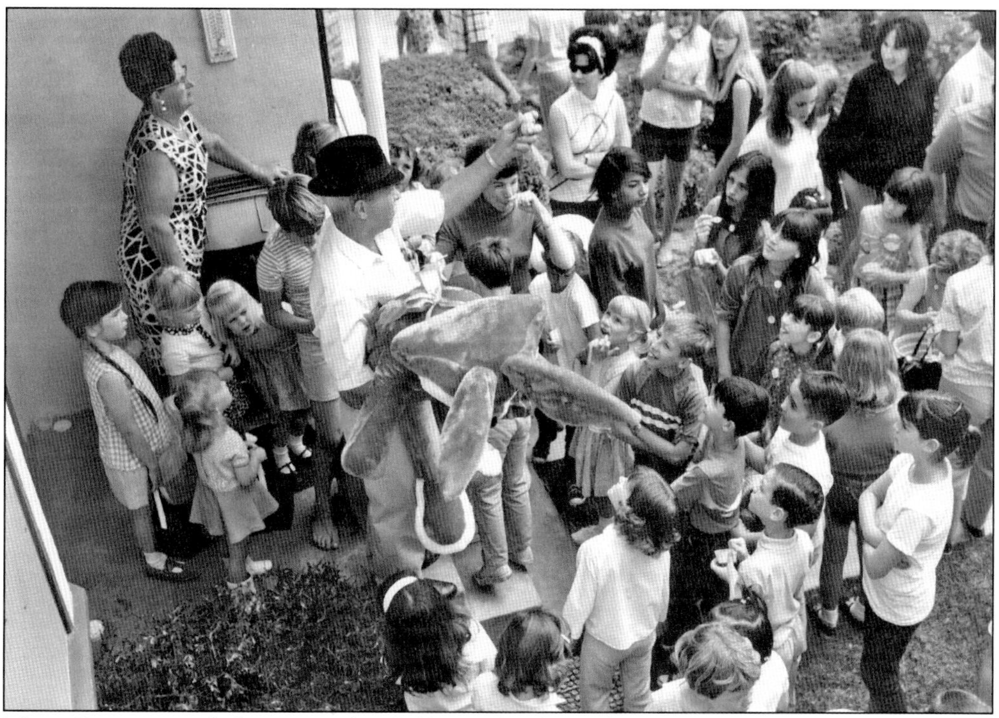

Mayor Bouma awarded prizes to the children. The day ended smoothly and everyone seemed to leave with a smile. (Courtesy of June and Don Plapp.)

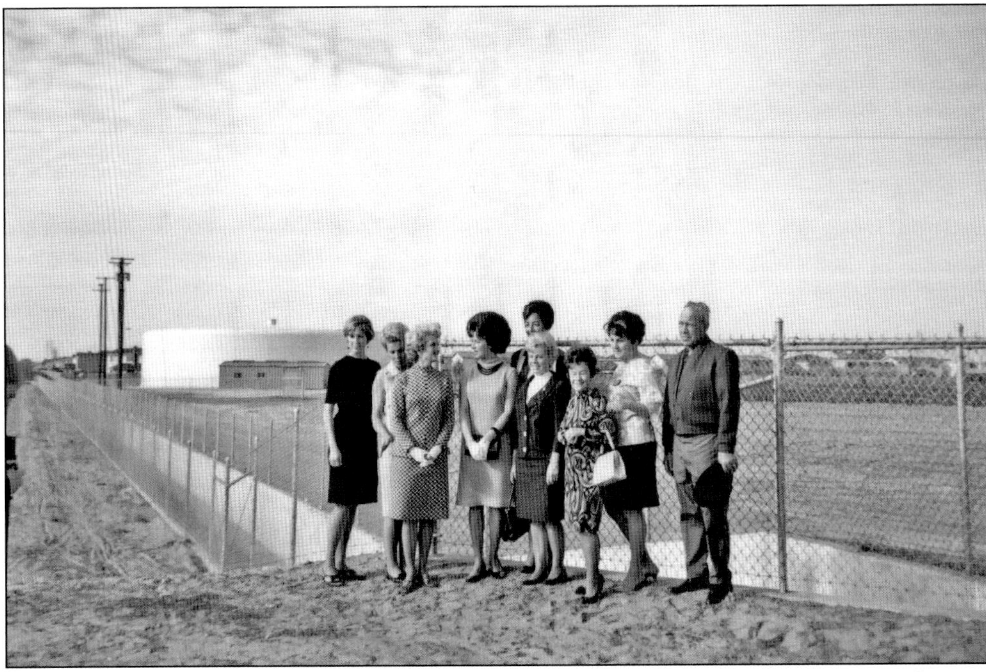

Celebrating the completion of another section of the storm drain and water reservoir on January 12, 1968, (see page 46) are, from left to right, Carolyn Patterson, unidentified, Bea Sorrells, June Plapp, Florine McNutt (behind June), Nadine Sherwood, Virginia Bonar, Mary Thrasher, and Mayor Pete Bouma. (Courtesy of June and Don Plapp.)

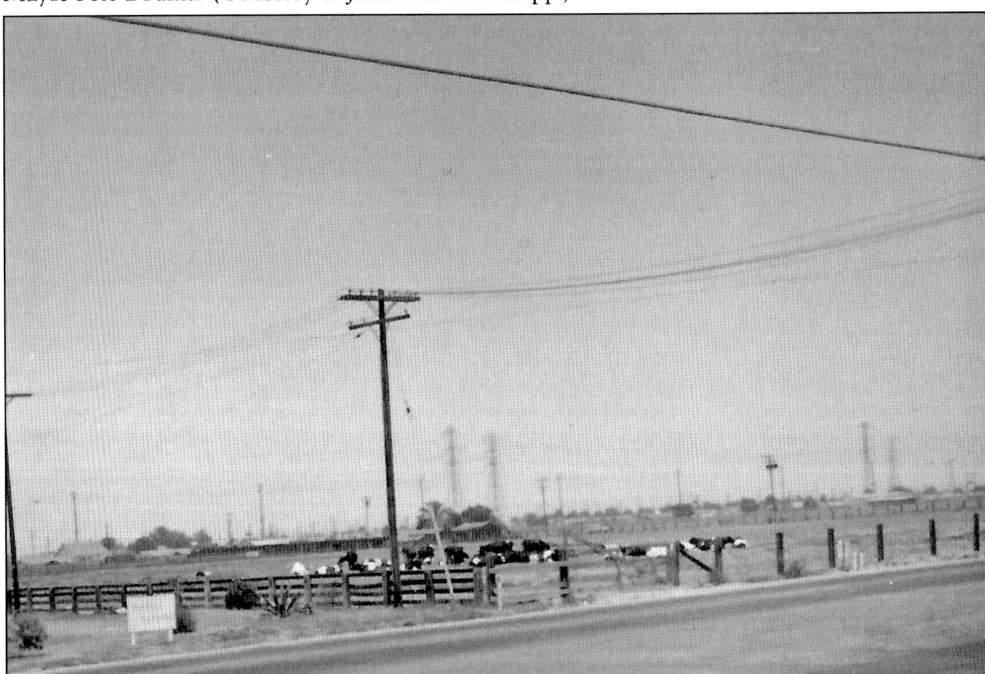

This is the site of the future Mullikin Medical Center looking north from de Vries Lane across La Palma Avenue, which runs east and west. (Courtesy of City of La Palma Archives.)

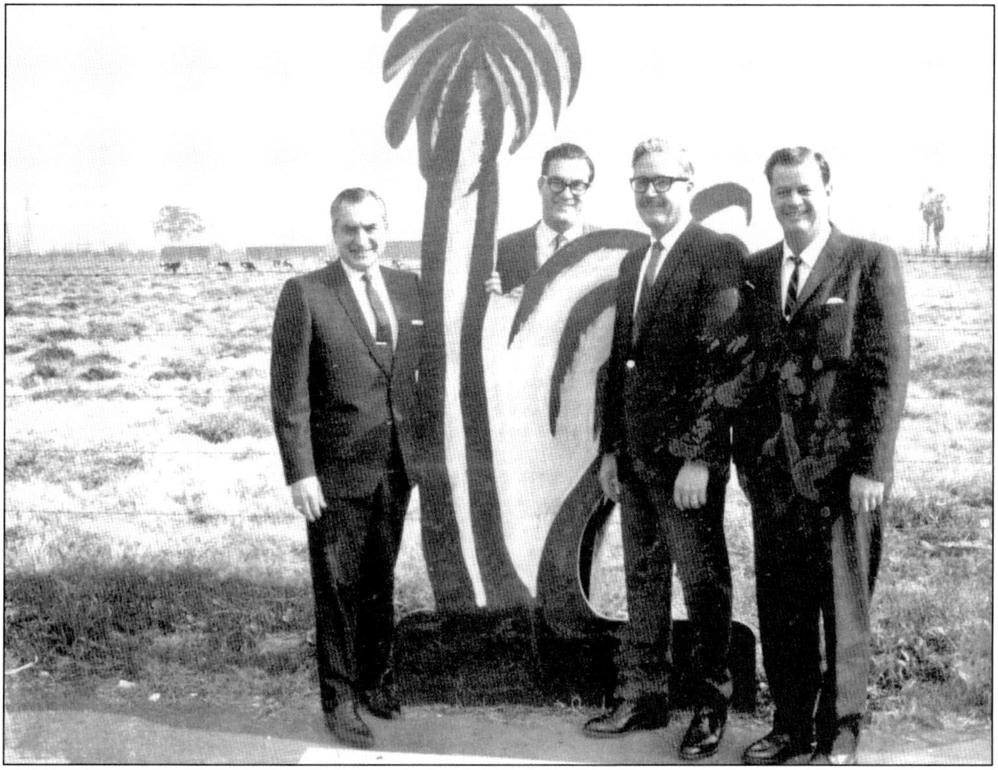

Unveiling the plans for the Mullikin Medical Center are, from left to right, Beri Saeli, M.D.; Alter T. Mullikin, M.D.; Jake J. Westra, councilman and former owner of the property; and Clyde McLaughlin, councilman. The palm trees in the background were designed and painted by Dixie Abrahamson, Les Sorrels, and June Plapp. (Courtesy of June and Don Plapp.)

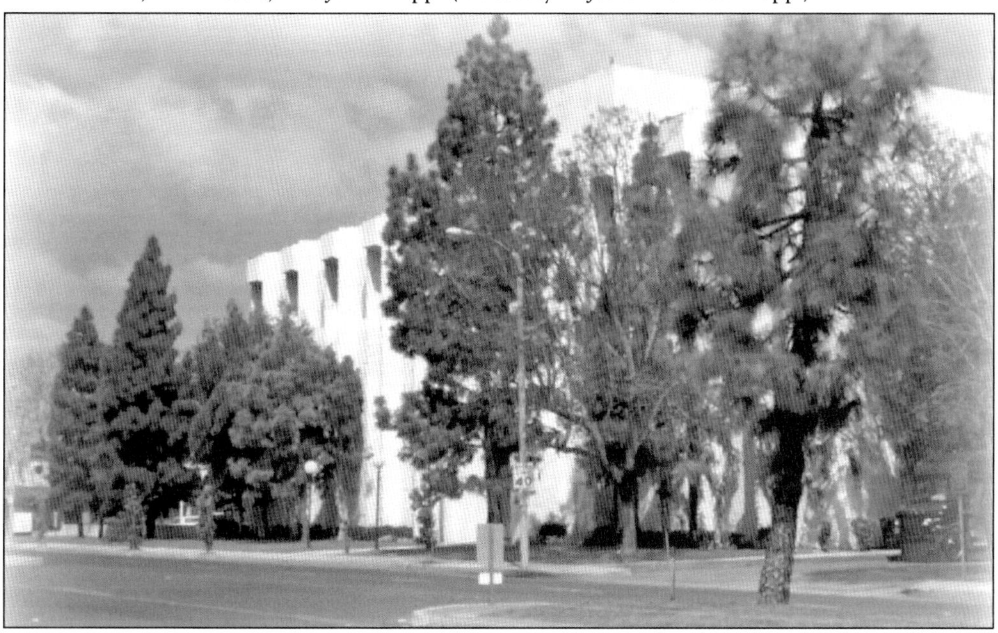

This is the Mullikin Medical Center in 2004. (Courtesy of Ron and Elfriede Mac Iver.)

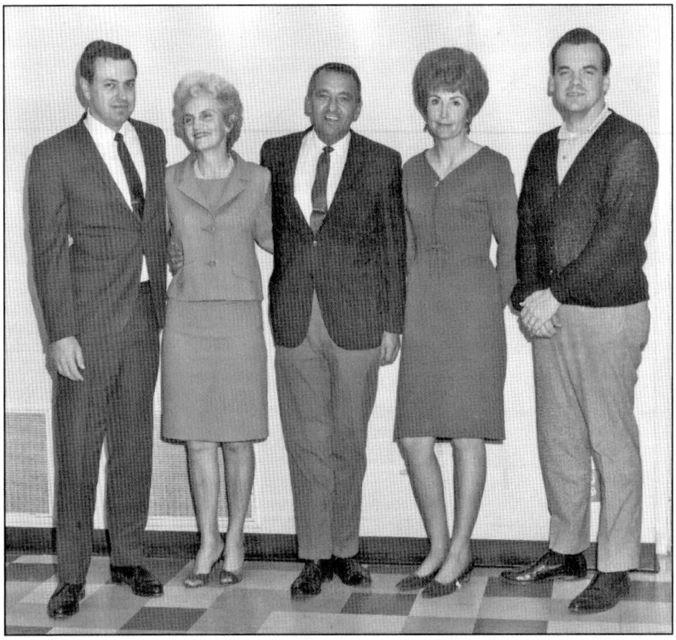

New directors were elected to the La Palma Chamber of Commerce. From left to right are Don Plapp and Bea Sorrells, charter members of the chamber both stepping down after three years of service; and new directors Gerrit Fikse; Margaret McLaughlin, a charter member of the chamber; and George Luedeke, president of the Steve Luther School PTO. (Courtesy of June and Don Plapp.)

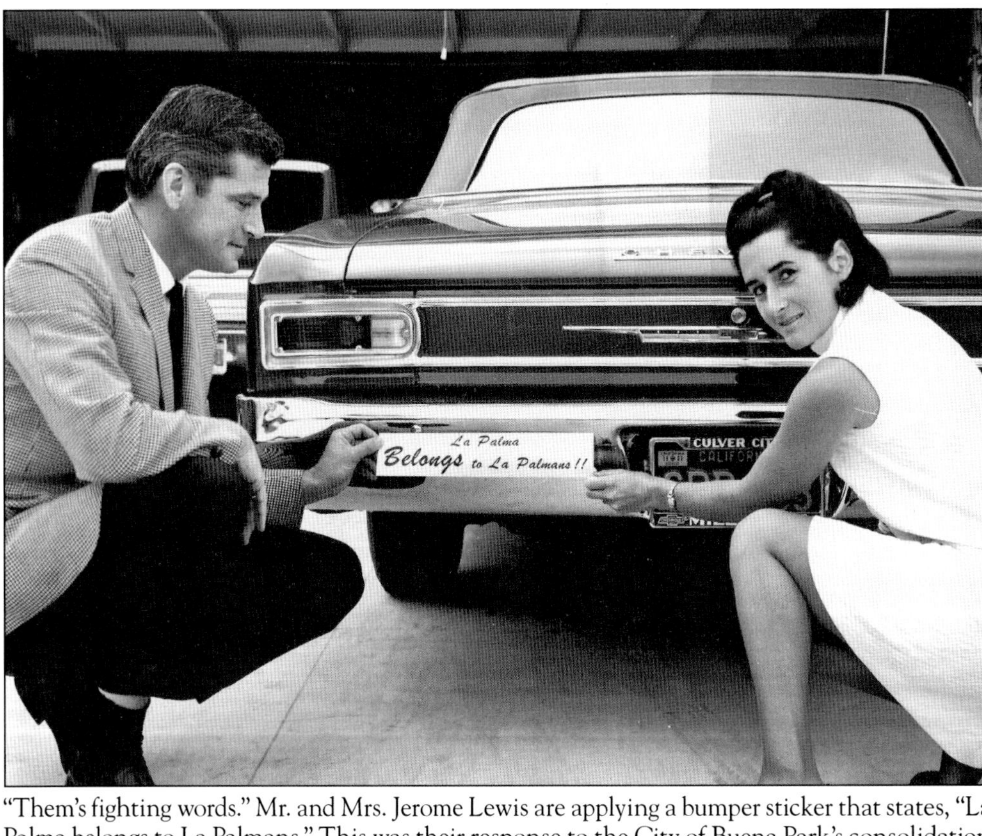

"Them's fighting words." Mr. and Mrs. Jerome Lewis are applying a bumper sticker that states, "La Palma belongs to La Palmans." This was their response to the City of Buena Park's consolidation plan, which was Buena Park's second attempt to acquire La Palma. (Courtesy of June and Don Plapp.)

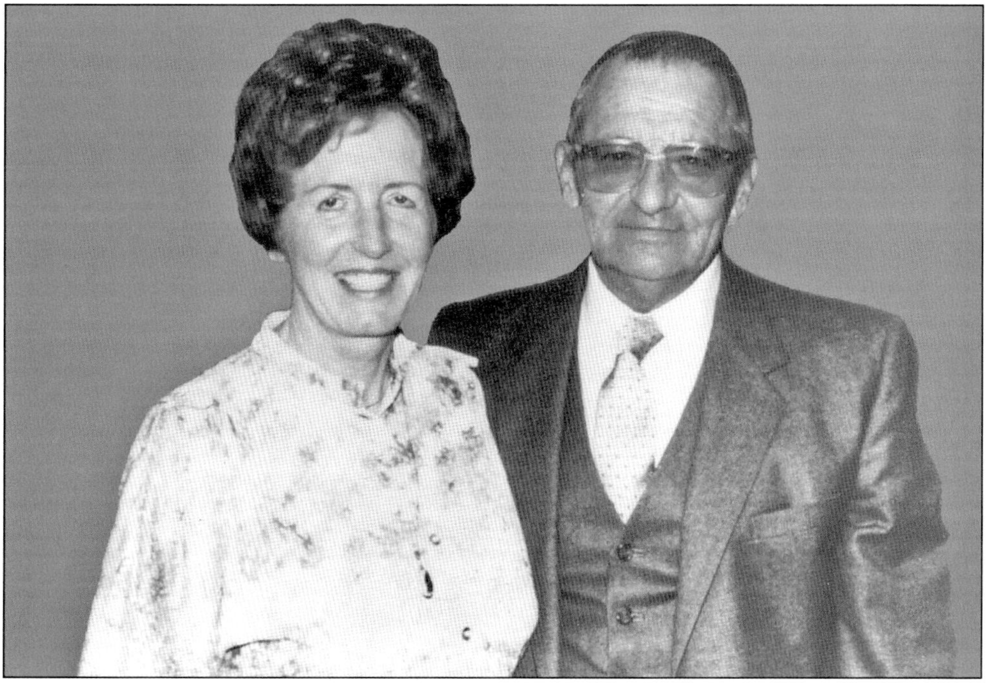

Hoppy and Gerrit Fikse lived in Cypress in the 1950s. Gerrit and his brother Tymen owned a hay business in Orangethorpe and Moody, where McDonald's is now located. They sold hay brought in by truck from the Imperial Valley and the San Joaquin Valley. The farmers would come to the hay lot, agree on a price, and drivers would then deliver to their dairies. When the hay business ended, Hoppy and Gerrit decided to stay in La Palma. The Mushegain Dairy had been taken by eminent domain to build Kennedy High School. (The map below shows the two houses with the barn in the middle.) The Fikse's bought these two homes and had them moved to Thelma Avenue, where they stand today. Gerrit became a realtor and a very active member/director of the newly formed La Palma Chamber of Commerce. (Above, courtesy Hoppy Fikse; below, courtesy Ron and Elfriede Mac Iver.)

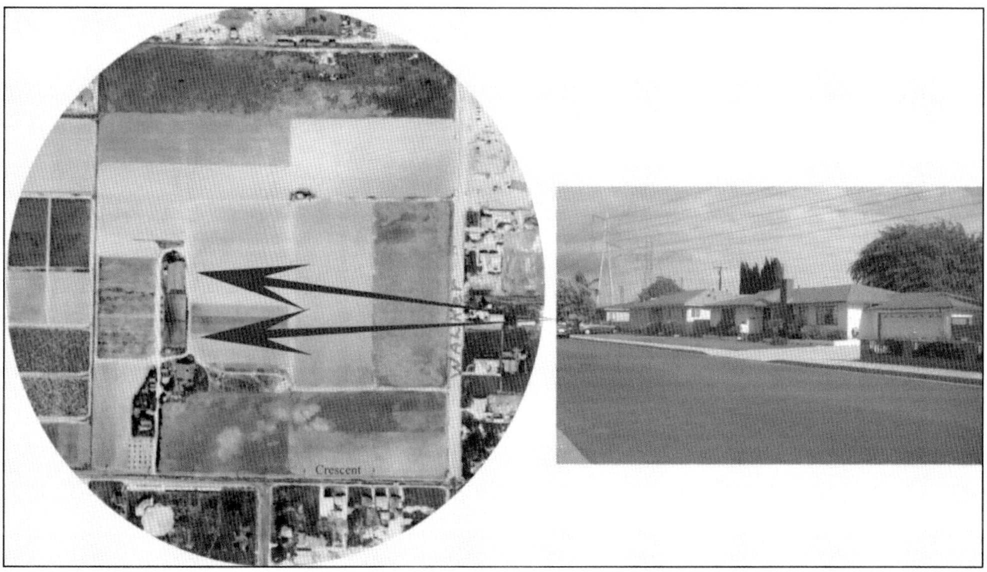

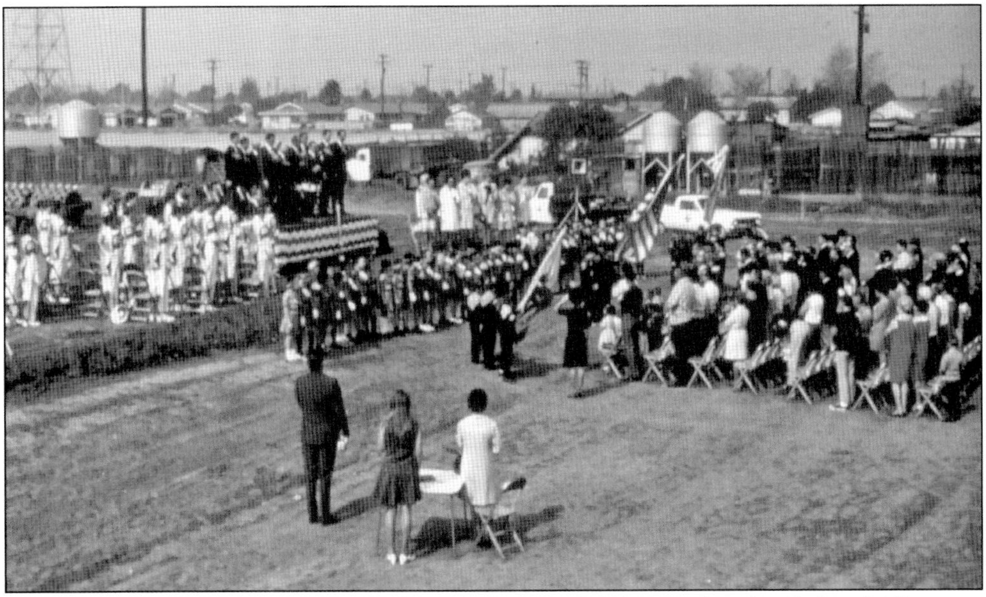

Nappy Sekiguchi, president of the chamber of commerce, led the crowd in the Pledge of Allegiance during the ground-breaking ceremony for the new civic center on November 2, 1968. The civic center is located at 7822 Walker Street. (Courtesy of City of La Palma Archives.)

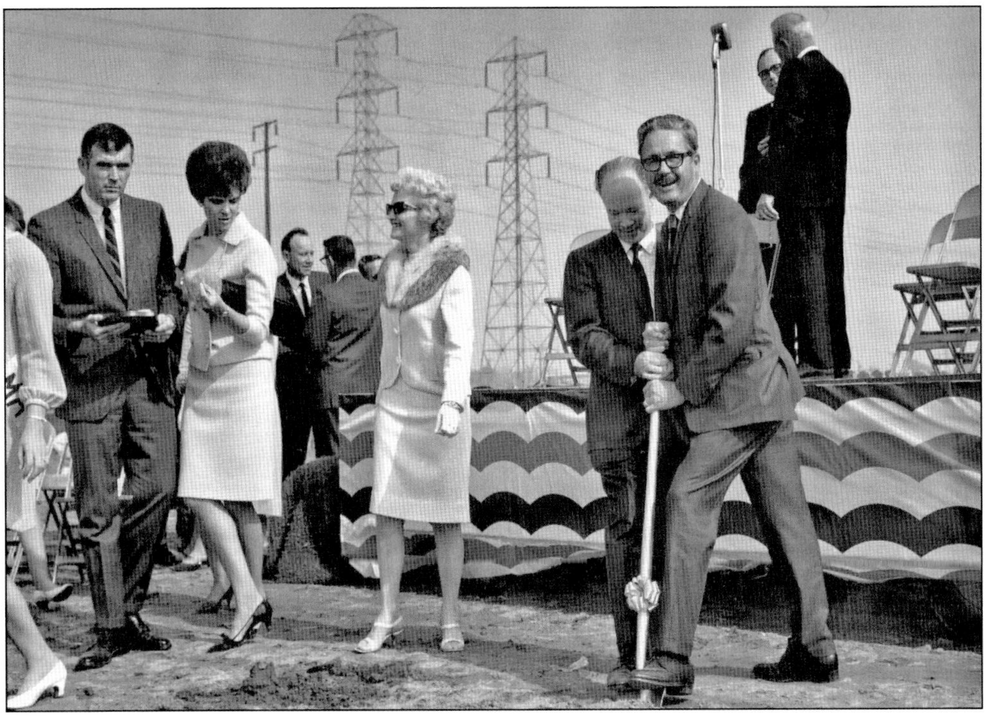

Posing for the ground-breaking ceremony picture are, from left to right, (in the foreground) councilman John Berton with his wife, Joy, Bea Sorrells, and Burt Wesenberg and Mayor Jake Westra sharing the ceremonial shovel; (in the background) unidentified speaking with councilman Paul Furman (back to camera, left background) and (on the podium) unidentified speaking with councilman Pete Bouma (back to camera). (Courtesy of City of La Palma Archives.)

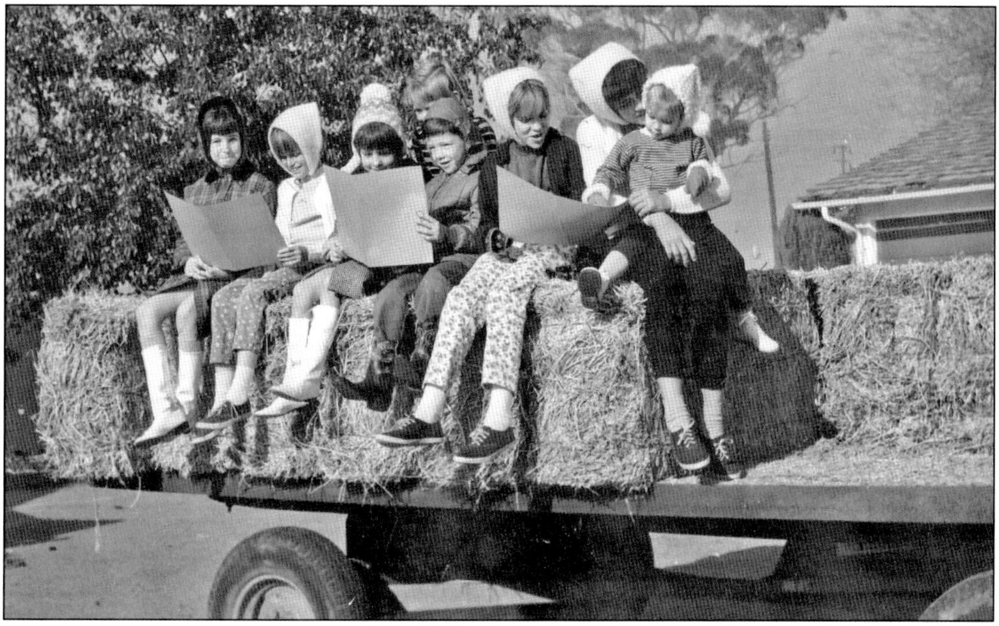

The tree-lighting ceremonies in 1968 included Christmas caroling at the Bank of America building and community hay rides to Cypress Park, where Santa was waiting to chat with the youngsters and his elves were serving refreshments. This picture appeared in the *News Enterprise* on Thursday, December 12, 1968. From left to right are Susan Thrasher, Kathy Berton, Kathy Thrasher, Brenda Westra, Jan Berton, Denise Berton, Mrs. John Berton, and Christine Berton. (Courtesy of John and Joy Berton.)

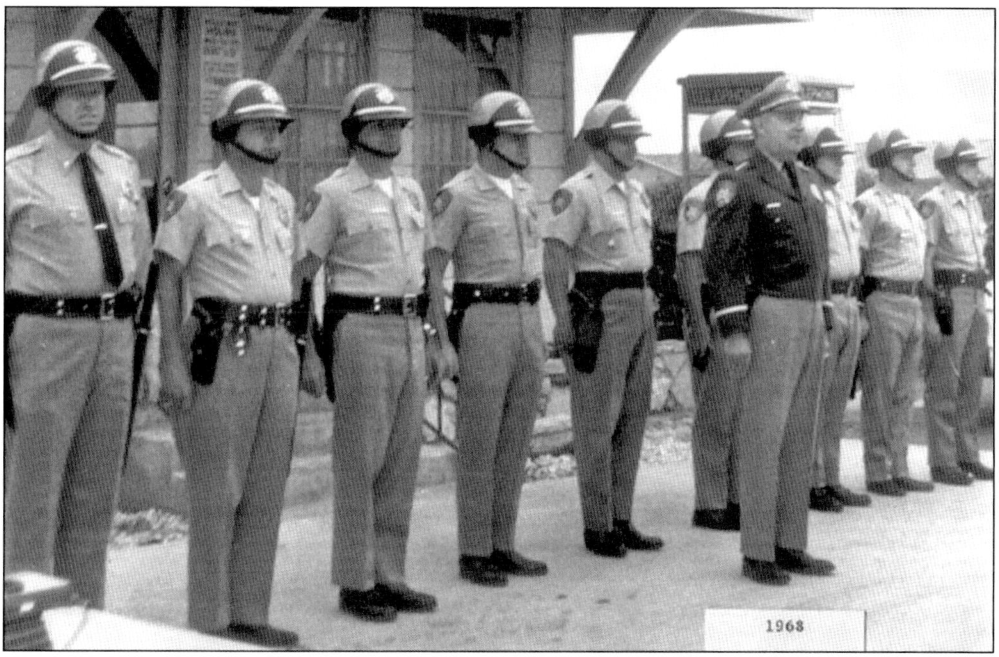

The police department stands at attention behind police chief John Sheppard. Chief Sheppard served from March 1964 through December 1969. Orbrey Duke, the officer standing on the left of the picture, became chief in January 1970. (Courtesy of La Palma Police Department Archives.)

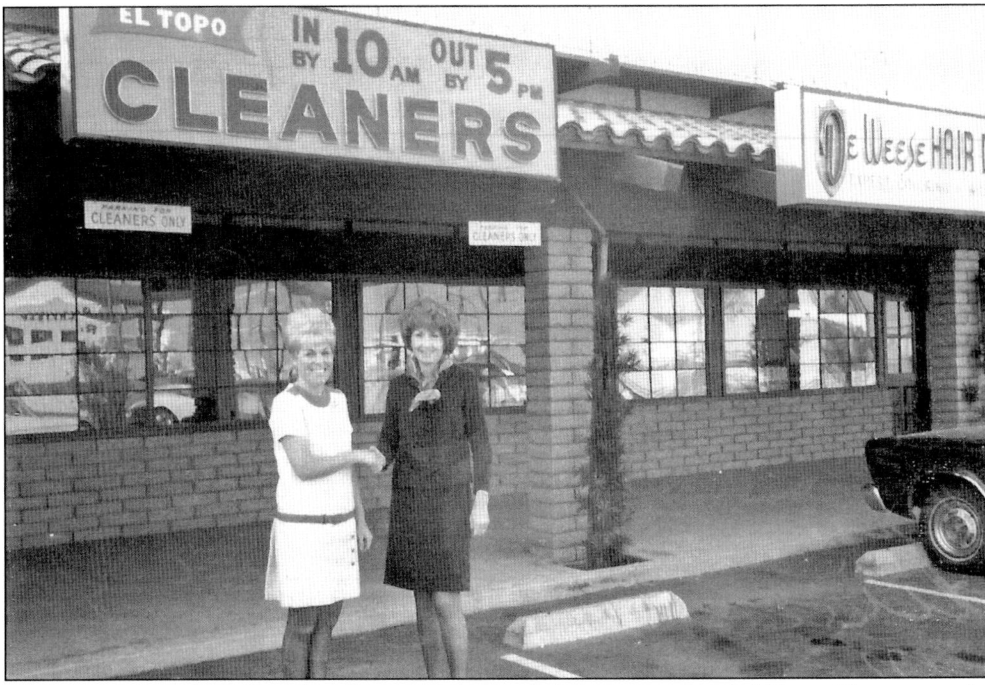

Margaret McLaughlin (right) welcomes Judy Guglielmana, owner of El Topo Cleaners, to La Palma. According to the May 1969 *La Palma Review*, the early chamber of commerce consisted of business owners and citizens who volunteered their time for various civic activities, such as the Easter egg hunt, tree lighting at Christmas, and the La Palma parades. Also welcomed that day was John Reinhart, "John the Barber." (Courtesy of June and Don Plapp.)

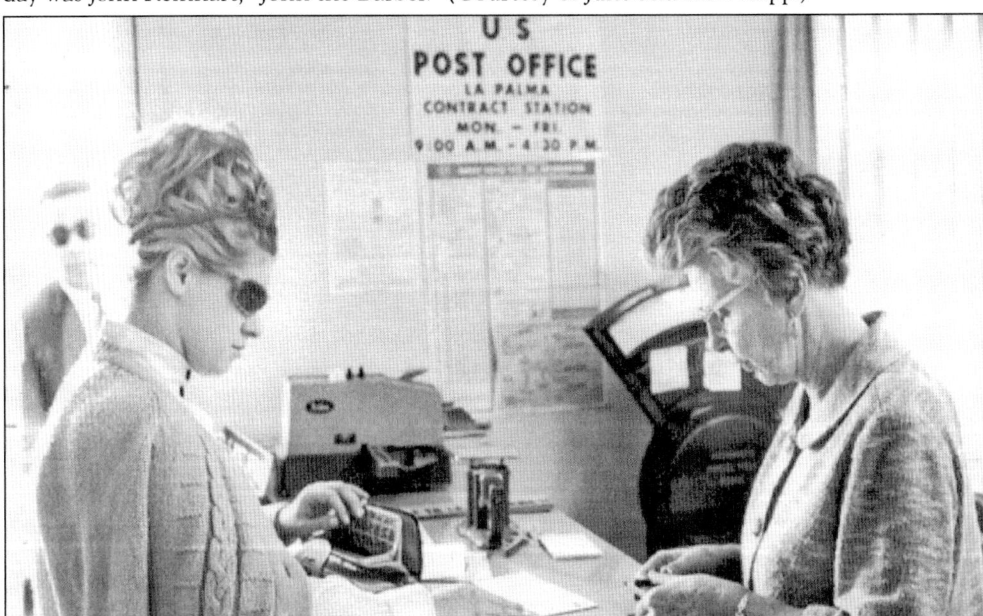

Madge Wasson is at work in the newly opened U.S. Post Office, La Palma Contract Station, in the city hall annex in March 1969. The La Palma Post Office did not last long. (Courtesy of City of La Palma Archives.)

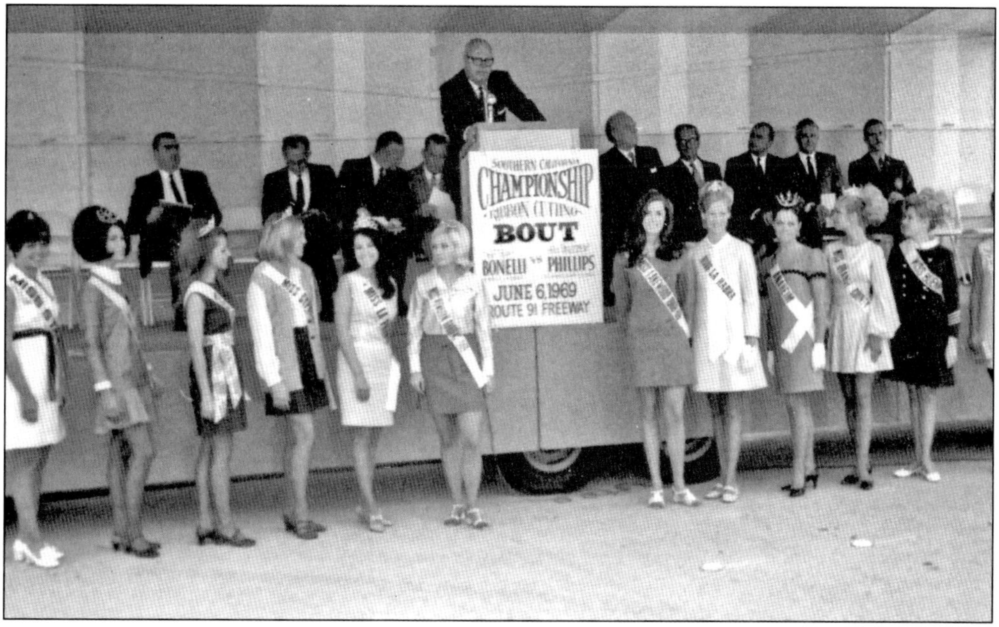

The opening of the Route 91 Freeway link through La Palma on June 6, 1969, was a well-attended, festive occasion. Supervisor Frank G. Bonelli of Los Angeles and William Phillips of Orange County participated. Miss La Palma, Norma Arias, and other beauty queens representing neighboring cities in the ribbon-cutting ceremony helped with the event. The sign at the podium advertised a "Southern California Championship Ribbon Cutting Bout, Route 91 Freeway" between the two supervisors. After the ceremonies, there were games for young and old. (Both, courtesy of City of La Palma Archives.)

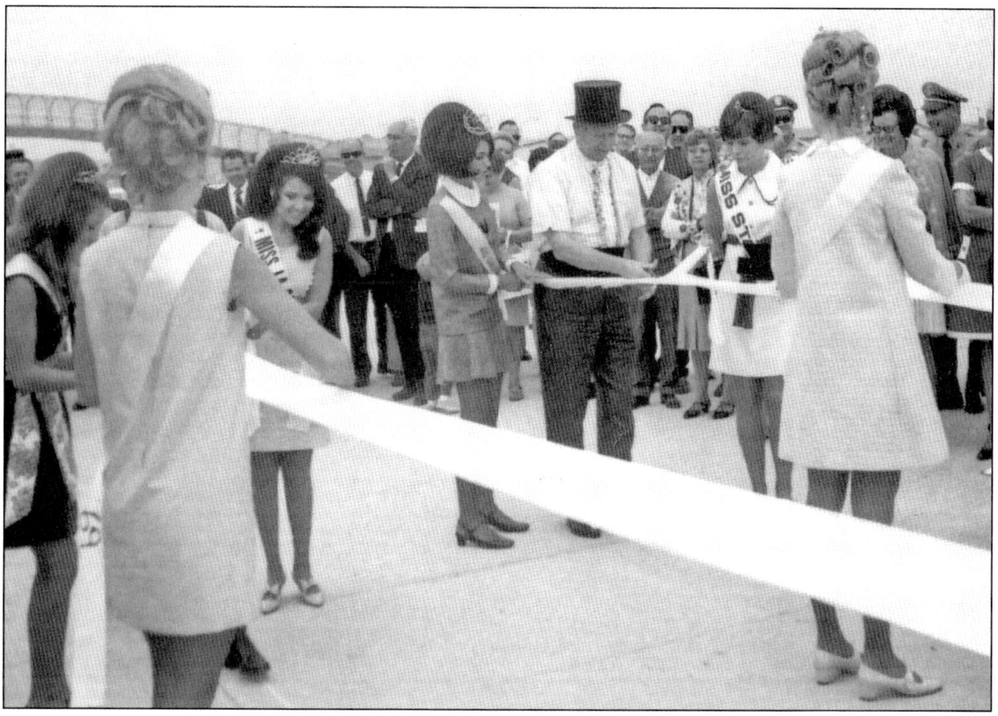

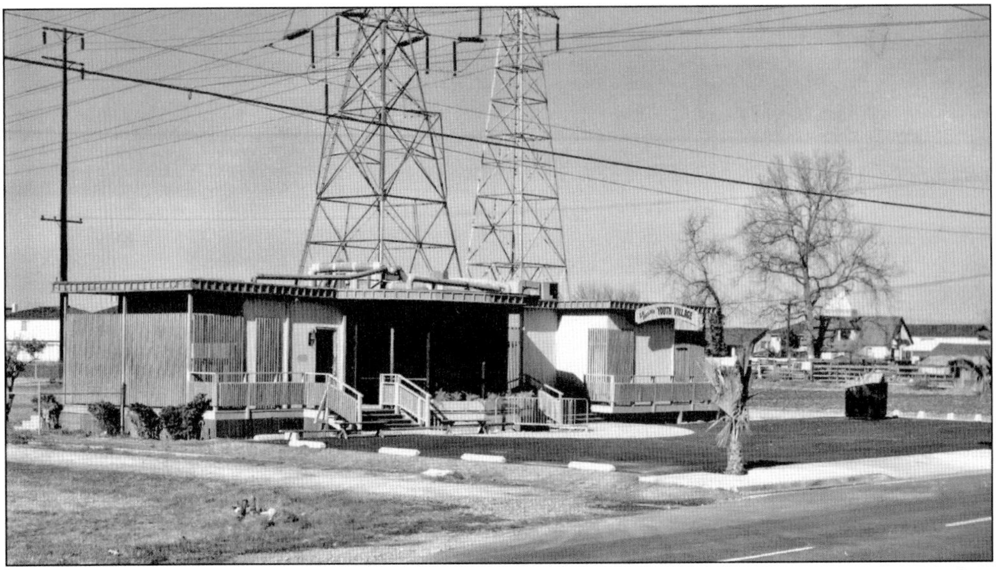

La Palma Youth Village was purchased for $5,000 from the Robert H. Grant sales office for Stardust Homes. The sales office was originally in the area north of Orangethorpe Avenue and Moody Street. It was moved to Walker Street, south of the Edison right-of-way, and the three-fourths acre of land was leased from the Centralia School District for $1 a year in 1969. (Courtesy of City of La Palma Archives.)

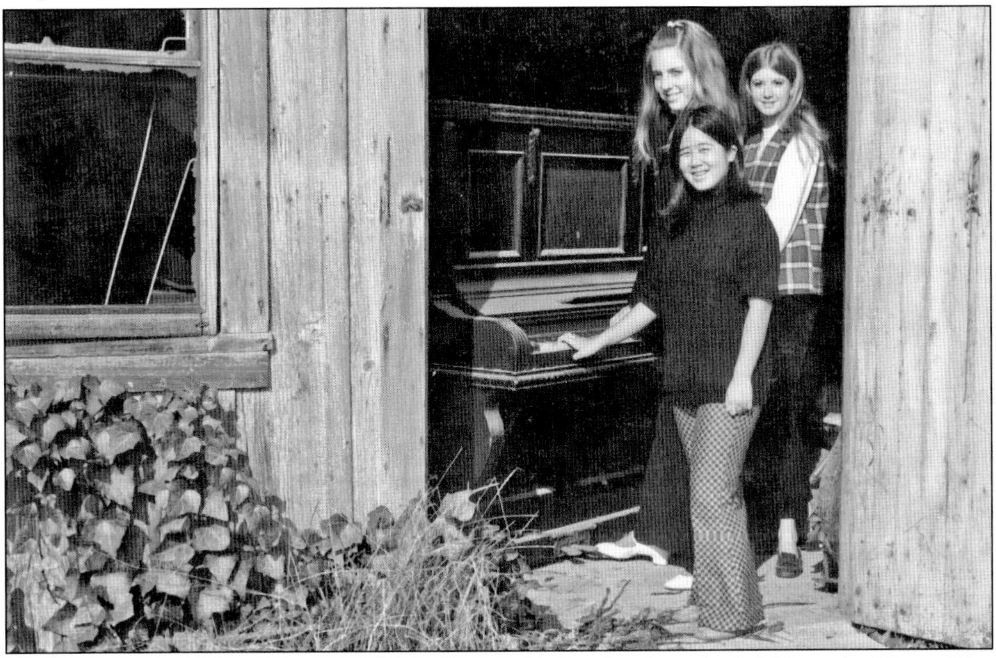

To prepare the land for the new Youth Village, it had to be cleared of old farm buildings. The teenagers, future beneficiaries of the village, were enlisted to help. In the process, a piano was discovered in one of the buildings to be demolished. From left to right, the "finders" are Robin Sekiguchi, Carol Sorrells, and Linda McLaughlin. The piano was dirty and rusty, but was able to be reconditioned and returned to its original purpose in the Youth Village. (Courtesy of City of La Palma Archives.)

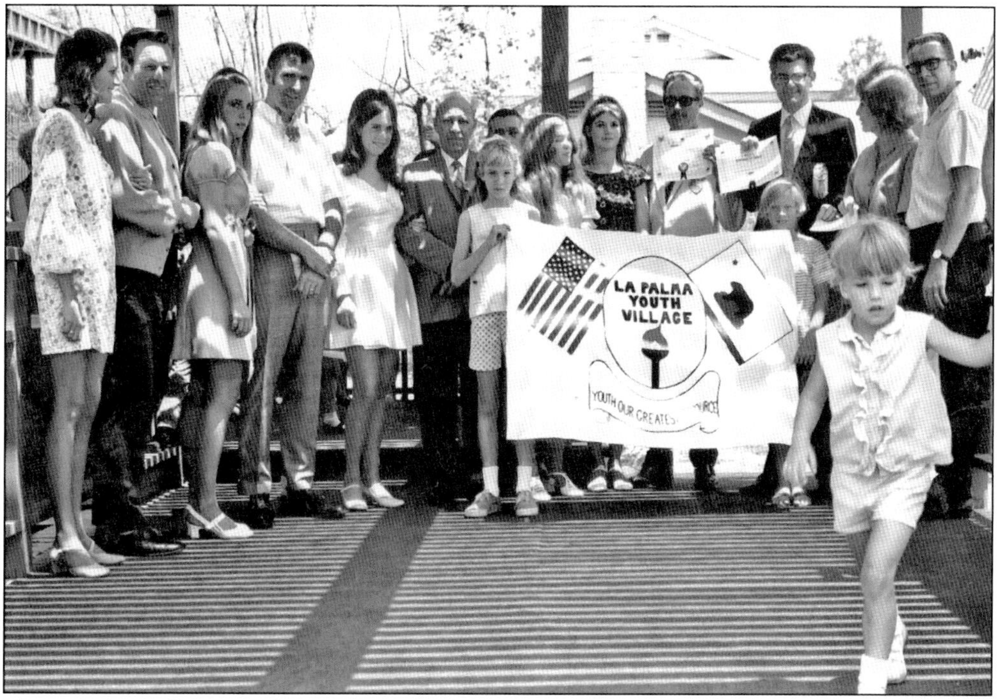

The La Palma Village grand opening was held July 20, 1969, the day of the Apollo 11 moonwalk. The audience watched the momentous event on a small screen. Everyone was hushed as they listened to Neil Armstrong proclaim, "That's one small step for man, one giant leap for mankind." From left to right are Gwen Bayes; Lt. Orbrey Duke, acting chief of La Palma Police Department; Carol Sorrells; councilman John Berton; Leslie Sorrells; councilman Peter G. Bouma; councilman Paul Furman; Laura Crick; Lynda McLaughlin; Mayor Jake J. Westra; Max Tipton, vice president Robert H. Grant Company; Margaret McLaughlin, president of Youth Village Corporation; and Jack Nelson, Youth Village vice president. The two girls holding the sign are Elizabeth Nelson (left) and Wendy Nelson. The small child in the front of the picture is unidentified. (Courtesy of Ron and Elfriede Mac Iver.)

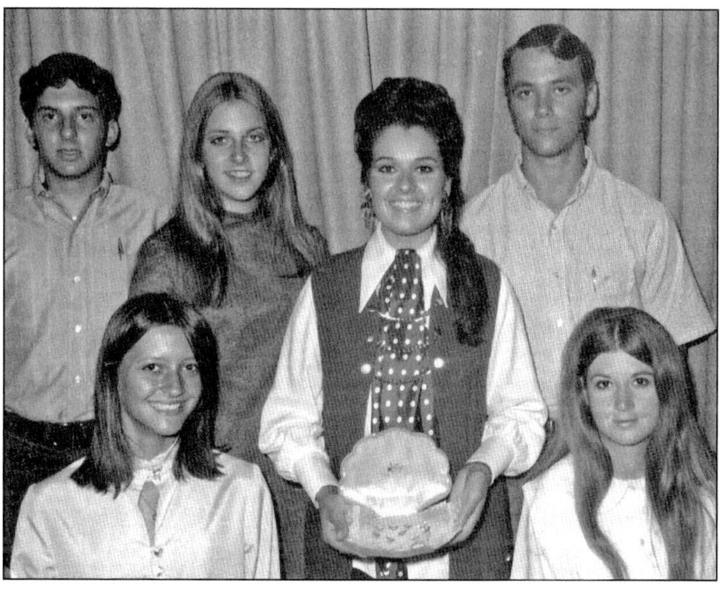

La Palma Youth Village officers accept pins of office on September 9, 1969. From left to right are (first row) Gwen Bayes, membership, and Lynda McLaughlin, president; (second row) Steve Levy, communications; Carol Sorrells, secretary; Norma Arias, Miss La Palma; and Bill De Forrest, vice president. (Courtesy of City of La Palma Archives.)

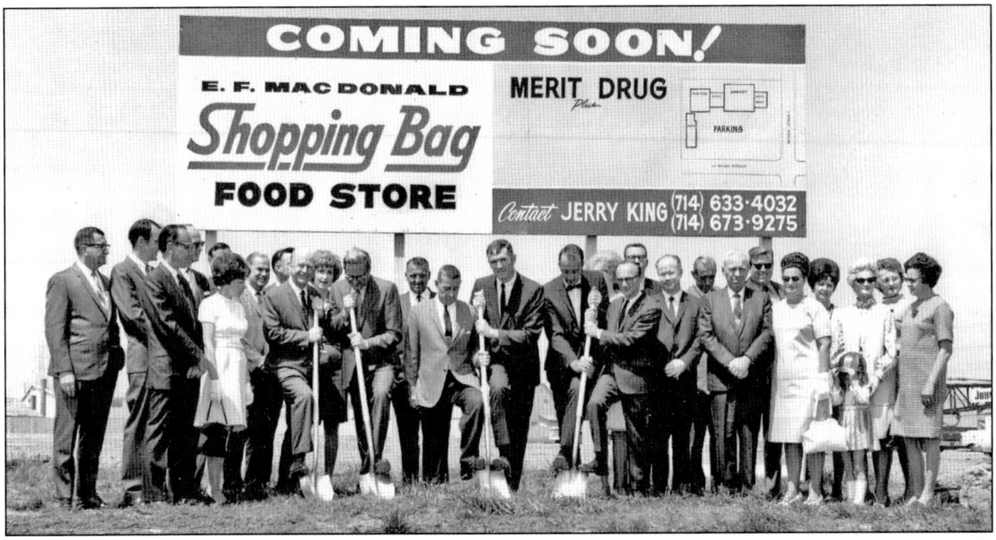

The ground-breaking ceremony for the Shopping Bag food store, located on the west side of Moody Street and La Palma Avenue, took place on April 7, 1969. According to the *La Palma Review* in May 1969, this was formerly the location of the De Groot dairy farm. Norman Bolstad, president of Shopping Bag, commented on how impressed he was by the La Palma turnout. The holders of shovels are, from left to right, Norman Bolstad, Jake Westra, Paul Furman, John Berton, Jerome Patterson, and Larry Freedman. The rest of the large audience is unidentified. (Courtesy of City of La Palma Archives.)

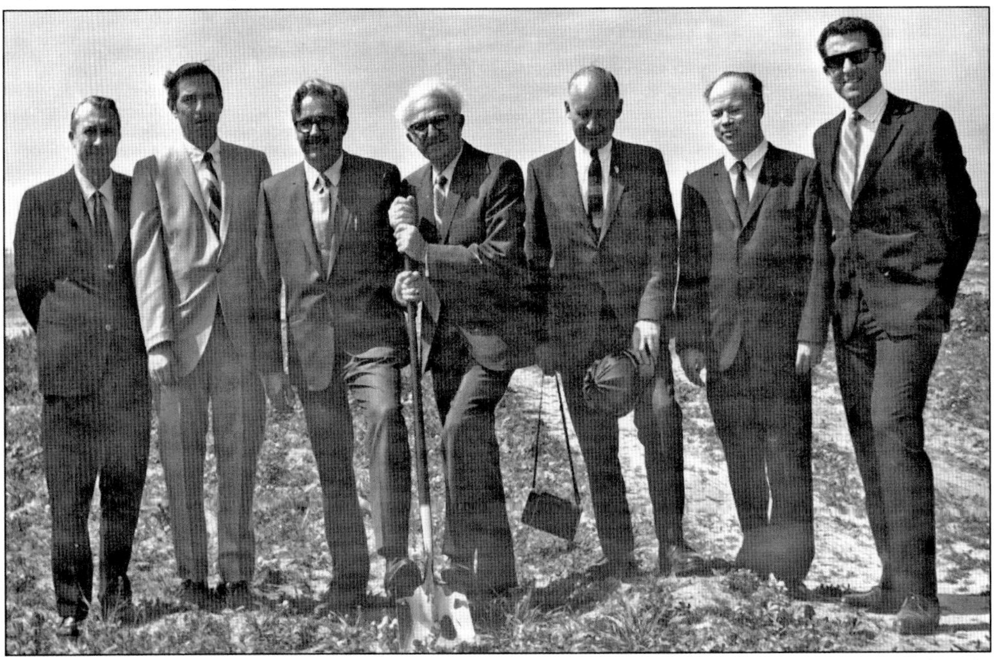

Orchid Products, Concel Incorporated was the first industry to build in La Palma's Industrial Park. The ground-breaking ceremony took place on March 17, 1969. Taking part in the ceremony are, from left to right, David Witherly, design engineer; ? Johnson, contractor's representative; Mayor Jake J. Westra; Al Melnick, president of Orchid Products; Blair Anderson; Burton Wesenberg, La Palma city manager; and Ned Wolfe, project engineer. (Courtesy of City of La Palma Archives.)

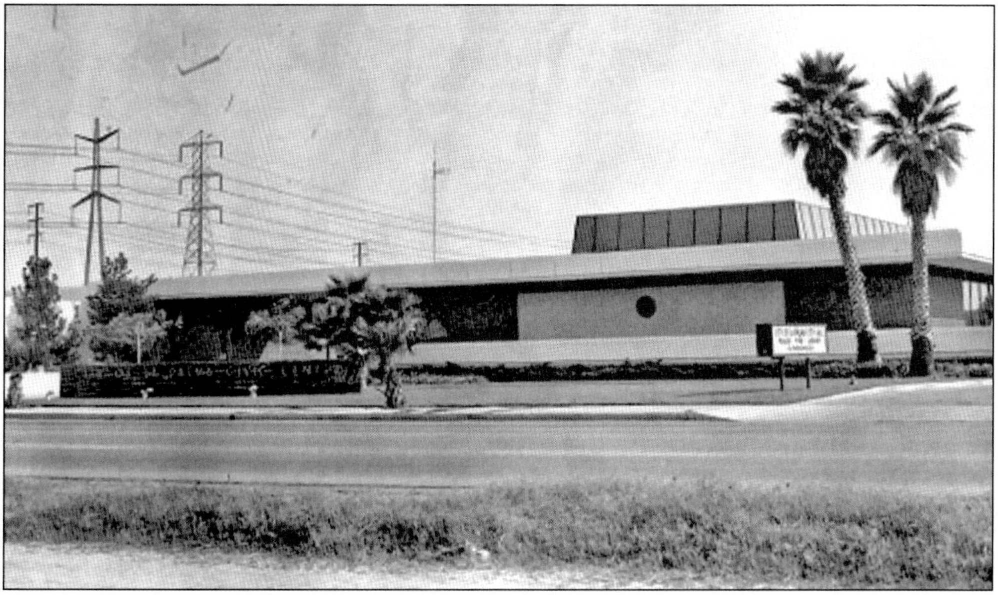

The La Palma City Hall dedication took place on Saturday, September 27, 1969. Central Park was scheduled to be constructed on the raw land behind the grassy patch visible in the foreground of the picture. (Courtesy of City of La Palma Archives.)

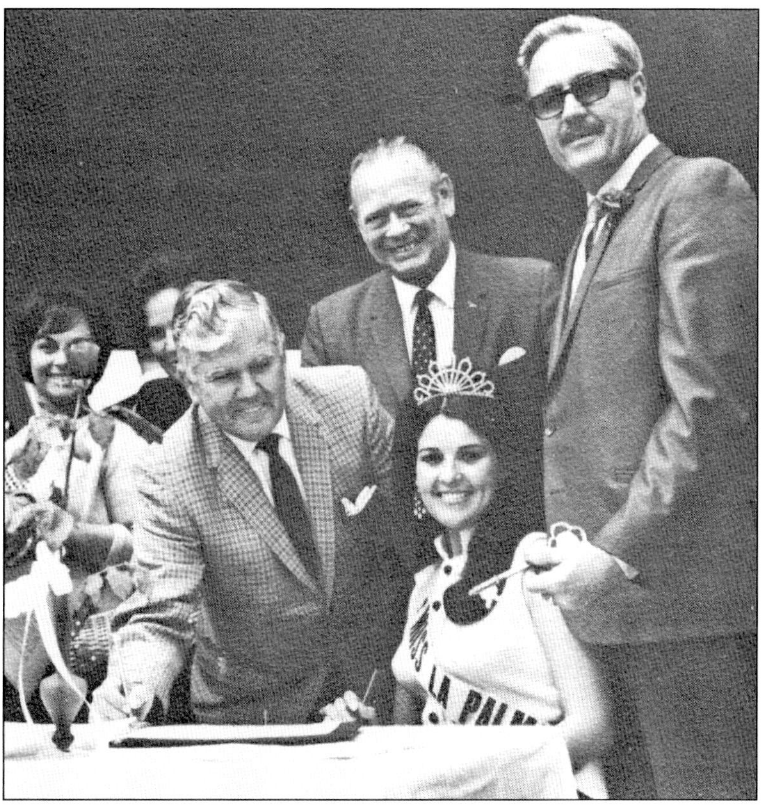

According to the *La Palma Review* in November 1969, the key to the civic center was presented to Mayor Jake Westra as, from left to right, congressman William Hanna, supervisor William Phillips, and Miss La Palma Norma Arias look on. (Courtesy of City of La Palma Archives.)

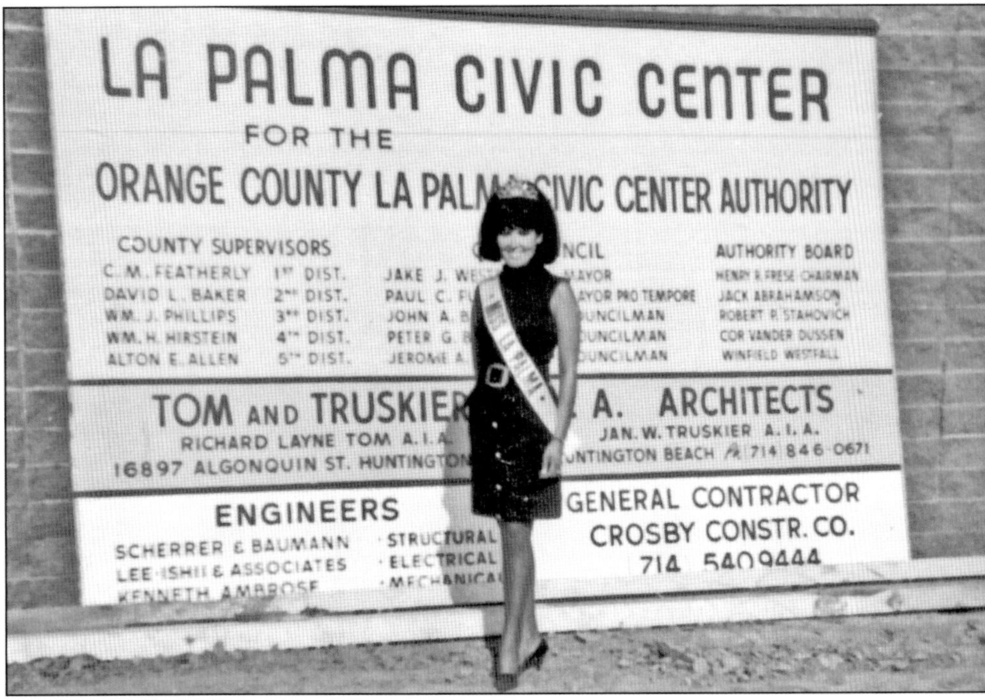

The La Palma Civic Center Authority recognizes the various entities responsible for the successful completion of La Palma's Civic Center. Norma Arias, Miss La Palma, stands in front of a sign listing their names during the grand opening celebration on September 27, 1969. (Courtesy of City of La Palma Archives.)

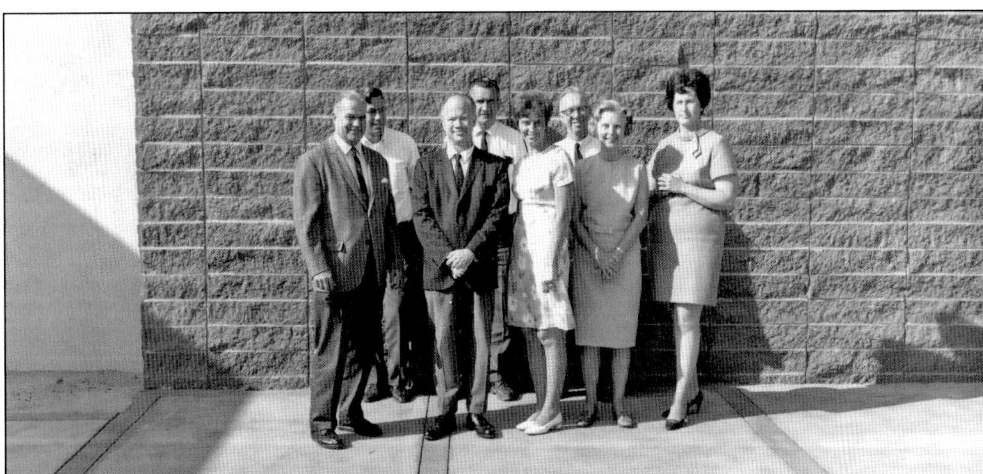

The first city hall staff is, from left to right, (first row) William Dieterle, building director; Burt Wesenberg, city manager; and secretaries Mary Happel, Madge Wasson, and Karen Poulson; (second row) Dale Patterson, civil engineer assistant; William Raymond, building inspector; and Joe Truxaw, city engineer. (Courtesy of City of La Palma Archives.)

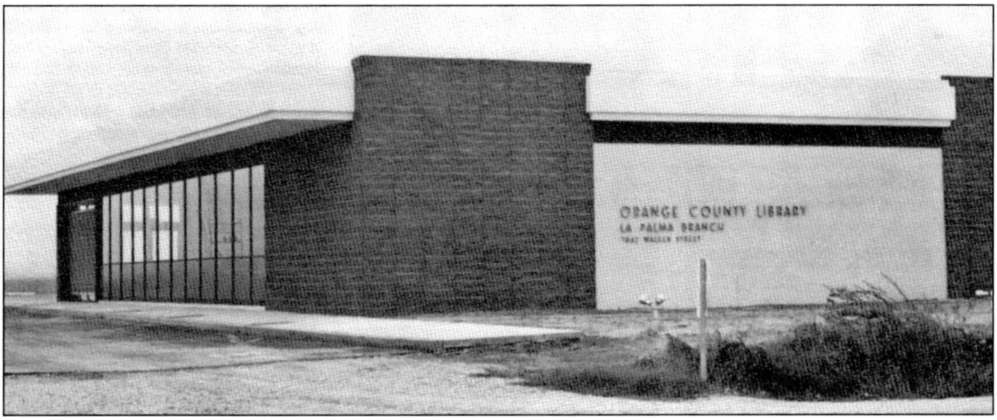

The La Palma library, next to city hall, opened its doors to the public on October 4, 1969. Mayor Jake Westra received library card number one from head librarian Lionel Ascher. The chairperson of the cultural committee, Bea Sorrells, and committee member Mavis Crick presented the key to the city to librarian Ascher. There were 180 library cards issued and 400 books borrowed on the library's first day. (Courtesy of La Palma Library Archives.)

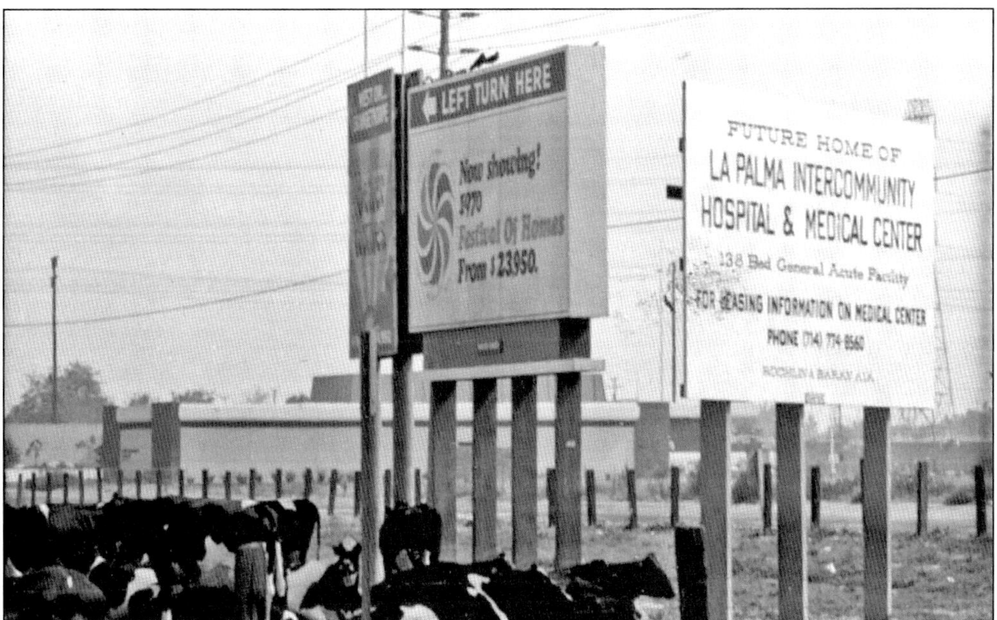

Cows still live in La Palma as part of the Westra Dairy. The sign announces the future home of the La Palma Intercommunity Hospital and Medical Center, which will be built on that property. The newly opened library and the civic center, slightly north, can be seen across Walker Street. (Courtesy of La Palma Library Archives.)

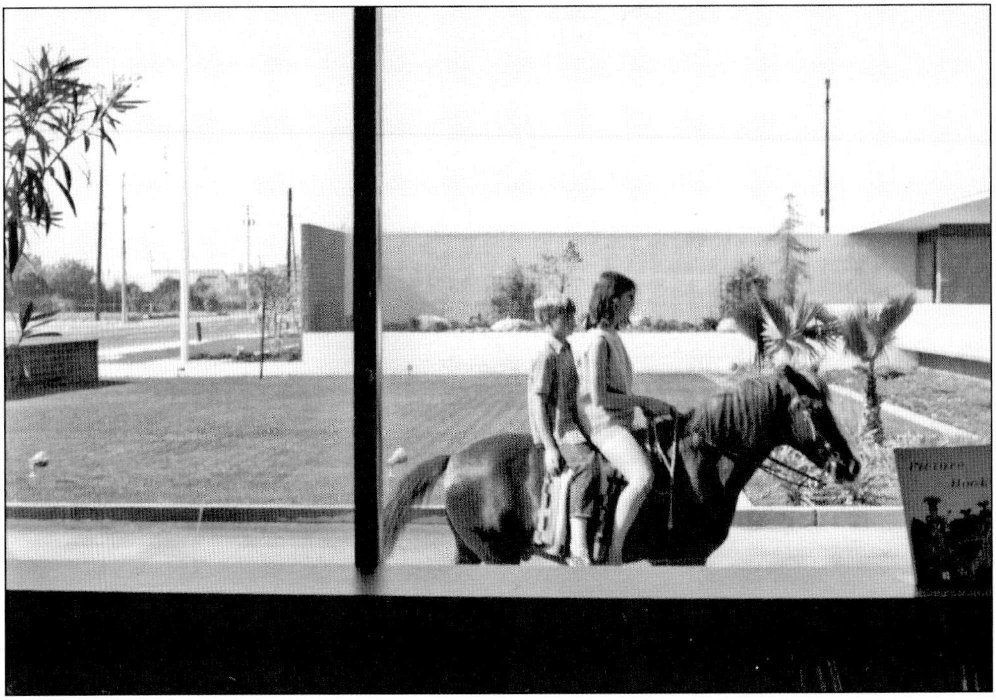

Riding a horse to the library was not uncommon in the rural, early days of the city. This picture of an unidentified equestrian was taken from inside the library. The picture below, taken from the front of the library building, shows the civic center at the top left of the picture. The road leading into both buildings is the white line, in front of the sign. The board and stakes are for the sidewalk, to be built as Walker Street. (Both, courtesy of La Palma Library Archives.)

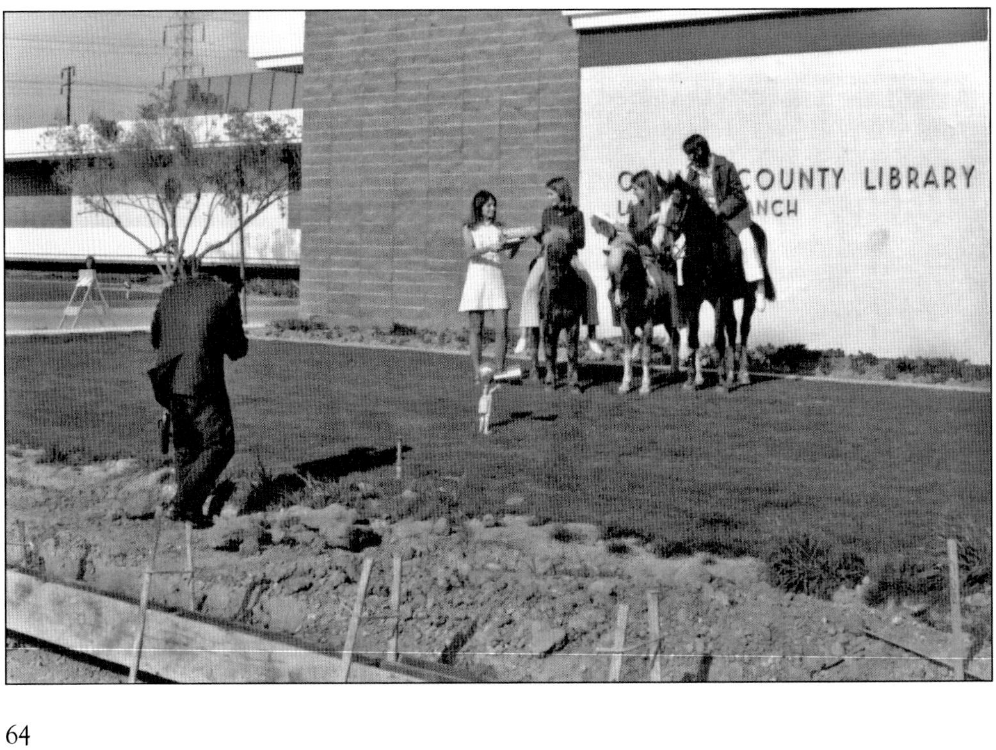

Head librarian Jesse Thompson brought fun to the early residents of La Palma. The children looked forward to her personal touch and displays that made everyone feel a welcome part of their library. (Courtesy of La Palma Library Archives.)

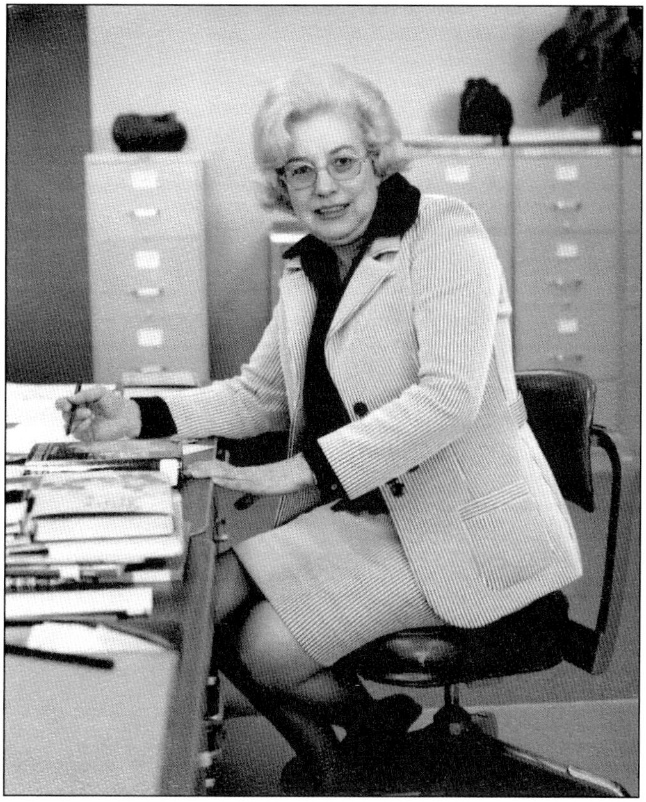

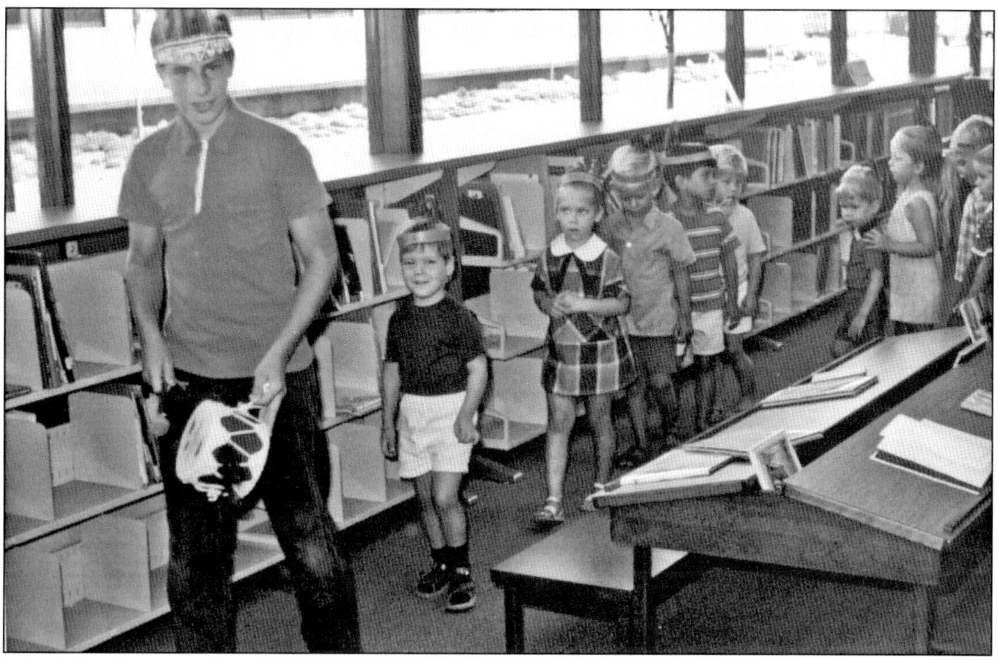

Chris Mac Iver marches preschoolers around the library dressed in Native American regalia. The youngsters looked to the library for special events, and teenagers participated in the activities held for them in the Youth Village. (Courtesy of City of La Palma Archives.)

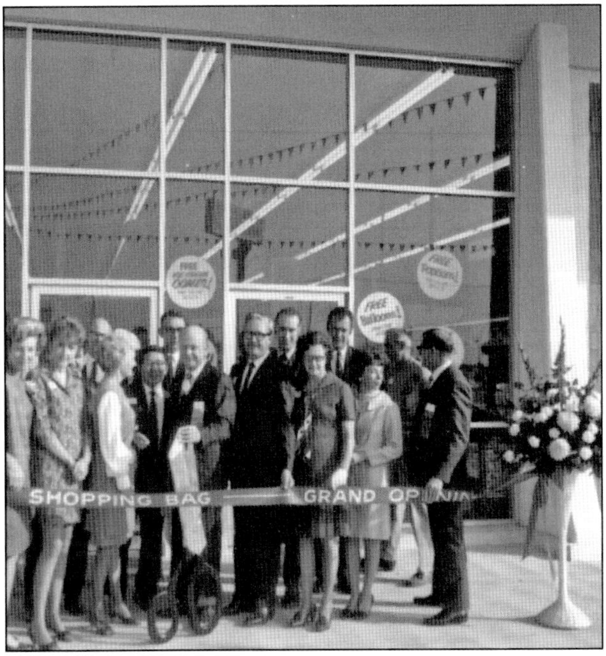

According to the *La Palma Review* in November 1969, the grand opening of Shopping Bag brought the city council and chamber of commerce together for a ribbon-cutting ceremony on October 1, 1969. Shopping Bag owner E. F. MacDonald cuts the ribbon, later treating everyone to ice cream and souvenirs. La Palma residents returned the favor with their enthusiastic shopping. Four other businesses were similarly welcomed that month: Camelot Drugs, Magic Thimble Fabric Shop, Ron's Draperies, and a coin laundry. (Courtesy of June and Don Plapp.)

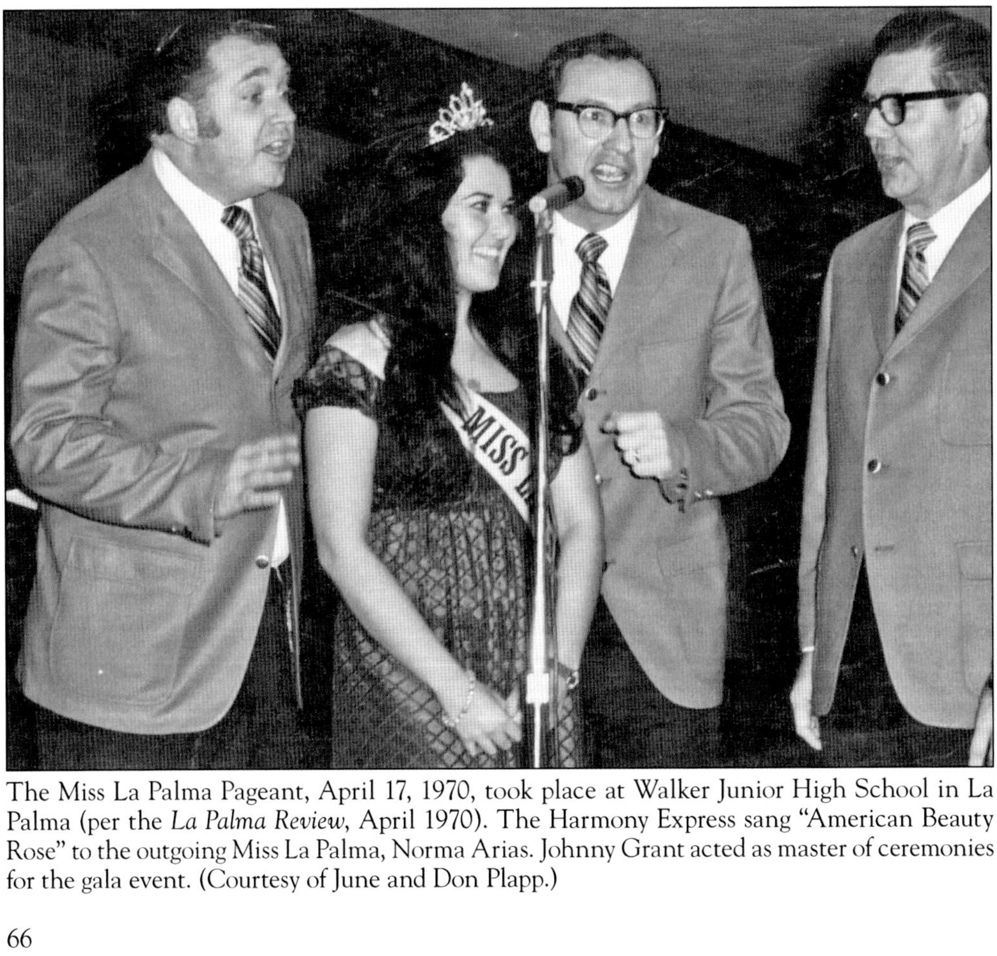

The Miss La Palma Pageant, April 17, 1970, took place at Walker Junior High School in La Palma (per the *La Palma Review*, April 1970). The Harmony Express sang "American Beauty Rose" to the outgoing Miss La Palma, Norma Arias. Johnny Grant acted as master of ceremonies for the gala event. (Courtesy of June and Don Plapp.)

Three

A Modern City

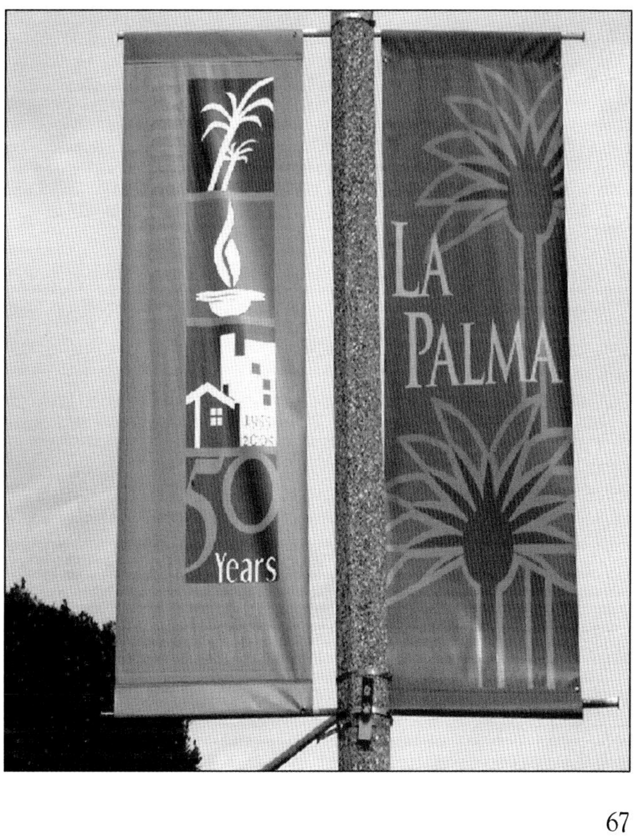

La Palma street banners, designed by graphic artist Liz Parker, are displayed throughout the city and are changed to reflect the seasons or special events. (Photograph by Ron and Elfriede Mac Iver.)

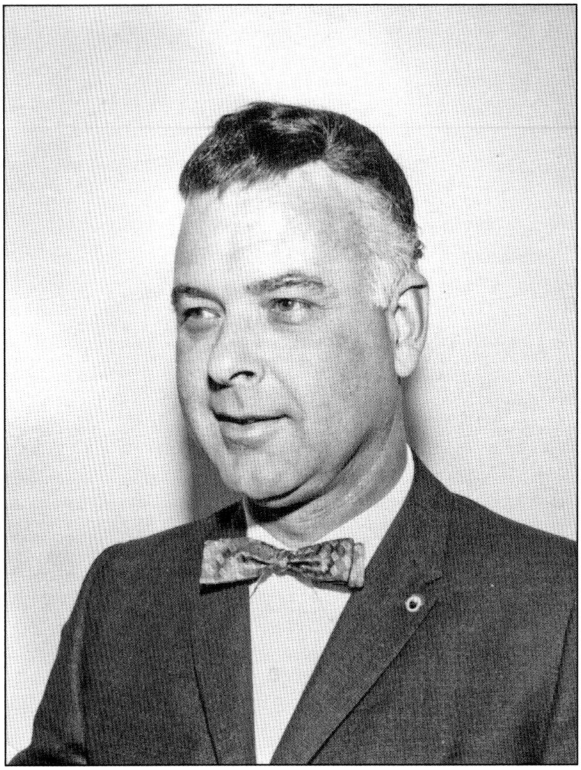

Pink McKay, charter president of the La Palma Chamber of Commerce, which was founded on October 25, 1965, served with Vice Pres. Don Plapp, secretary Bea Sorrells, treasurer Nathan Shuman, and directors James Fellows, Gerrit Fikse, Clyde McLaughlin, and Cor Vander Dussen. Community volunteers supported events and the fledgling businesses lent support as they joined the city. Citizens outnumbered the business community at its inception. (Courtesy of City of La Palma Archives.)

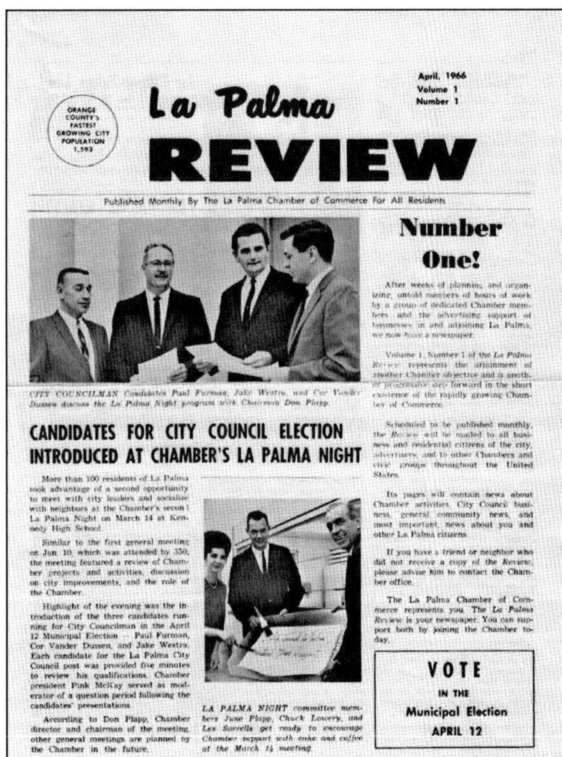

ORANGE COUNTY'S FASTEST GROWING CITY POPULATION 1,593

La Palma REVIEW

April, 1966
Volume 1
Number 1

Published Monthly By The La Palma Chamber of Commerce For All Residents

CITY COUNCILMAN Candidates Paul Furman, Jake Westra, and Cor Vander Dussen discuss the La Palma Night program with Chairman Don Plapp.

CANDIDATES FOR CITY COUNCIL ELECTION INTRODUCED AT CHAMBER'S LA PALMA NIGHT

More than 100 residents of La Palma took advantage of a second opportunity to meet with city leaders and socialize with neighbors at the Chamber's second La Palma Night on March 14 at Kennedy High School.

Similar to the first general meeting on Jan. 10, which was attended by 350, the meeting featured a review of Chamber projects and activities, discussion on city improvements, and the role of the Chamber.

Highlight of the evening was the introduction of the three candidates running for City Councilman in the April 12 Municipal Election — Paul Furman, Cor Vander Dussen, and Jake Westra. Each candidate for the La Palma City Council post was provided five minutes to review his qualifications. Chamber president Pink McKay served as moderator of a question period following the candidates' presentations.

According to Don Plapp, Chamber director and chairman of the meeting, other general meetings are planned by the Chamber in the future.

LA PALMA NIGHT committee members June Plapp, Chuck Lowery, and Les Sorrells get ready to encourage Chamber support with cake and coffee at the March 14 meeting.

Number One!

After weeks of planning and organizing, untold numbers of hours of work by a group of dedicated Chamber members and the advertising support of businesses in and adjoining La Palma, we now have a newspaper.

Volume 1, Number 1 of the *La Palma Review* represents the attainment of another Chamber objective and is another progressive step forward in the short existence of the rapidly growing Chamber of Commerce.

Scheduled to be published monthly, the *Review* will be mailed to all business and residential citizens of the city, advertisers, and to other Chambers and civic groups throughout the United States.

Its pages will contain news about Chamber activities, City Council business, general community news, and most important, news about you and other La Palma citizens.

If you have a friend or neighbor who did not receive a copy of the *Review*, please advise him to contact the Chamber office.

The La Palma Chamber of Commerce represents you. The *La Palma Review* is your newspaper. You can support both by joining the Chamber today.

VOTE
IN THE
Municipal Election
APRIL 12

La Palma Review, Volume 1, No. 1, first appeared in April 1966 as a monthly publication that was mailed to each home to inform the residents of activities and events in the community, such as ground-breaking ceremonies, grand openings, Easter egg hunts, tree lightings, and parades. Bill Worthen was its first editor and June Plapp was his assistant, later taking on the job of editor. Glen Travis was the long-serving photographer for the publication. Its photographs and stories have been an invaluable source of historical information. (Courtesy of City of La Palma Archives.)

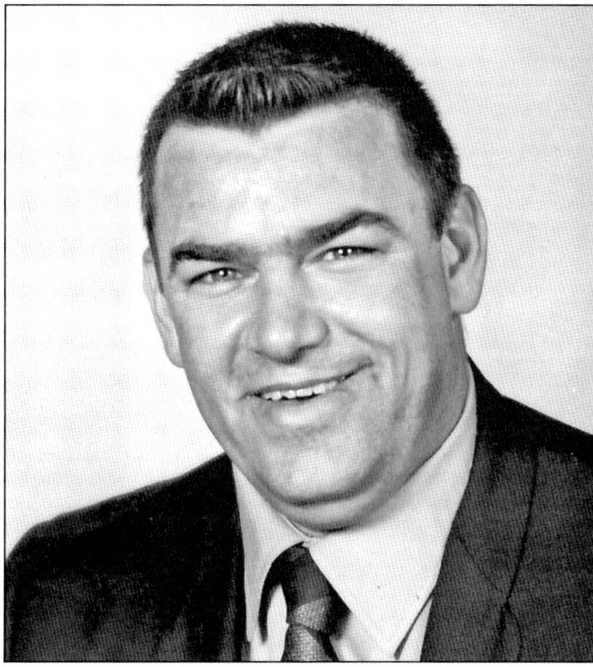

According to the *La Palma Review* in April 1970, James Fellows, one of the first residents in the Landmark tract, became a charter director for the La Palma Chamber of Commerce in 1965. He is credited with adopting the La Palma motto, "City of Vision." For his "day job," he was an associate professor at Los Angeles Trade-Technical College. (Courtesy of June and Don Plapp.)

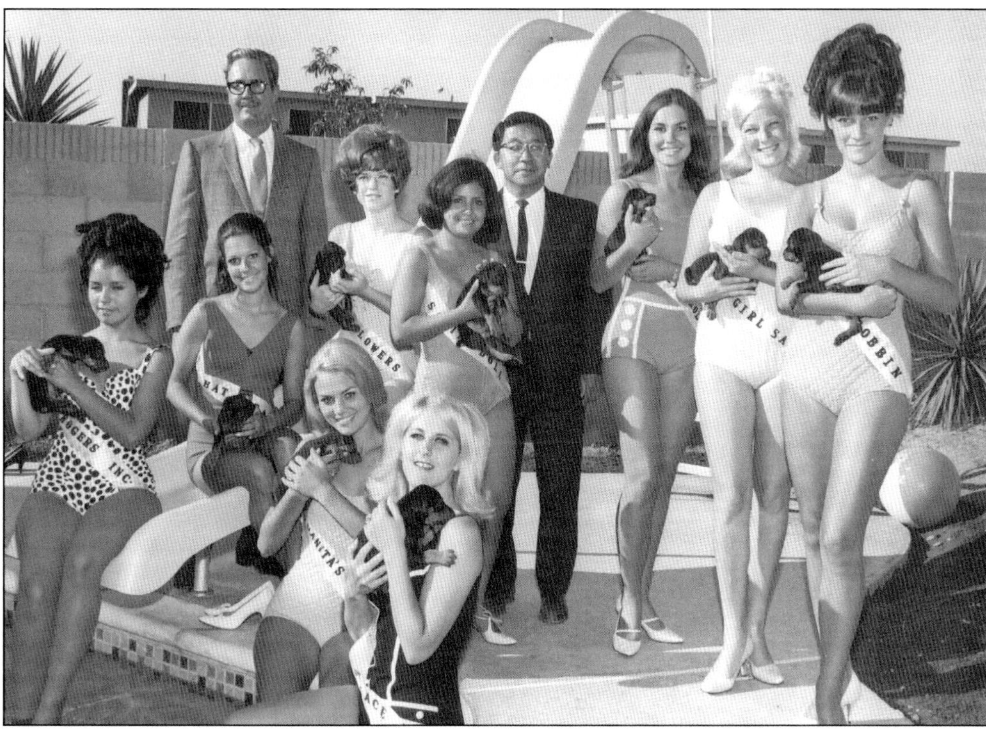

The Miss La Palma Pageant of 1968 became an event under the sponsorship of the La Palma Chamber of Commerce. Identified in this photograph are Mayor Jake Westra (far left); Nappy Sekiguchi (center with dark suit), president of the chamber; and standing next to him at right, Marilyn Truckey, who became Miss La Palma on June 27, 1968. The publicity picture was staged in Nappy's backyard. (Courtesy of City of La Palma Archives.)

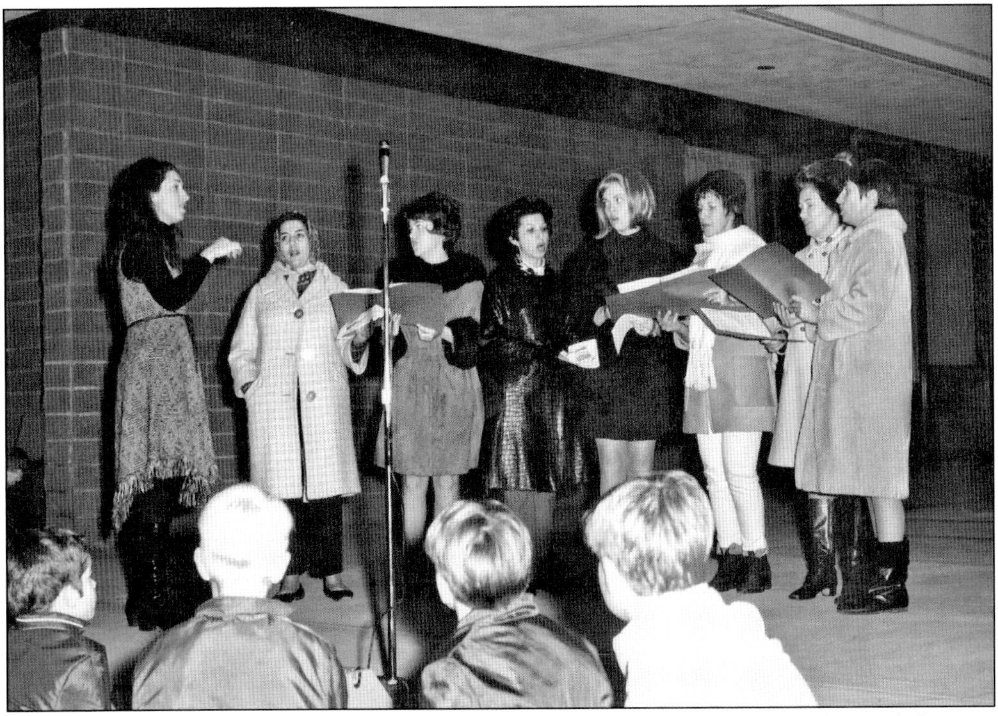

The 1970 tree lighting was another community event sponsored by the chamber and the city. The picture above captured the carolers singing for the large audience of residents. The picture below captured the special Butterfield Express train ride, which left from the parking lot of the city hall, toured to Cypress Park, and returned to give the next group of parents and children a ride. (Both, courtesy of June and Don Plapp.)

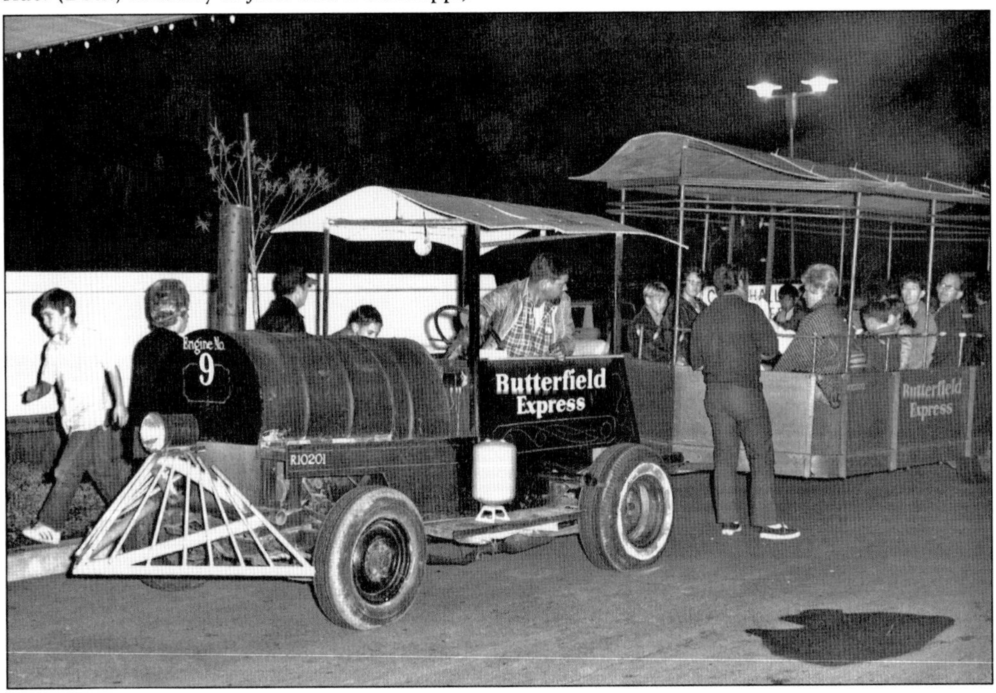

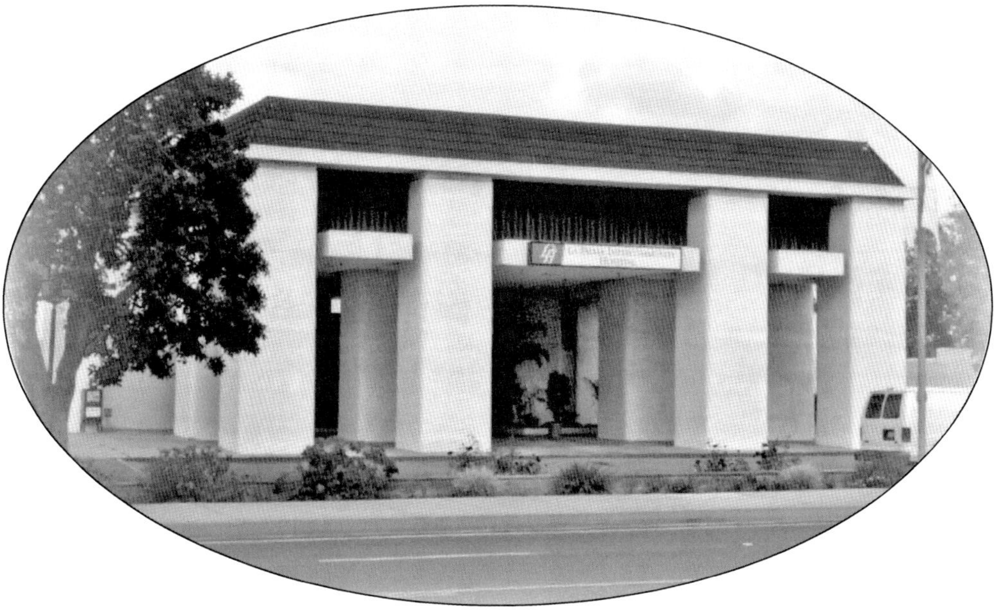

La Palma Intercommunity Hospital, located on Walker Street on the northwest side of La Palma Avenue, was built at a cost of $3 million. In 1971, as an acute care facility, it could accommodate 138 beds. (Courtesy of Ron and Elfriede Mac Iver.)

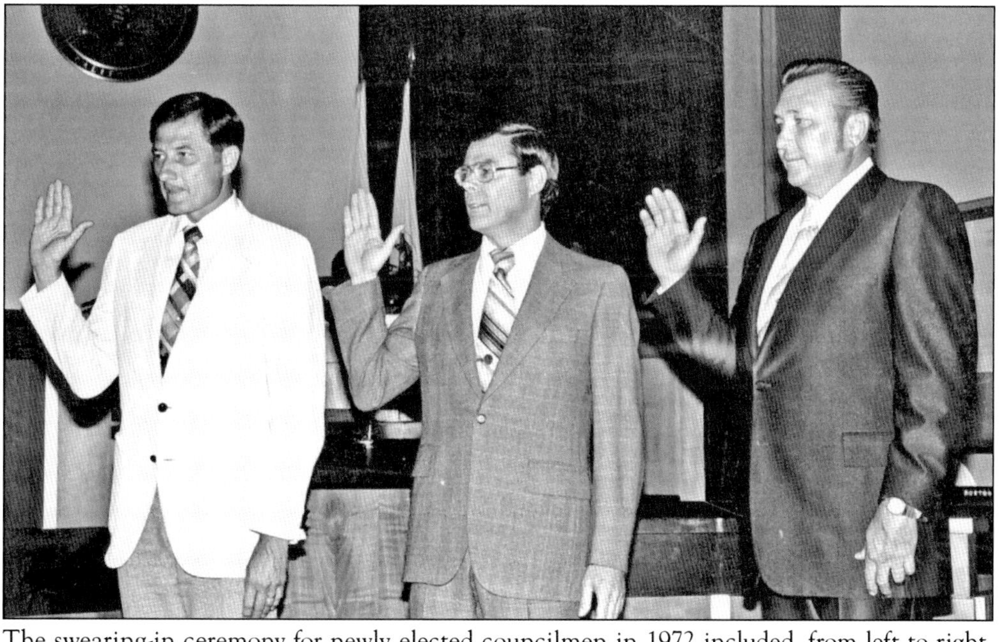

The swearing-in ceremony for newly elected councilmen in 1972 included, from left to right, Henry R. Frese, Edward J. Byrne, and Dan Collins. Ed Byrne was elected mayor. (Courtesy of City of La Palma Archives.)

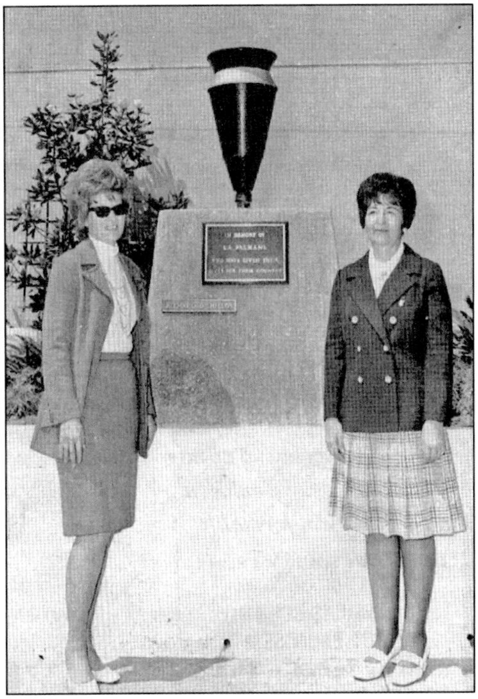

An article from the *News Enterprise* on Thursday, July 13, 1972, highlighted La Palma's long-standing commitment to honor its veterans. The Eternal Flame was dedicated in May 1972 to La Palma's fallen citizens. The first name on the plaque was Richard D. Shields. The donors to the memorial were the La Palma Woman's Club, the Junior Women's Club, the Kiwanis Club, and American Legion Eisenhower Post No. 99. Members of the La Palma Garden Club were the caretakers of the planted area around the flame. The second picture was taken from the back of the torch looking out at the city hall steps. (Both, courtesy of City of La Palma Archives.)

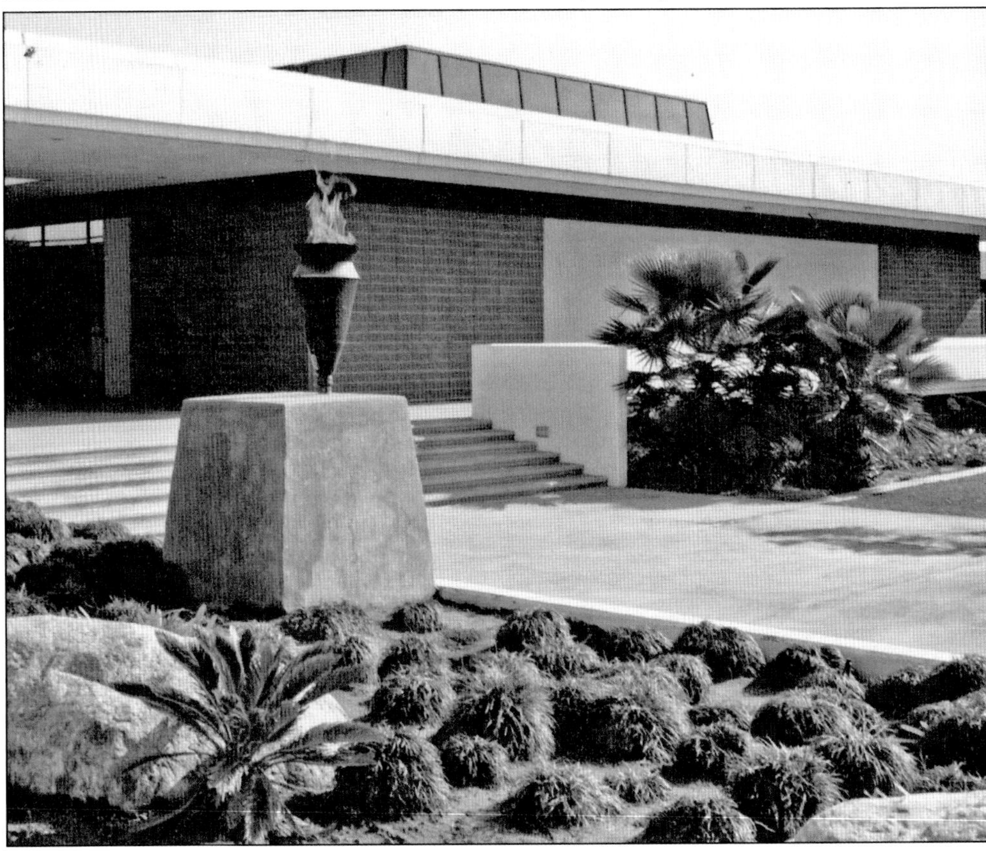

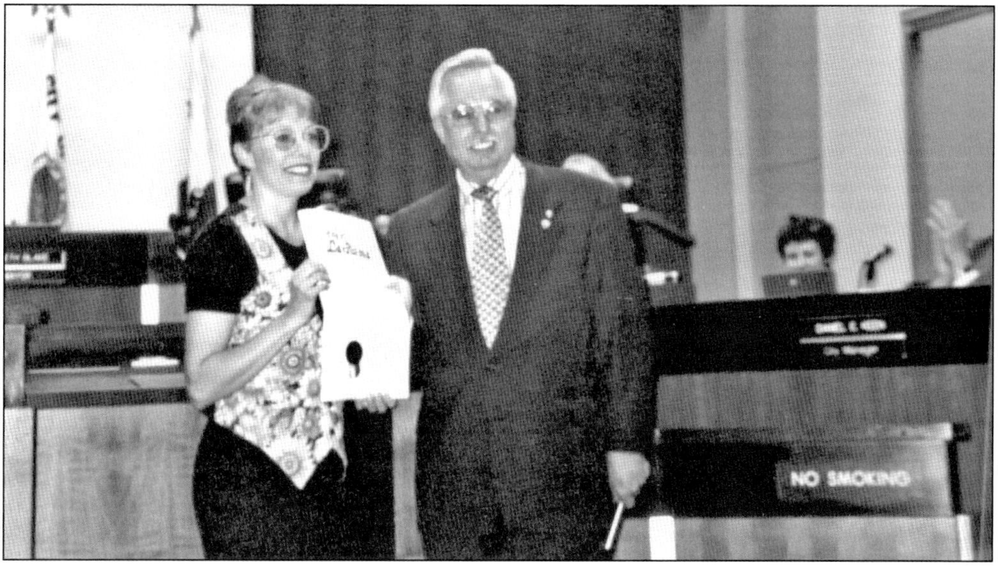

A proclamation marking Garden Week, June 1–7, 1997, was presented to the La Palma Garden Club honoring their efforts as members of the Orange County District Garden Club and efforts on behalf of La Palma. Vicky Morgan accepted the award from Mayor Ken Blake on behalf of the club. (Courtesy of City of La Palma Archives.)

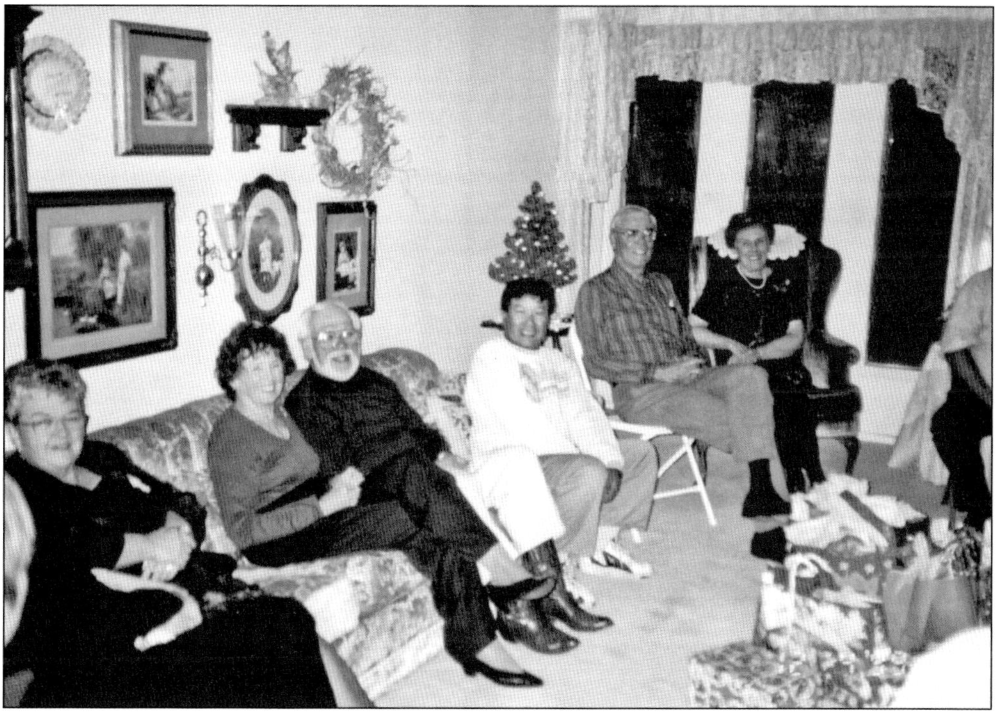

Members of the Garden Club enjoyed a holiday get-together in December 1999. From left to right are Betty Stevens, Bertie and Lowell Overture, Doris Arakaki, and Ed and Marilyn Byrne. Marilyn Byrne was president of the club from 1998 to 2000. The club was disbanded in 2006. (Courtesy of City of La Palma Archives.)

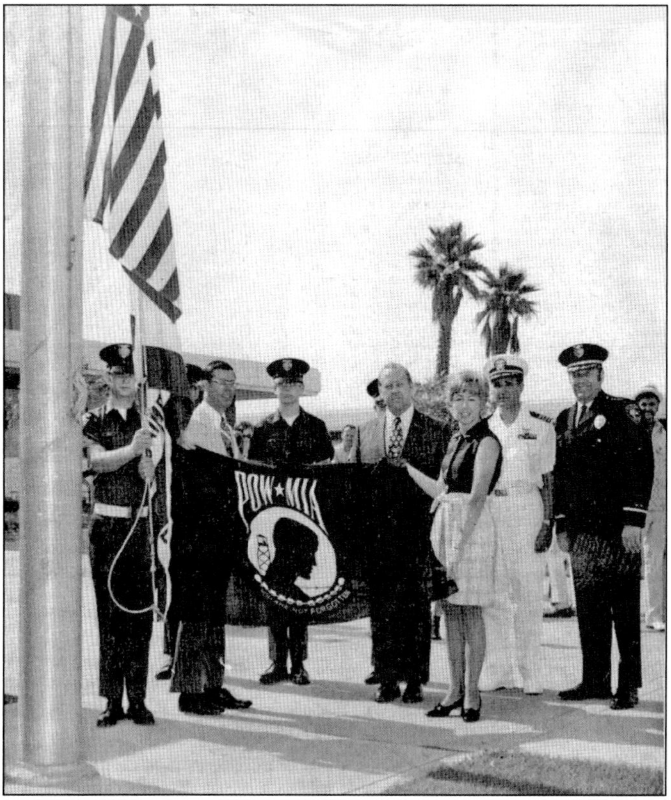

According to a July 13, 1972, *News Enterprise* article, the Junior Women's Club presented the Prisoner of War–Missing in Action flag (POW–MIA flag) to the city on July 4, 1972, at a very impressive ceremony. The flag is to fly until all prisoners and those missing in action have been accounted for. (Courtesy of *News Enterprise*.)

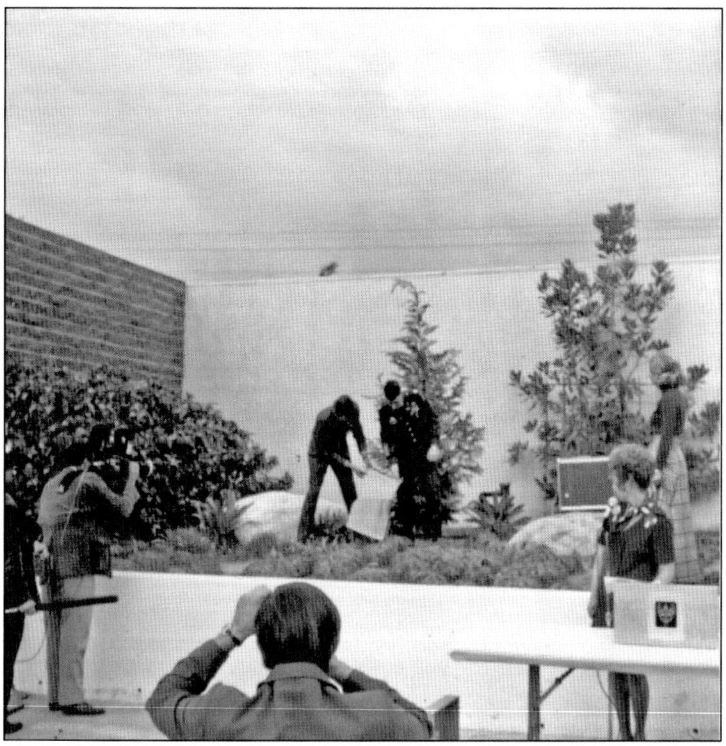

The freedom tree, planted behind the torch on March 10, 1973, honors S.Sgt. Roger Hallberg and all service persons still unaccounted. Capt. Mark Smith, a returned POW, was an honored guest. Joy Paul and Carol Salisbury of the La Palma Junior Women's Club hosted the ceremony. The Kennedy band performed from the top of the steps for the large audience seated in front. (Courtesy of Ron and Elfriede Mac Iver.)

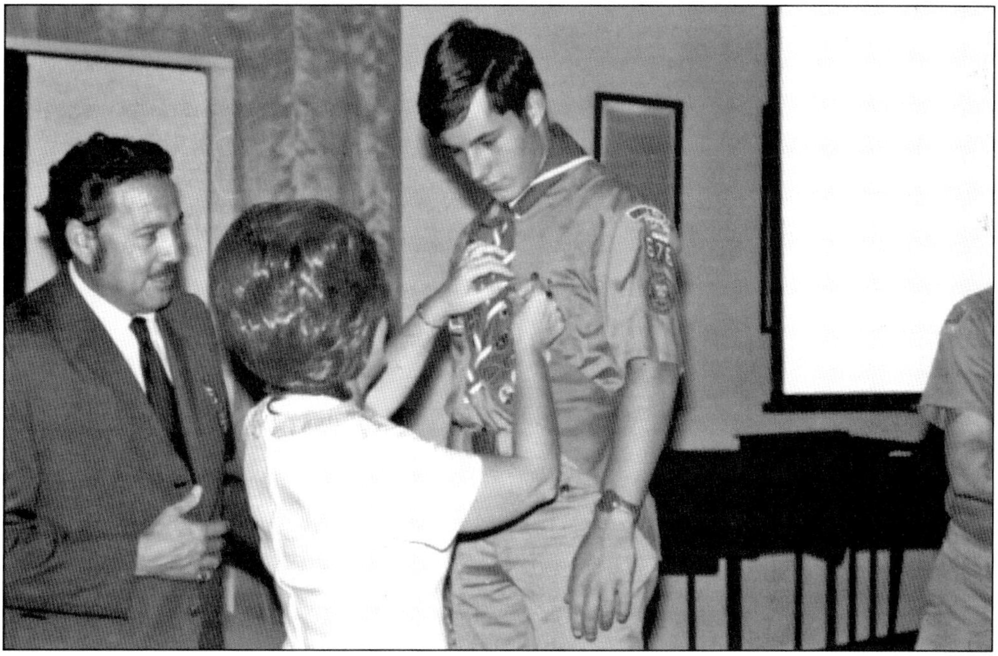

Herbert I. Sutherland III has the distinction of being La Palma's first Eagle Scout, recognized with a proclamation from the city council on September 8, 1970. His court of honor was on September 30, 1970, with Mayor John Berton and scout executive Al Gaudio of Sunset District among the dignitaries present. Millie Sutherland, Herb's mother, pinned his Eagle Award, while Al Gaudio looked on. Herb was president of the Kennedy High School Band, a member of the swim team and yearbook staff, active in his church and community activities, and a member of the U.S. Naval Reserve, Los Alamitos Air Station. (Courtesy of Herb Sutherland.)

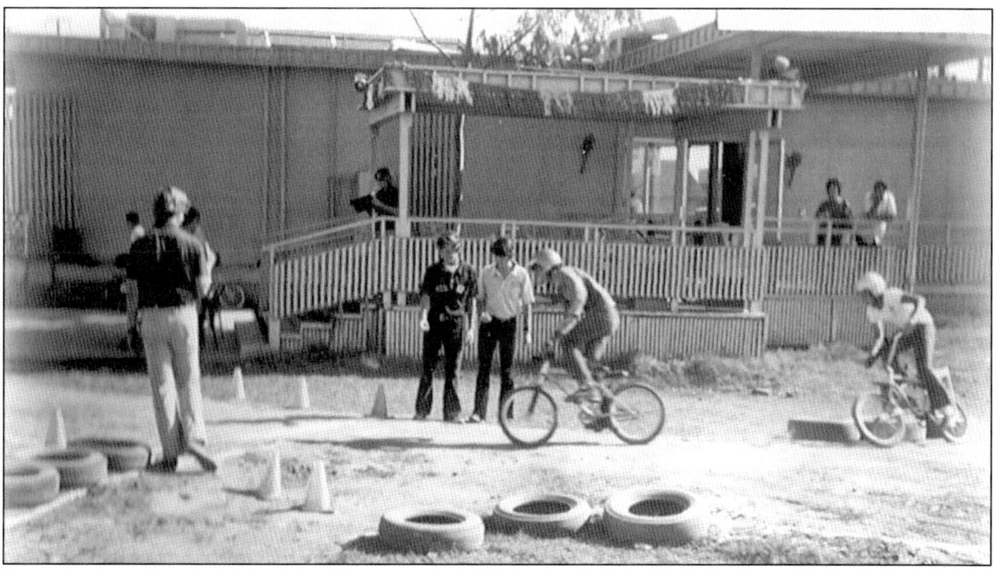

La Palma's bicycle motocross was developed in 1974 on land around Youth Village, which was destined to become Central Park. The La Palma City Council gave the group $1,000 for its development. The more advanced paths were in the back of the village. (Courtesy of Ron and Elfriede Mac Iver.)

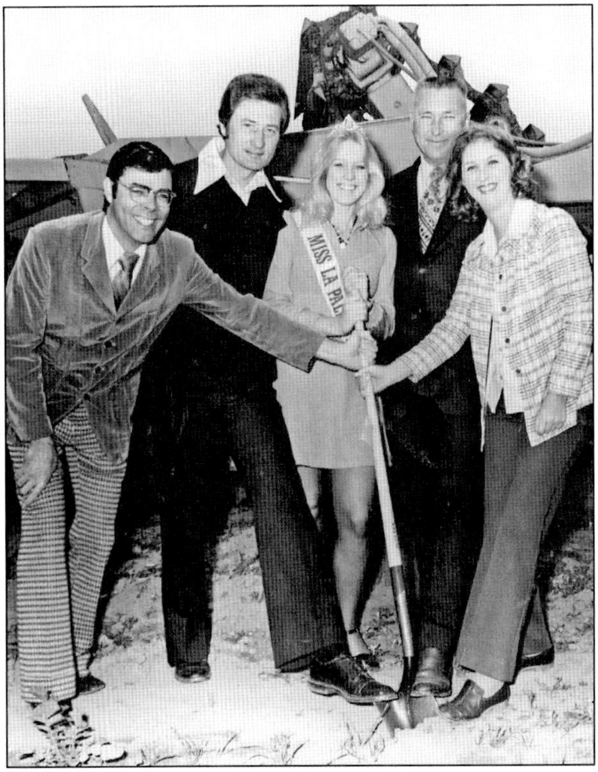

The long-awaited ground-breaking ceremony for Central Park occurred on March 1, 1975. From left to right are Mayor Ed Byrne, councilman Hank Frese, Miss La Palma Cheri Duke, Mayor Pro Tem Dan Collins, and council person Mary Williams. (Courtesy of City of La Palma Archives.)

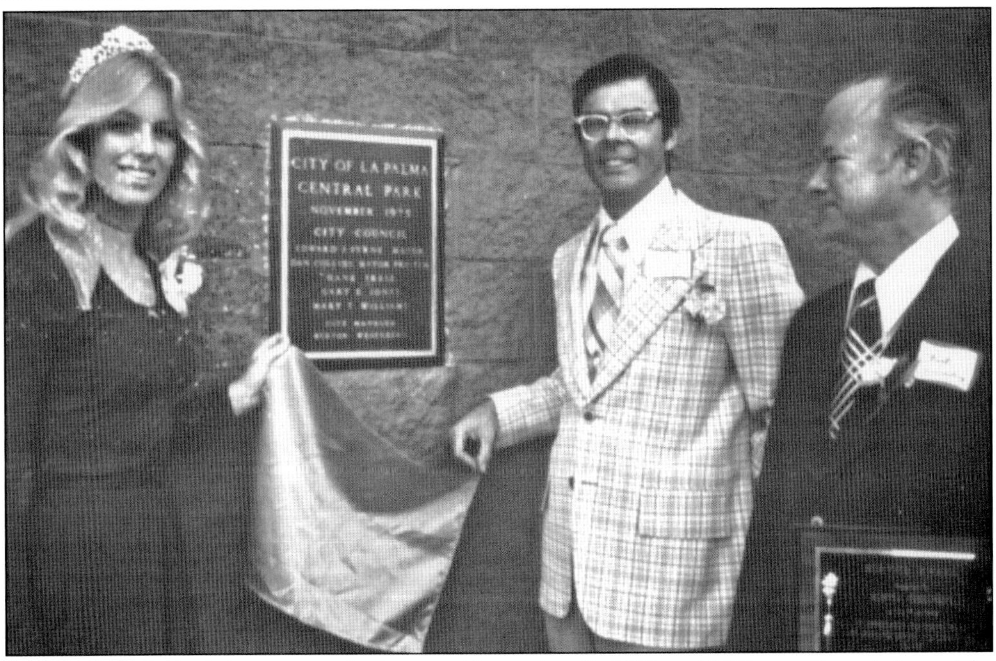

The Central Park dedication took place on November 8, 1975, at 11:00 a.m. From left to right are Cheri Duke, Miss La Palma; Mayor Ed Byrne; and city manager Burt Wesenberg. Following the dedication, there was a reception hosted by the city with community displays, exhibits, and recreational activities, which lasted until 5:00 p.m. (Courtesy of Ed and Marilyn Byrne.)

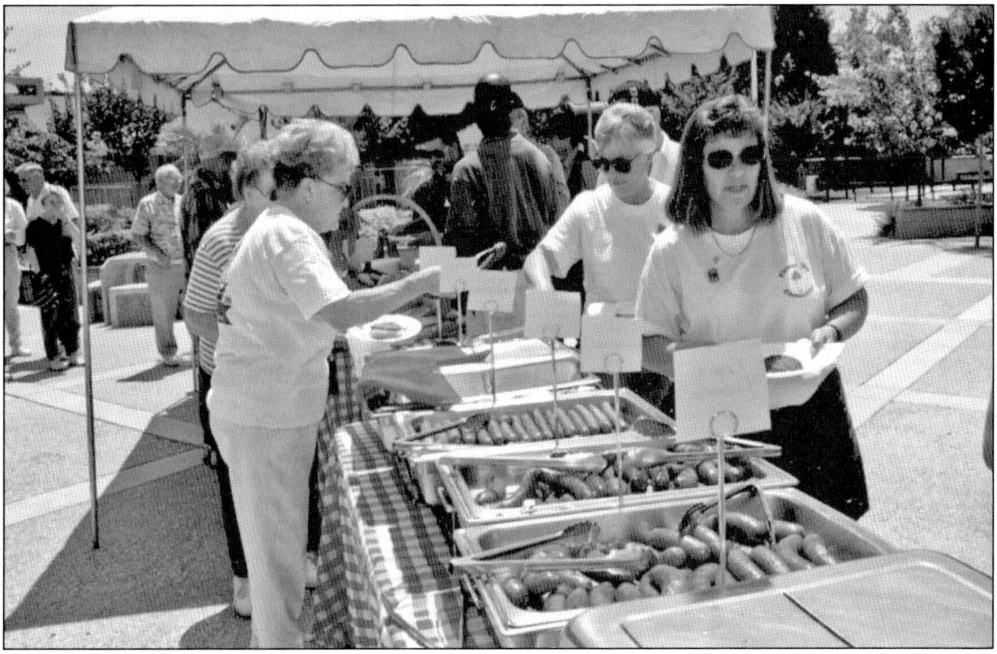

Central Park became an immediate success. Events such as the cookout pictured above are popular, and barbecue pits are available for family gatherings as well. La Palma offers a wide variety of family activities, such as Halloween carnivals, tree lightings, movies, concerts in the park, activities for tiny tots, team sports, and an assortment of classes. The staff is friendly, enthusiastic, hardworking, and never short on ideas for community fun. (Courtesy of City of La Palma Archives.)

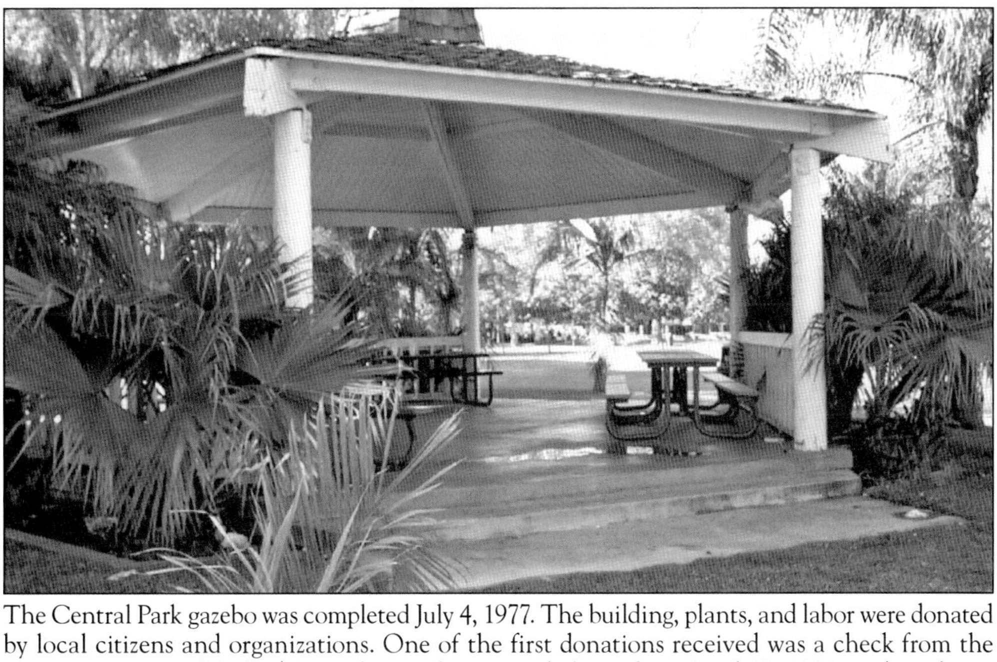

The Central Park gazebo was completed July 4, 1977. The building, plants, and labor were donated by local citizens and organizations. One of the first donations received was a check from the Junior Women's Club for $500. The gazebo was rededicated on April 27, 1994, with a plaque honoring all those who contributed money and labor to its construction. (Courtesy of Ron and Elfriede Mac Iver.)

La Palma will score a stamp collecting first

The City of La Palma will score a "first" for stamp collectors on the 4th of July, according to Mayor Hank Frese.

"We will be the first city in the United States to release a first day use the same day the United States Postal Service issues a commemorative stamp," Frese said.

The "first day of issue" by USPS in another city on the 4th of July is a block of four stamps depicting civilian skills in support of the Continental troops in the field. The skills are blacksmiths, wheelwrights, leatherworkers, and seamstresses. Thus the annual 4th of July City of Vision Day theme "Skilled Hands for Independence."

The La Palma perfins pattern will be the initials LP and will be made available to the public on the "first day of use," July 4, 1977, at booths in the City Park. Arrangements have been made to share this Philatelic first with the Nation where in any one can acquire a first day of issue of the "Skilled Hands" perforated with the LP design on a first day of use cover. City of Vision Day chairman stated details will be announced soon how to acquire the covers.

What is a PERFIN?

Perfins are stamps that have been perforated with designs, initials, or numerals by private businesses and governmental agencies to discourage theft and misuse. Within the last two to four years it is again gaining vast usage by governmental agencies and organizations for identification and control purposes. The word PERFINS comes from PERForated INSignia. Perfins originated in Great Brittain in the 1860's and were authorized for use on United States stamps on May 8, 1908. Perfins have appeared on the postal paper of more than 200 nations.

In the United States alone, 6000 patterns are known to have been used. Estimates of the number of patterns used around the world range as high as 40,000.

The Perfins Club with members throughout the world, an affiliate of the American Philatelic Society with over 50,000 members, sanctions the action taken by the City of La Palma. It is only fitting a City in California have this philatelic first when for the first time the National Perfin Exhibit will be held in California. It will be in Los Angeles in October.

There will be rare perfins from the United States and other countries of the world, the largest exhibit of perfins ever held world wide.

The American First Day Cover Society has designated "Skilled Hands" the issue to conduct their National guessing contest of the number of First Day Covers processed by USPS.

The City of Vision Day is also conducting such a contest. Beside being eligible for the local prize an entry will place your guess into the National Contest. The guessing must be made on July 4th at the City Park for the local contest. The National contest will continue through 30 July, 1977.

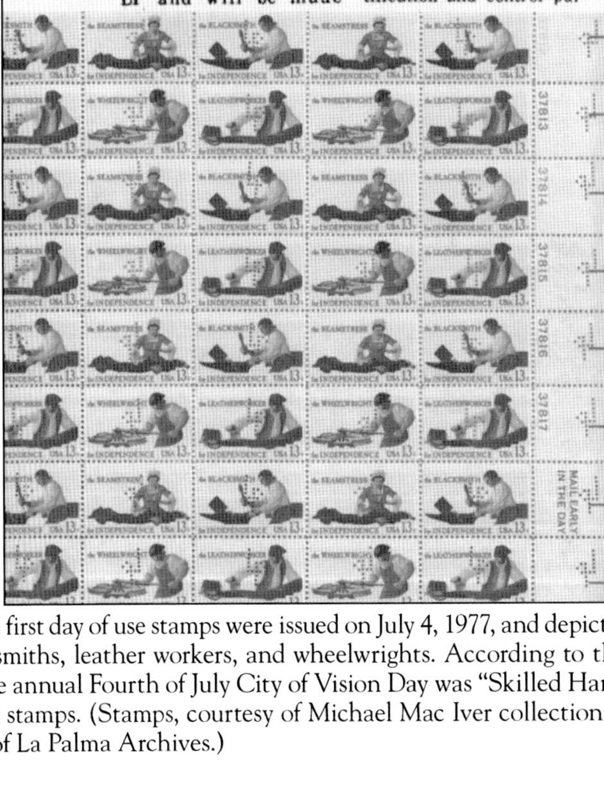

These first day of use stamps were issued on July 4, 1977, and depict various job skills: seamstresses, blacksmiths, leather workers, and wheelwrights. According to the article, the theme that year for the annual Fourth of July City of Vision Day was "Skilled Hands for Independence," because of the stamps. (Stamps, courtesy of Michael Mac Iver collection; newspaper article, courtesy of City of La Palma Archives.)

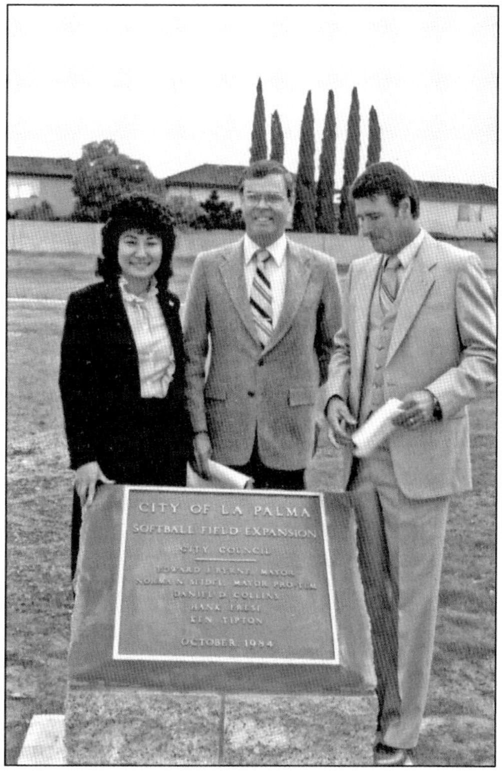

The softball field on the north side of Walker Junior High School was expanded in October 1984. The city council turned out to unveil the plaque commemorating the event. From left to right are Mayor Pro Tem Norma Seidel, Mayor Ed Byrne, and councilman Ken Tipton. Below, Mayor Pro Tem Seidel tries out the new ball field. (Both, courtesy of City of La Palma Archives.)

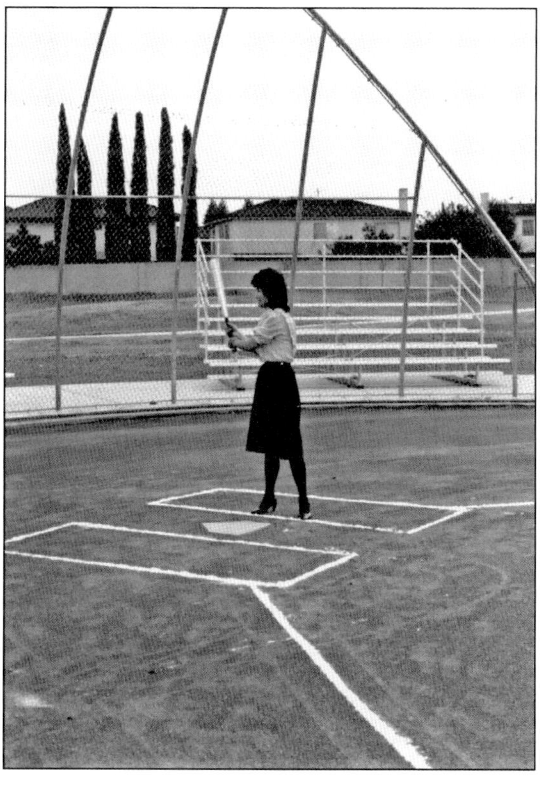

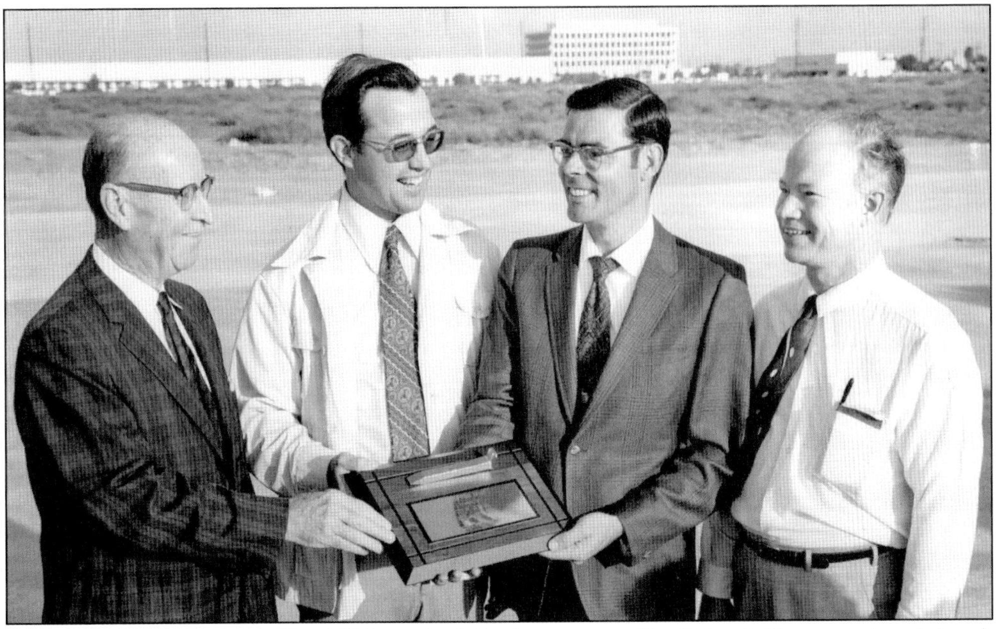

This picture, taken in October 1972, marked the beginning of La Palma's 35-acre industrial park at Fresca Drive. Mayor Byrne received a "golden spike" award, indicative of the two railroad spur lines on either side of Fullerton Creek, from the general partners of Sequoia Pacific, Ronald E. and Arthur B. Birchter (not shown). From left to right are city clerk Ron Dallas, the project manager (unidentified), Mayor Ed Byrne, and city manager Burt Wesenberg. (Courtesy of City of La Palma Archives and Ed and Marilyn Byrne.)

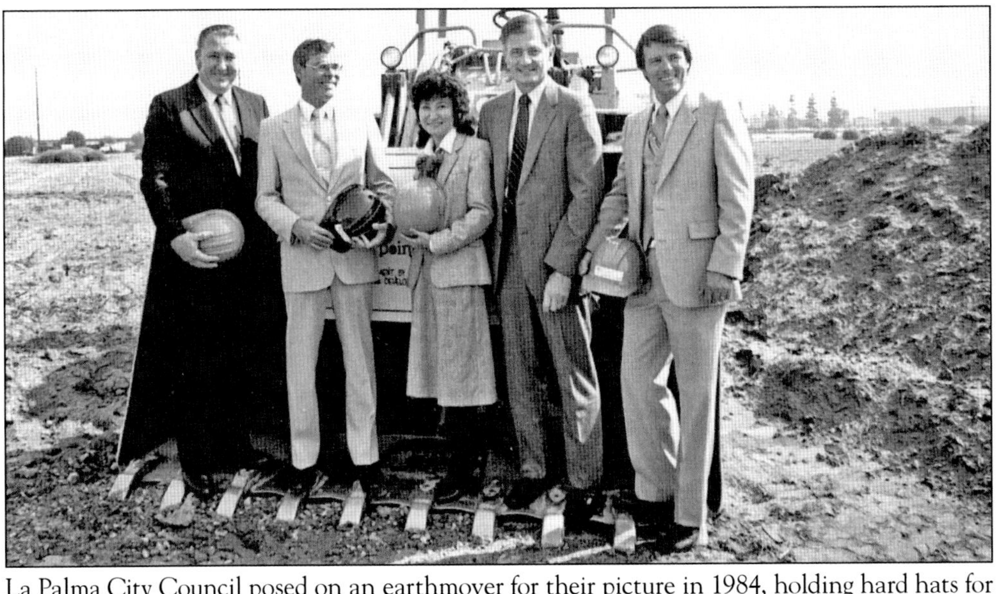

La Palma City Council posed on an earthmover for their picture in 1984, holding hard hats for effect. From left to right are council members Dan Collins, Ed Byrne, Norma Seidel, Hank Frese, and Ken Tipton. They were at the northwest corner of Orangethorpe Avenue and Valley View Street at the Artesia/Riverside (Route 91) Freeway. On the far right, at the top of the picture, is a building on Valley View Street (north and south). (Courtesy of City of La Palma Archives and Ed and Marilyn Byrne.)

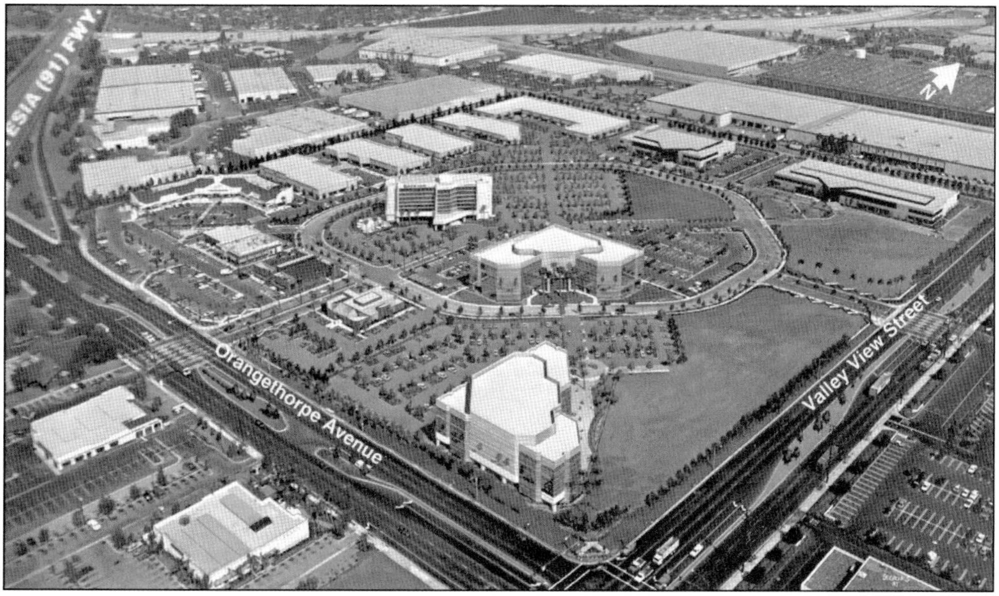

The aerial view taken in 1987 and the architect's rendering are early depictions of the area of Centerpointe. Many new buildings have been added since the grand opening. (Above, courtesy of Larry and Ulla Herman collection; below, courtesy of Ed and Marilyn Byrne.)

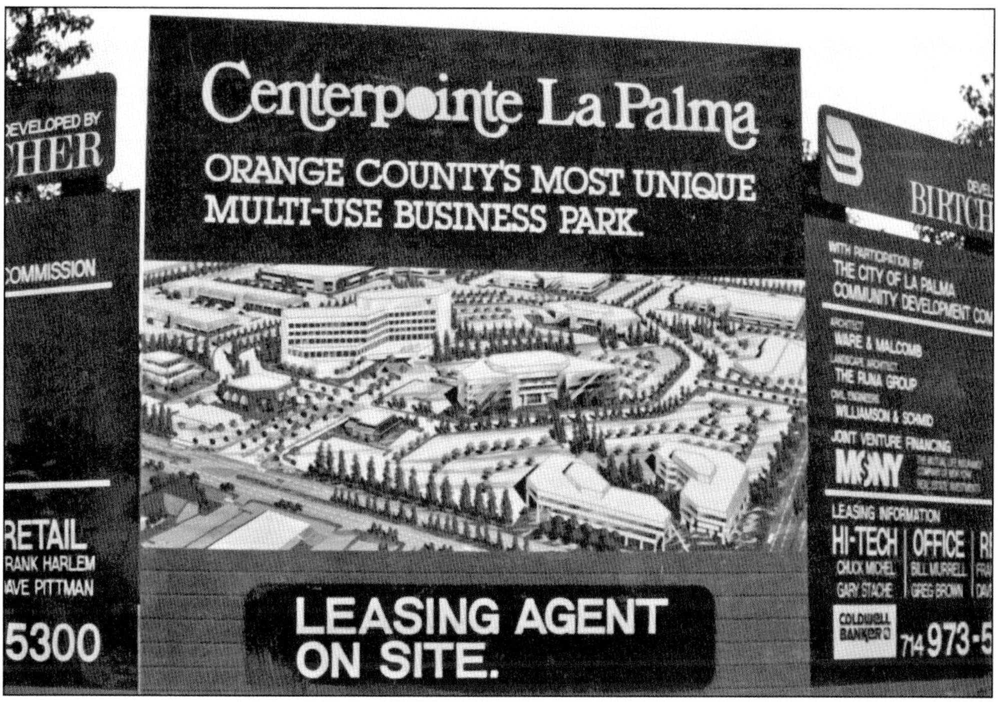

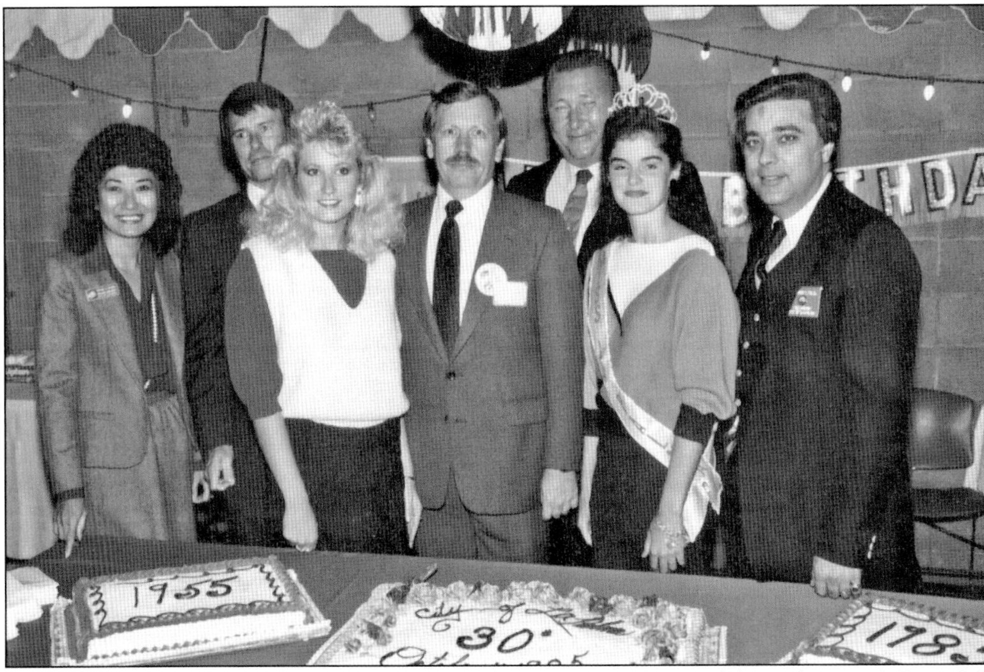

The 13th anniversary celebration of La Palma's incorporation was celebrated in 1985. From left to right are council members Norma Seidel and Ken Tipton; former Miss La Palma, Deborah Wissink; council member Keith Nelson; Mayor Dan Collins; Alane Azevedo, Miss La Palma; and council member Rick Polis. (Courtesy of City of La Palma Archives.)

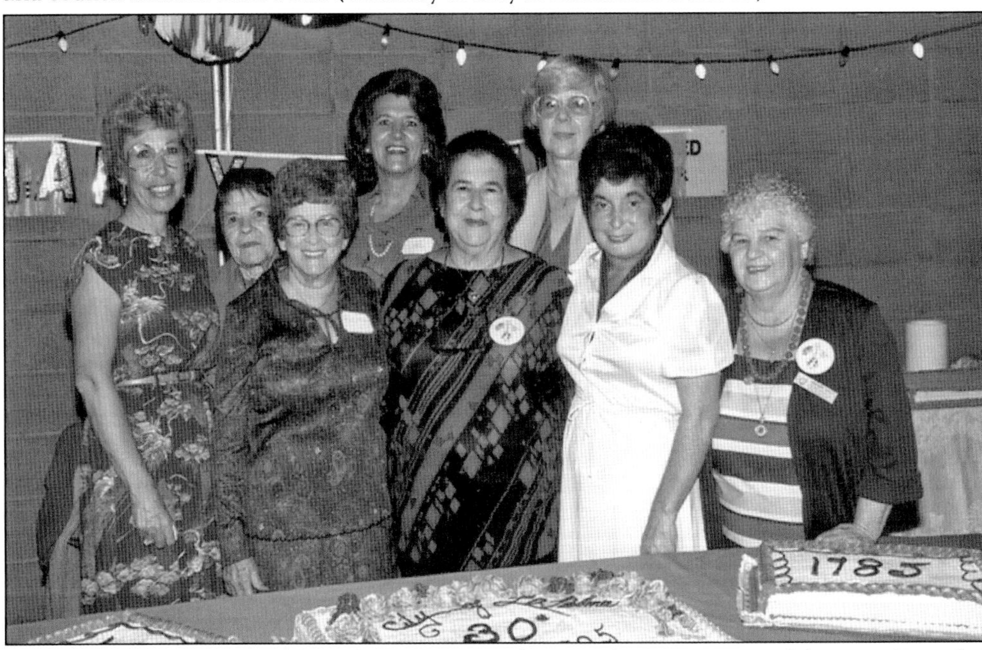

The La Palma Women's Club took part in La Palma's 13th anniversary celebration. From left to right are (first row) Pat Benjamin, Rose Holman, Mary Manning, Rose Reilly, and Lenore Cheeseman; (second row) Elsie Kaufman, Virginia Rust, and Ulla Herman. (Courtesy of City of La Palma Archives.)

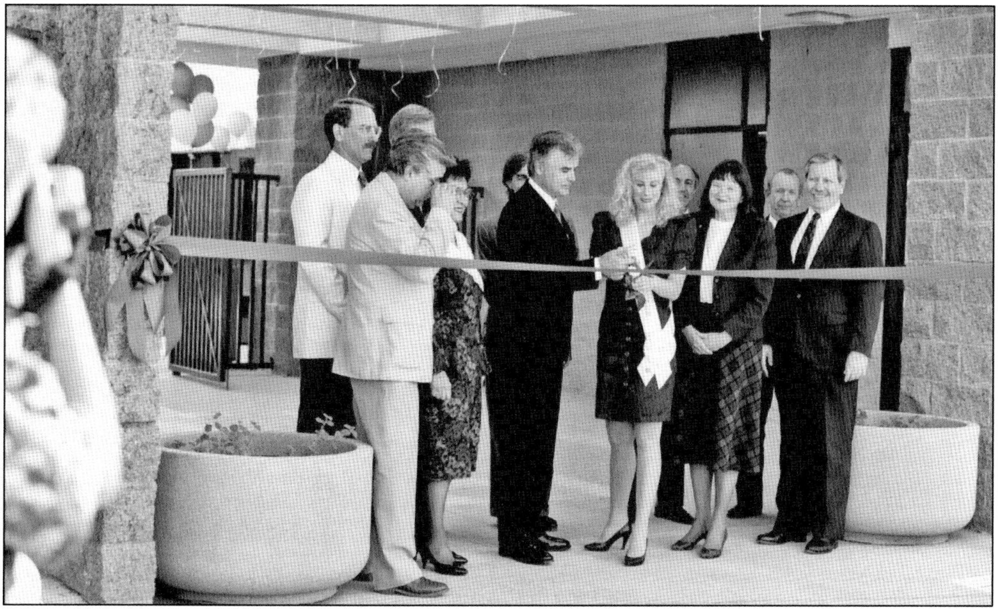

The community center dedication took place on April 22, 1992, at 4:00 p.m. The original complex was built in 1975. The community center was added in 1979, and the current expansion has added 4,100 square feet to accommodate the expanding needs of the city. From left to right are council member Richard Polis (closest to the ribbon on left), council member Eva Miner, Mayor Larry Herman, Miss La Palma Debra Wissink, city manager Pamela Gibson, and councilman Keith Nelson; (second row) Ron Kenny, director of recreation and community services; two unidentified; Ismile Noorbaksh, director of public works and city engineer; and building inspector Paul Pitts. (Courtesy of La Palma Recreation and Community Services.)

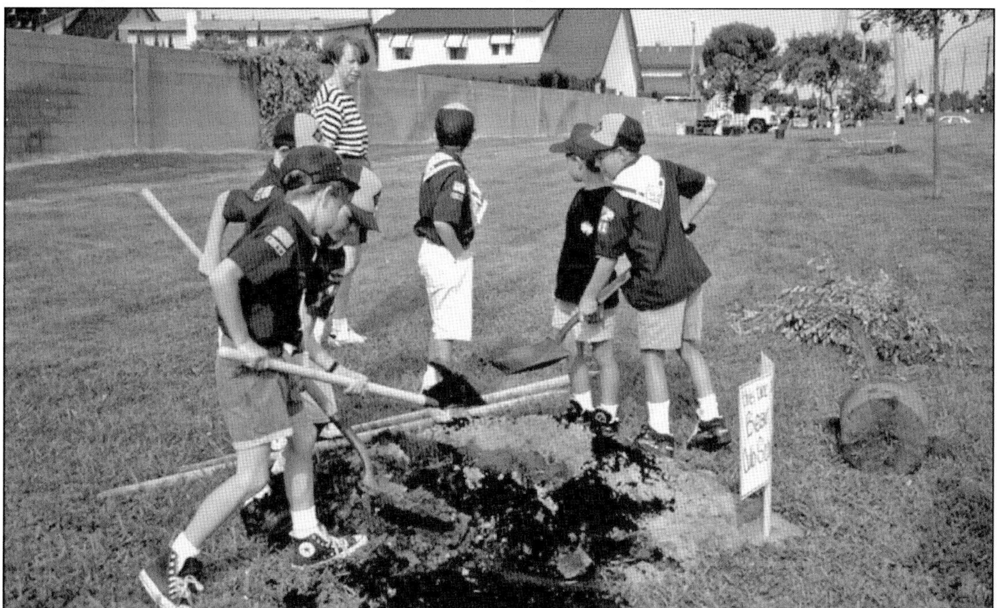

Cub Scout leader Karen Blake looks on as her group observes Arbor Day by planting a Laurelwood tree in the greenbelt in 1992. (Courtesy of City of La Palma Archives.)

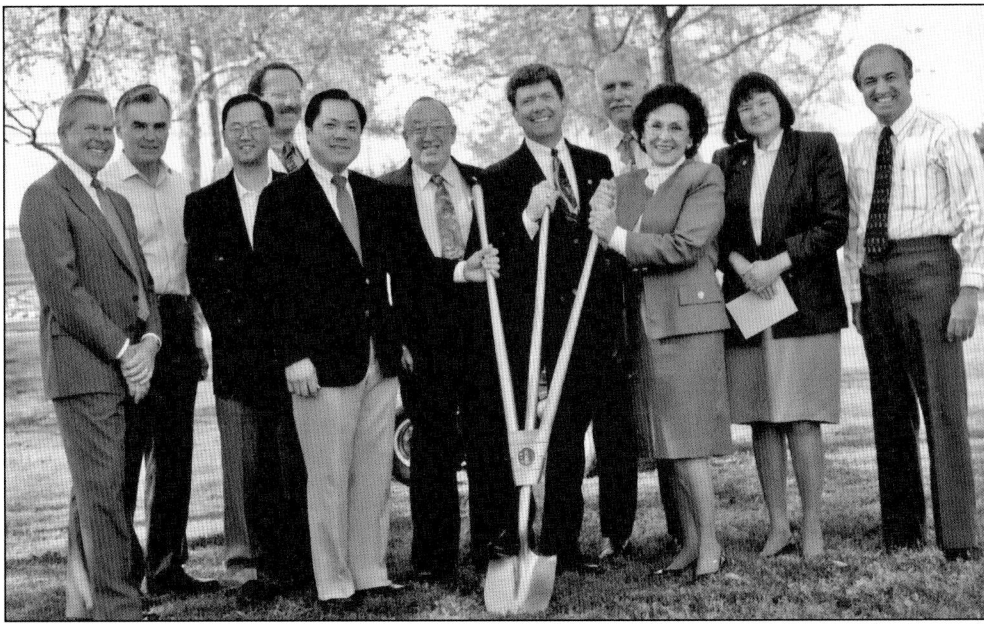

City officials, staff, and organizational representatives marked the beginning of the Central Park renovation in January 1994. From left to right are (first row) Dean Olson, Larry Herman, William Wu, David Lim, Duane Schuster, Wally Lin, Eva Miner Bradford, Pam Gibson, and Ismile Noorbaksh; (second row) Ron Kenny and Pat Hirsch. (Courtesy of La Palma Recreation and Community Services.)

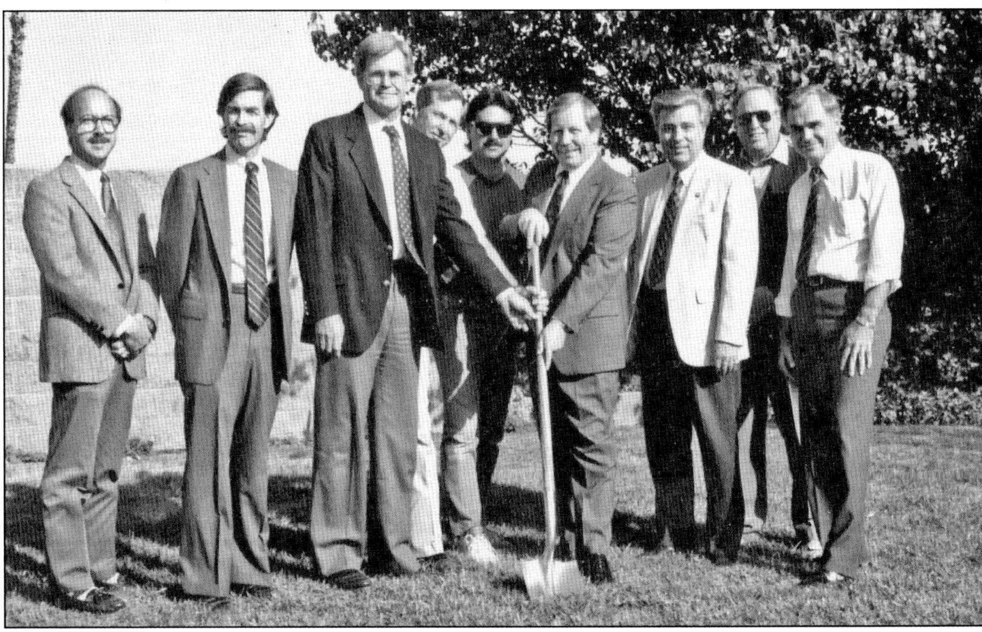

Central Park continues to upgrade and ceremonies mark the event. From left to right are Ron Kramer, Miracle Recreation Equipment; former council member Ron Nyborg; three unidentified contractor representatives; Mayor Keith Nelson (with shovel); council member Richard Polis; police chief Orbrey Duke; and council member Larry Herman. (Courtesy of La Palma Recreation and Community Services.)

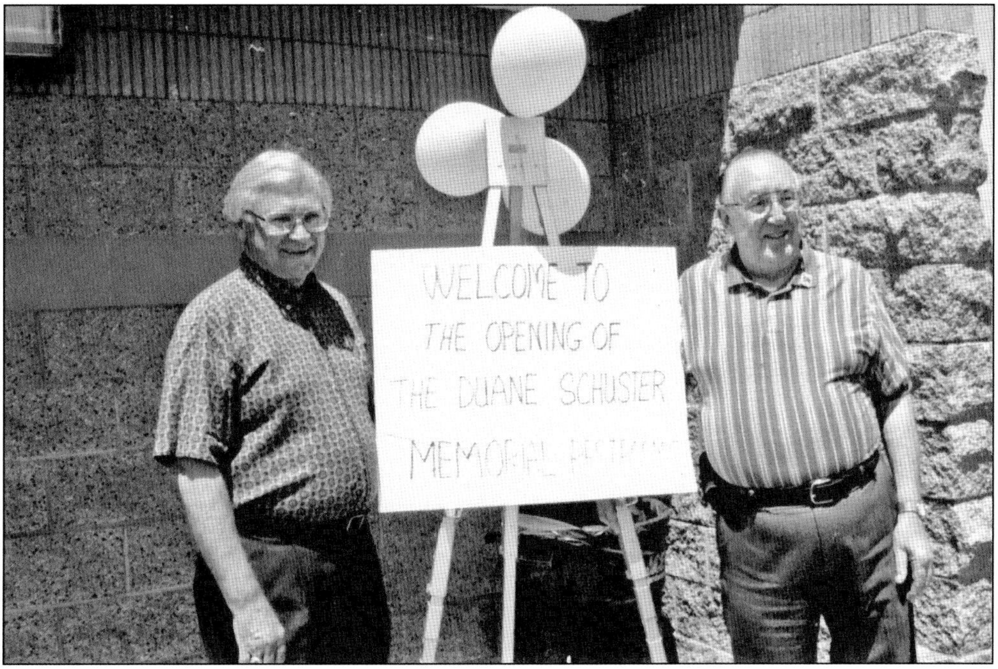

A ribbon-cutting event marked the unveiling of the Duane Schuster Memorial Restrooms in May 1997. From left to right above are Orange County supervisor William "Bill" Steiner and former mayor Duane Schuster; the restrooms were built at Duane's urging for the convenience of after-hours park users. Supervisor Steiner was a good friend of La Palma Projects in conjunction with the La Palma City Council and city volunteers. The restroom dedication was part of a celebration held for La Palma to recognize its volunteers. Below, enjoying the sunny day are, from left to right, police chief Vince Giampa, Duane Schuster, former police chief David Barr, and his wife, Edda, chatting with Rose Holman. (Both, courtesy of La Palma Recreation and Community Services.)

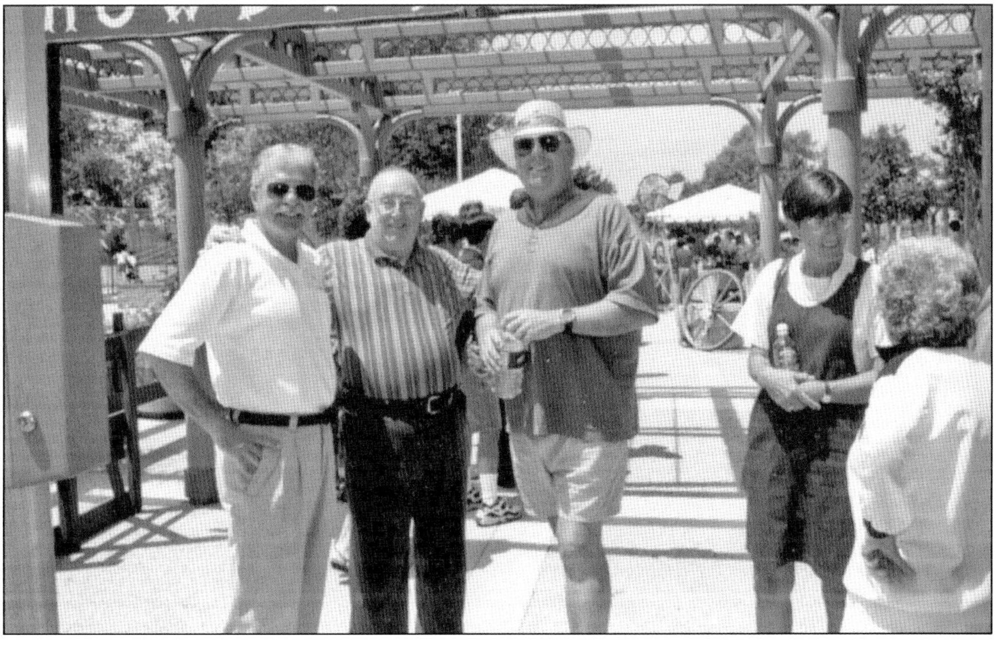

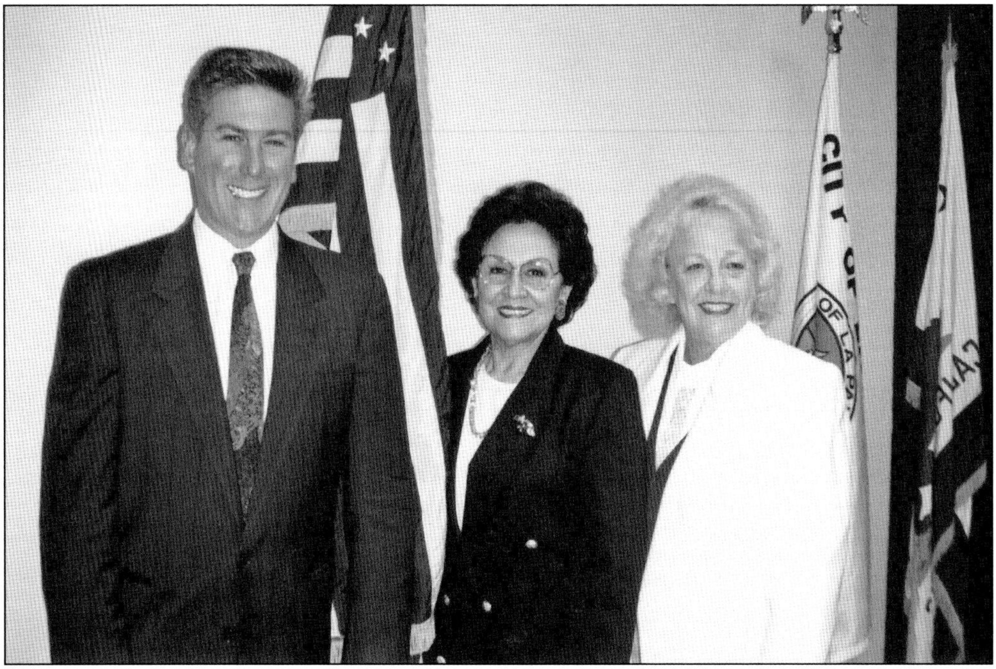

Attending the swearing-in ceremonies for the newly elected city council are, from left to right, Paul F. Walker, Eva Miner Bradford, and Alta E. Duke. (Courtesy of Paul and Lisa Walker Archives.)

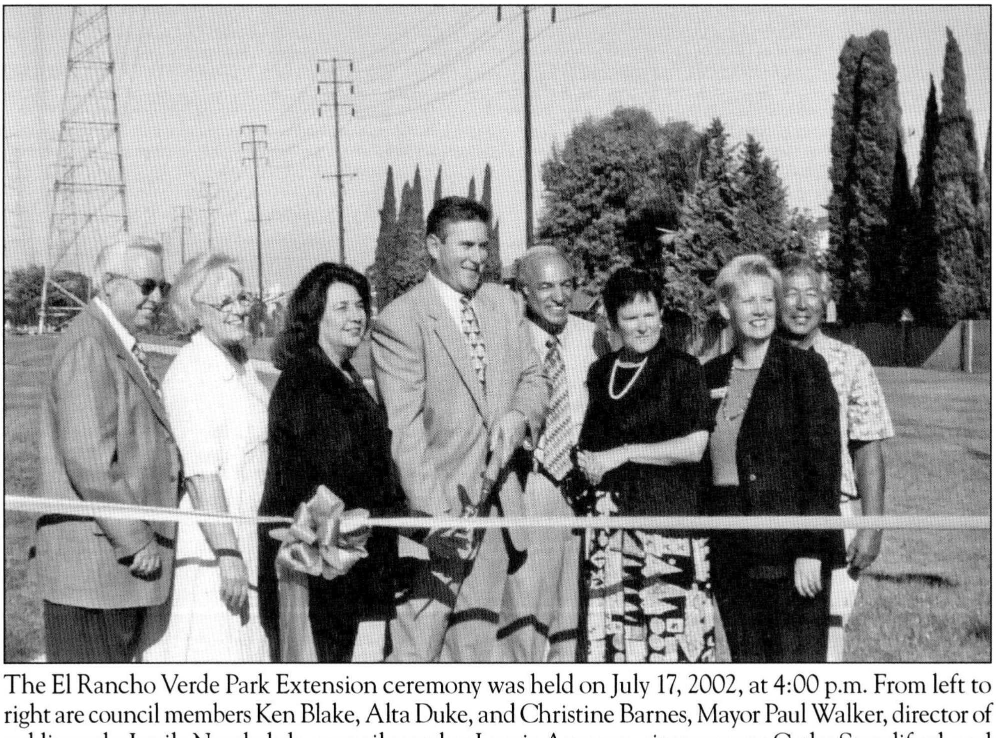

The El Rancho Verde Park Extension ceremony was held on July 17, 2002, at 4:00 p.m. From left to right are council members Ken Blake, Alta Duke, and Christine Barnes, Mayor Paul Walker, director of public works Ismile Noorbaksh, council member Laurie Aragona, city manager Cathy Standiford, and landscape architect Roger Kobota. (Courtesy of Ismile Noorbaksh Public Works Archives.)

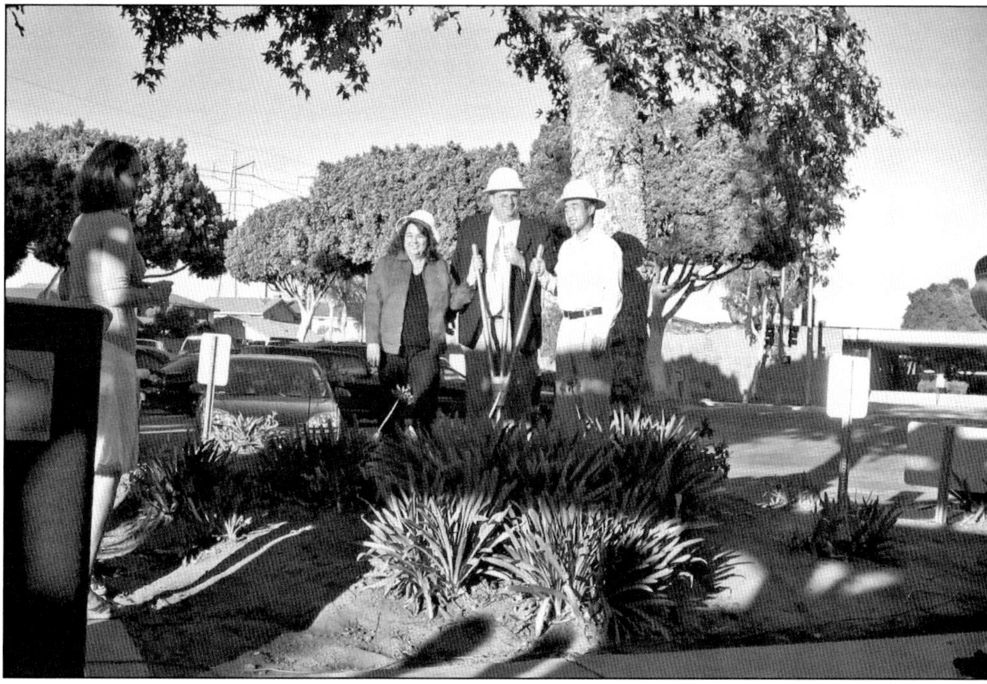

The ground-breaking ceremony for community center expansion was held on September 4, 2007. From left to right are council member Christine Barnes, Mayor Make Waldman, and Mayor Pro Tem Henry Charoen, with shovels ready. (Courtesy of La Palma Recreation and Community Services.)

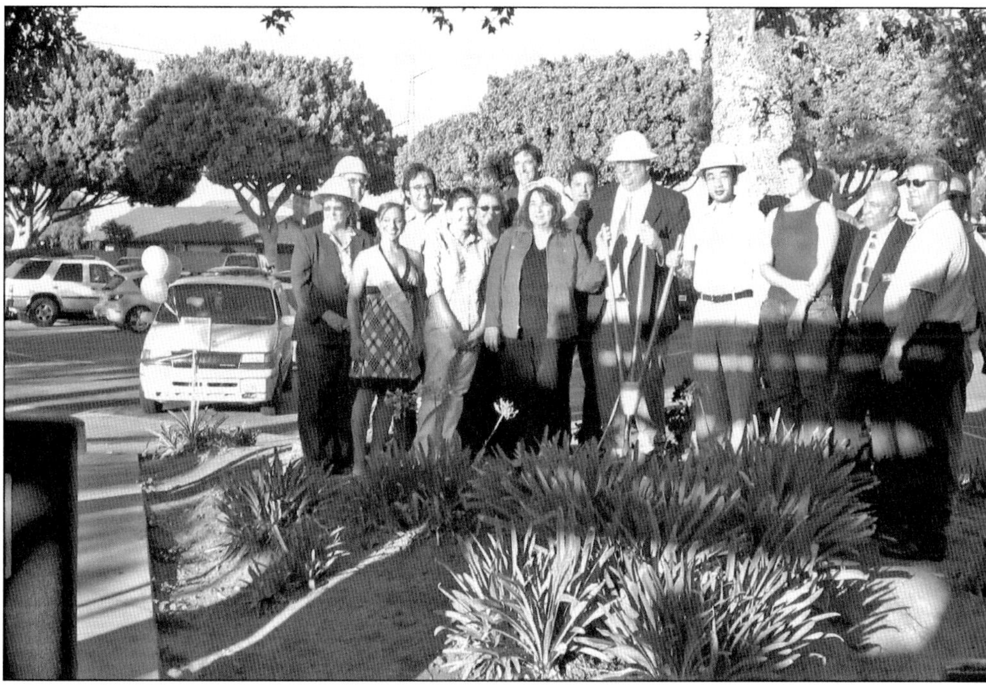

City departments, members of the council, city manager, Miss La Palma, and representatives of the rehabilitation project assemble above. La Palma citizens, as always, turned out in support of this city event. (Courtesy of La Palma Recreation and Community Services.)

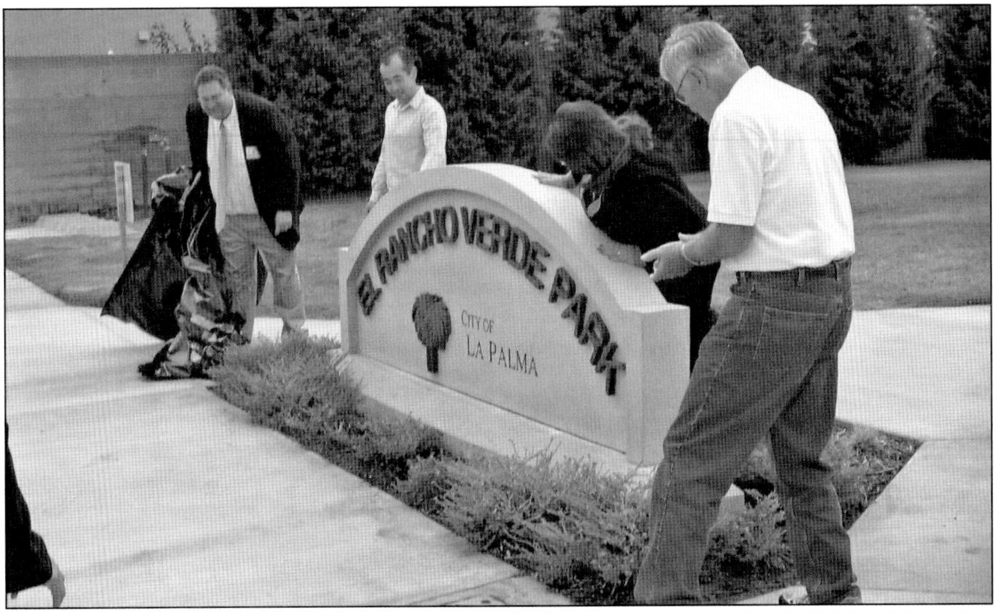

The unveiling of the new El Rancho Verde sign took place on September 28, 2007. The old wooden sign had bravely withstood the elements since June 1967 and finally needed to be retired. The appointed members of the cultural/educational committee coined the Spanish name for the park, with the blessing of the first city council. They consulted the Spanish teacher of Kennedy High School for translations of the names they had in mind for the park. June Plapp, a member of the committee, came up with the winning name in 1967. Pictured above are, from left to right, Mayor Waldman holding the sign cover, Mayor Pro Tem Henry Charoen, council member Christine Barnes reading the sign, and council member Larry Herman. Picture below, from left to right, are attendees Ric Maurice, Duane Schuster, Ulla Herman, Lauree Aragona, Larry Herman, and Mark Waldman. (Both, courtesy of Ron and Elfriede Mac Iver.)

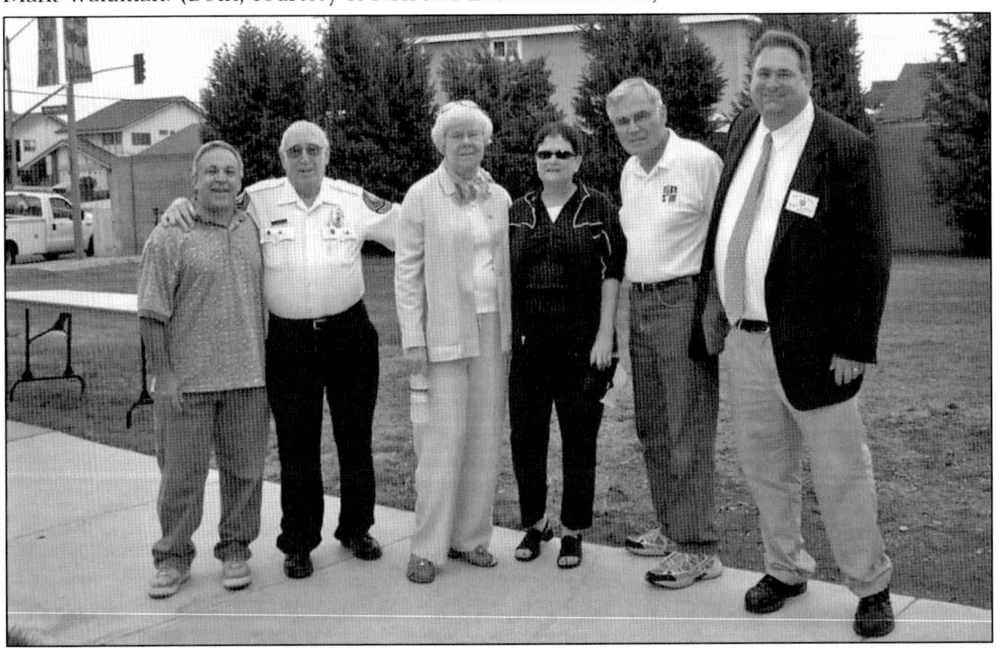

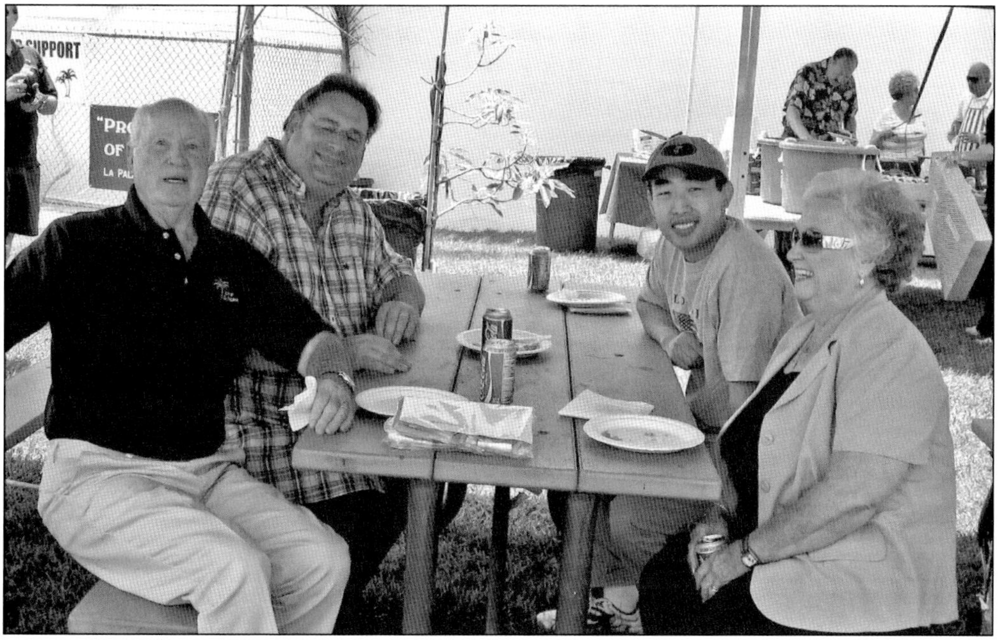

La Palma's Public Work's open house, a yearly event, was held on May 19, 2007, and included good food and good company. Seated above are, from left to right, Claude Coker, Mark Waldman, Henry Charoen, and Marynell Coker. In the background at the right side of the picture are Glenn Karter, Judy Singleton, and Ismile Noorbaksh. Pictured below from left to right are (first table) Duane and Jesse Schuster with Jay Goldberg; (background) Glenn Karter, unidentified, and Jimmie Hambelton (standing); (far back) Claude Coker, unidentified, Ismile Noorbaksh, Judy Singleton, Michelle Rusu, and two unidentified girls. (Both, courtesy of Ismile Noorbaksh Public Works Archives.)

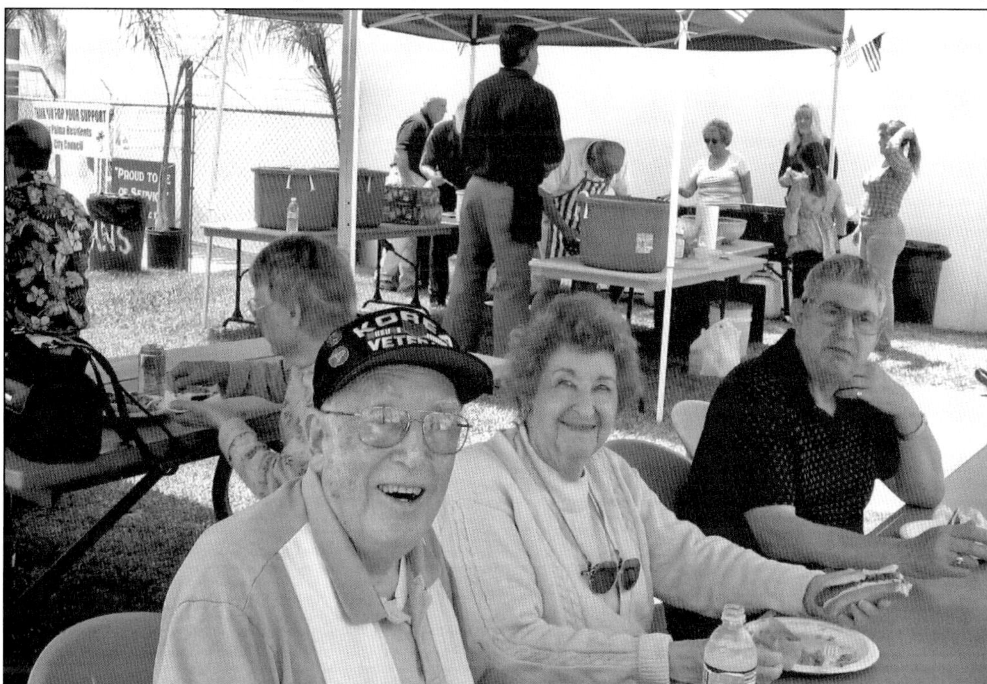

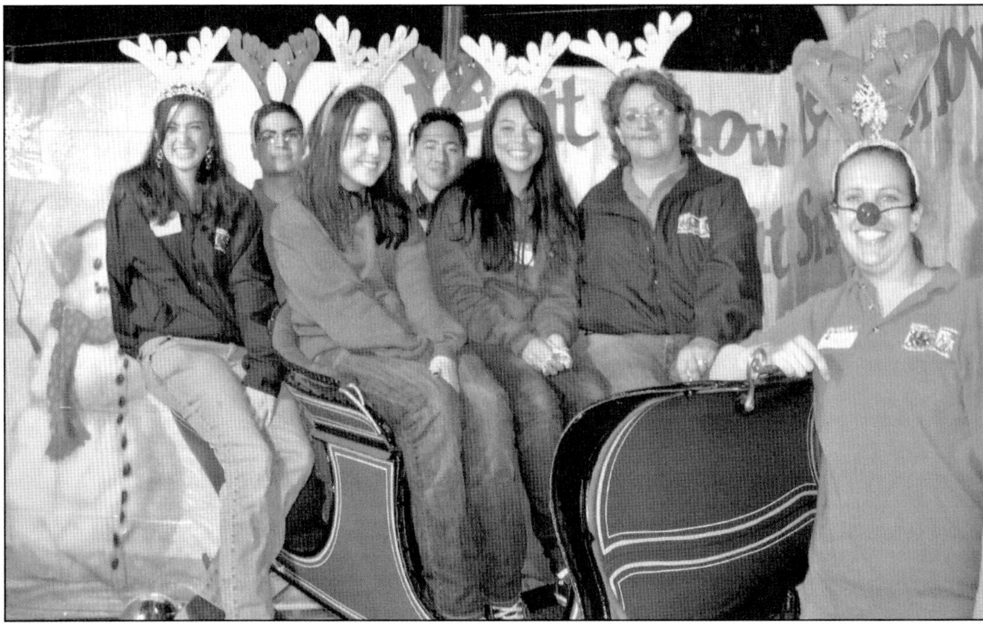

Santa's helpers at the tree-lighting ceremony in 2007 included, from left to right, Erin Peters, Bryan Amezquita, Vanessa Haning, Tony Kim, Tara Williams, Janet Cates, and Cindy Robinson. The tree-lighting ceremony has been held every year since 1967. (Courtesy of La Palma Recreation and Community Services.)

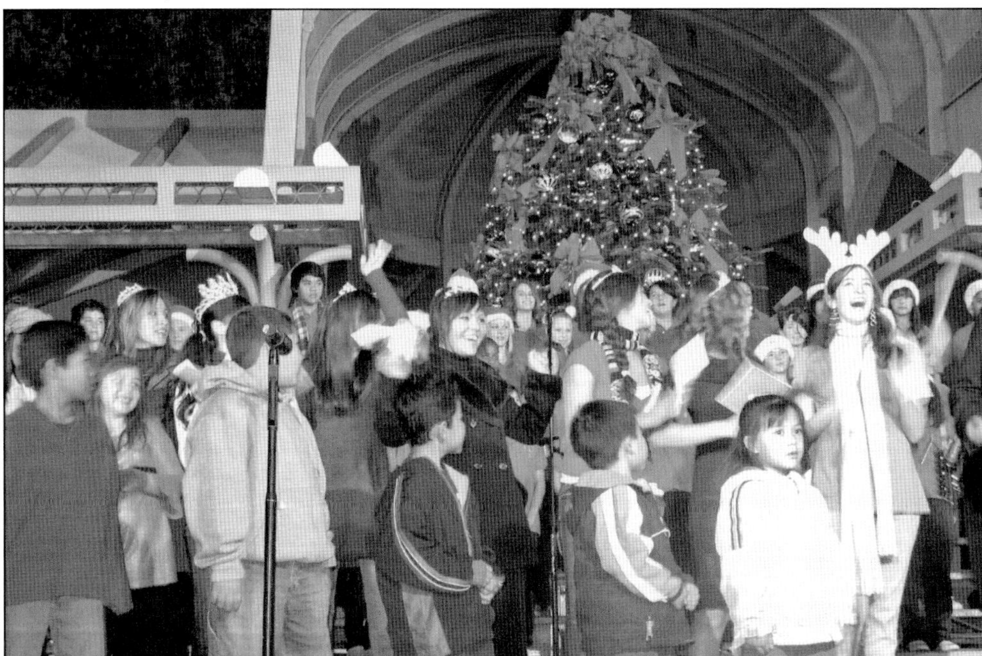

Group participation at the annual tree lighting includes park staff; city council members; city staff, including the city manager and department heads; Miss La Palma and her court; school groups with teachers who sing for the audience; parents; grandparents; and members of the local community. (Courtesy of La Palma Recreation and Community Services.)

Four

City Pride

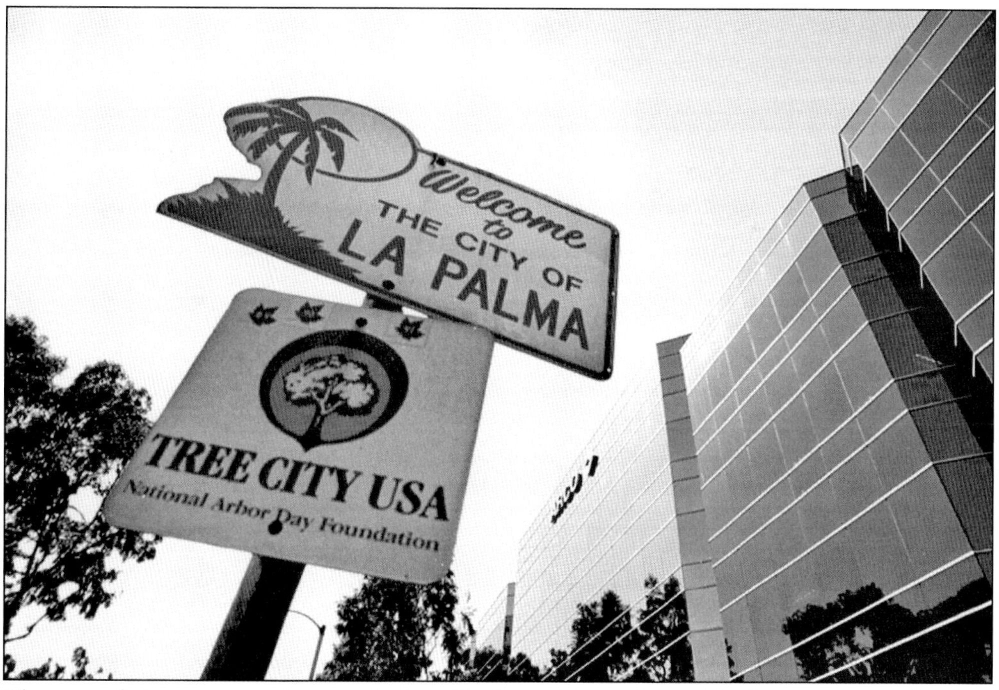

The second city entrance sign was designed by Janet Cates, Central Park supervisor, as her first assignment upon joining the city staff and has been in use since January 1982. Janet Cates was responsible for restoring the last original city sign, which came into use on February 4, 1967, designed by Ron Mac Iver and now displayed on City of Vision Day in November. It was a large sign that became too expensive to replace after it was stolen by souvenir hunters. (Courtesy of City of La Palma Archives.)

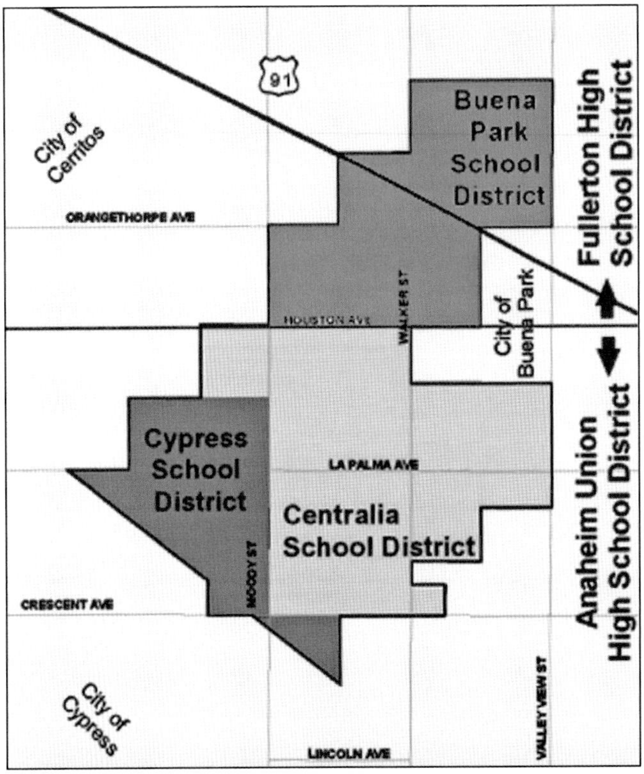

This map of five school districts within the 1.8 square mile boundary of the city of La Palma shows three elementary and two high school districts. The two districts north of Houston Street are Buena Park Elementary and Fullerton High School District. Students within those boundaries are bussed out of the city because no schools exist within the city. Centralia School District has two elementary schools within the city, George B. Miller and Los Coyotes. Cypress has one school, Steven Luther, and Anaheim Union High School District has Walker Junior High School and John F. Kennedy High School. (Courtesy of City of La Palma Archives.)

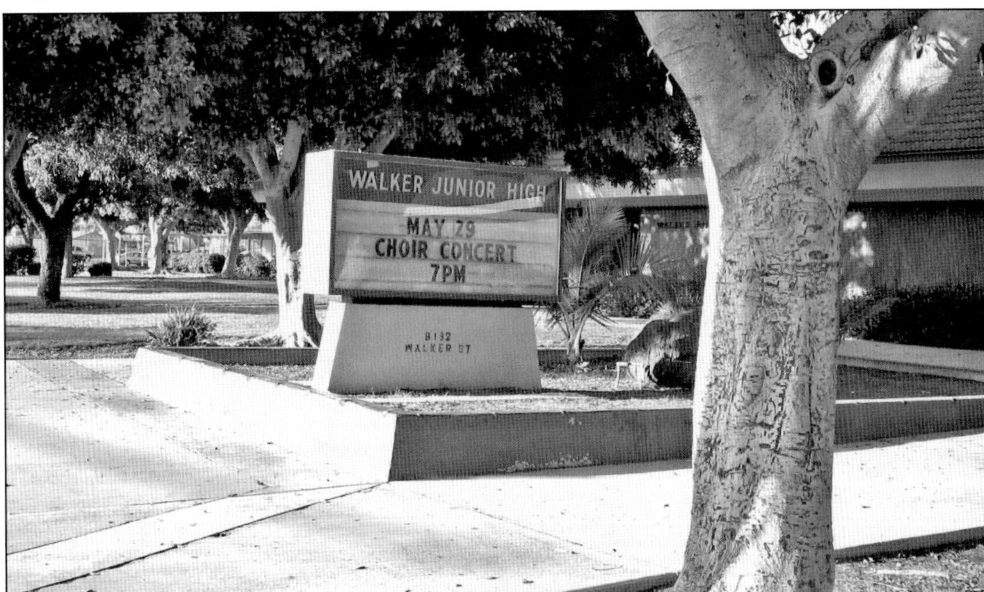

Walker Junior High School was the first school built while the city was still Dairyland. It opened in the fall of 1959 for seventh graders only. The school is located on Walker Street and named for O. S. Walker. Walker, an oil well borer, was an early resident of the Cypress area and served on the school board from 1898 to 1902. (Courtesy of Linda Bird, Walker Junior High School, and the 35th Anniversary Edition, Cypress Chamber of Commerce.)

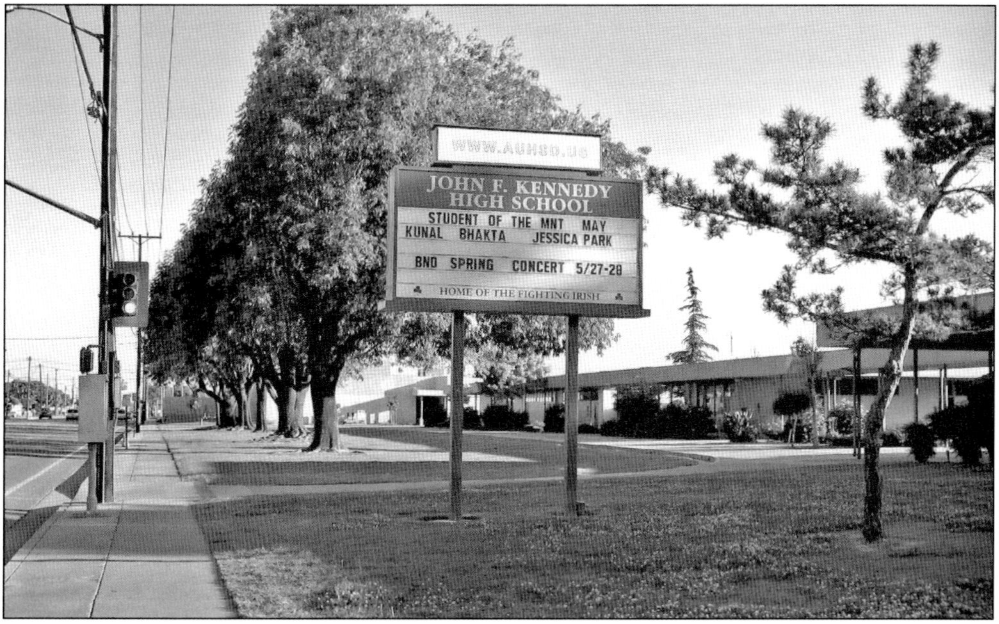

John F. Kennedy High School, the second school to be built in La Palma, opened in September 1964 as Centralia High School, in keeping with the practice of naming the high school after the local elementary school district. Monaco Mallory, a ninth-grade student at Walker Junior High School successfully presented a petition with 400 names to the school board asking that the high school be renamed in honor of President Kennedy, who had been assassinated in 1963. (Courtesy of Sharon Gutjahr, the Kennedy Shillelagh.)

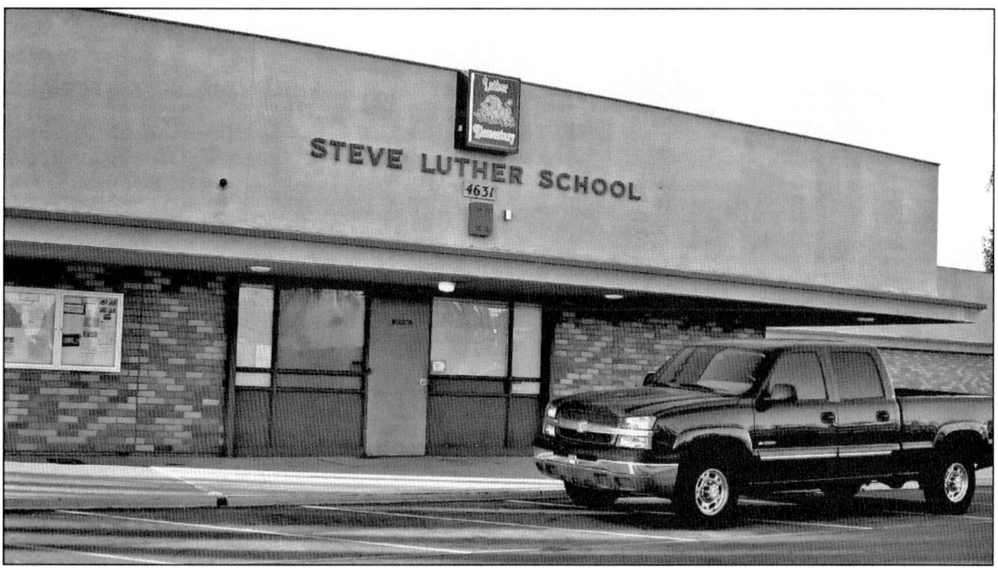

Steve Luther School was formally dedicated on May 3, 1970. It is the only school in the Cypress School District located within La Palma. Per a thesis written by Jaime and Mary Ellen Dickerson in June 1969, it was named for Steven Luther, a board member from 1934 to 1937. Luther is credited with continuing students' schooling in tents after the destructive earthquake of 1933. The earthquake occurred during the height of the Depression when funds to rebuild were not immediately available. (Courtesy of Cypress School District.)

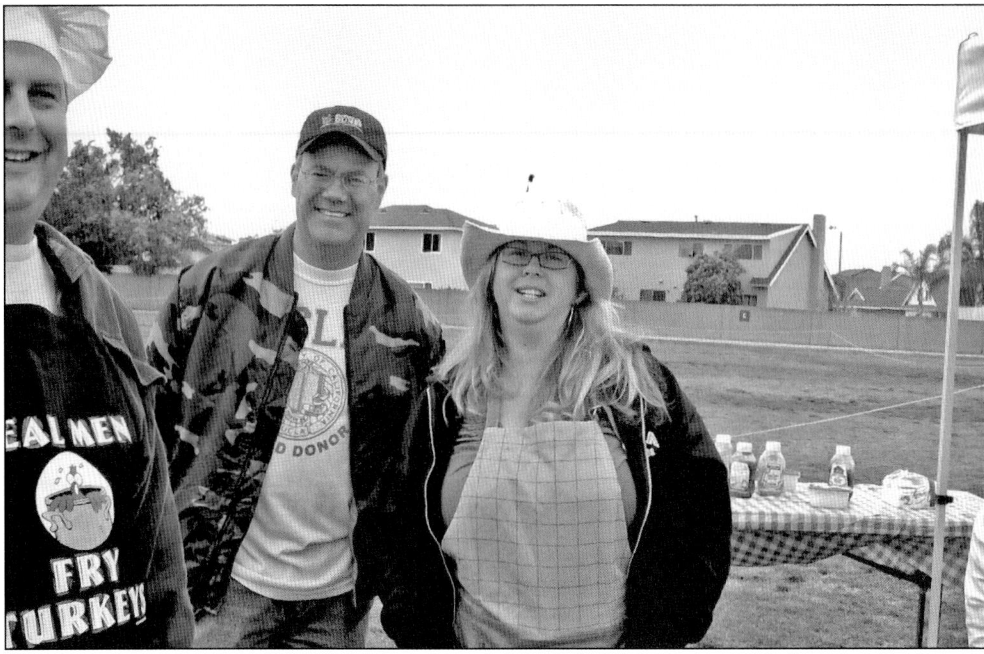

The Kennedy Band Boosters held a fund-raiser for the Kennedy Band on April 7, 2007, that, in addition to food sales, hosted a contest with five live cows trucked in by dairy farmer Art Boster, from Chino. The contest was rather unique. The field was sectioned in quadrants and guests were challenged to predict the next area the cows would use for nature's call. No interaction or lobbying was permitted for this fun contest. Prizes were awarded to the guests, with the cows determining the "winner" in their own time! Above, from left to right, are James Dinwiddie II, Steve Mass, and Lori Dinwiddie. The picture below shows, from left to right, an unidentified girl, Billie Bixlay, and Art Boster with one of his friendly cows. (Both, courtesy of Ron and Elfriede Mac Iver.)

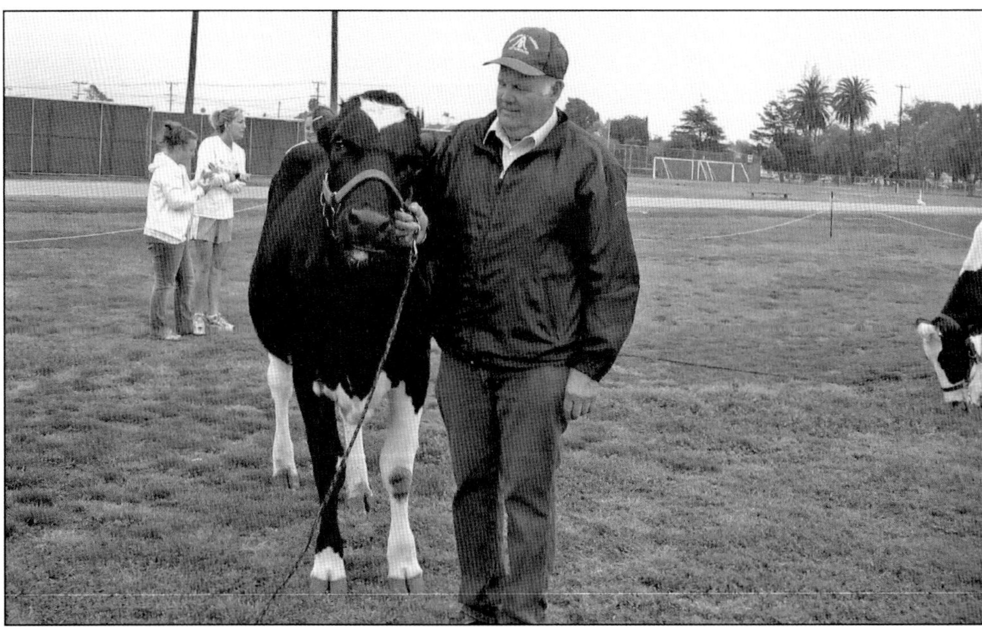

George B. Miller Elementary School opened for the 1961–1962 school year when the city was still called Dairyland. It was the first elementary school built in the city, named in honor of George B. Miller, who served on the Centralia School Board from 1902 to 1909. In 1904, Miller and the Centralia School Board set a precedent for California by providing free textbooks and paper for the students in the district. The rest of the country soon adopted this practice. Miller is called the "Father of Cypress" for his contributions to the city. Until the mid-1950s, Valley View Street was named Miller Street. (Both, courtesy of George B. Miller School, Centralia School District.)

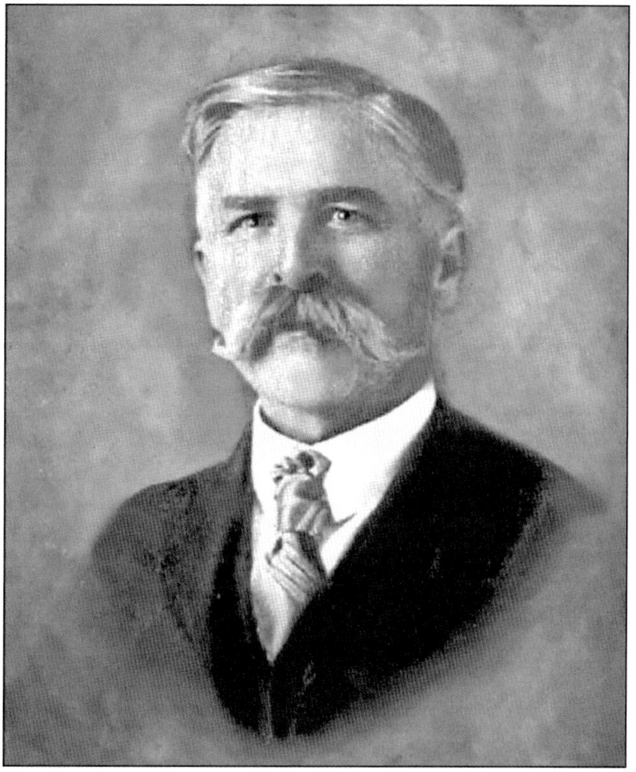

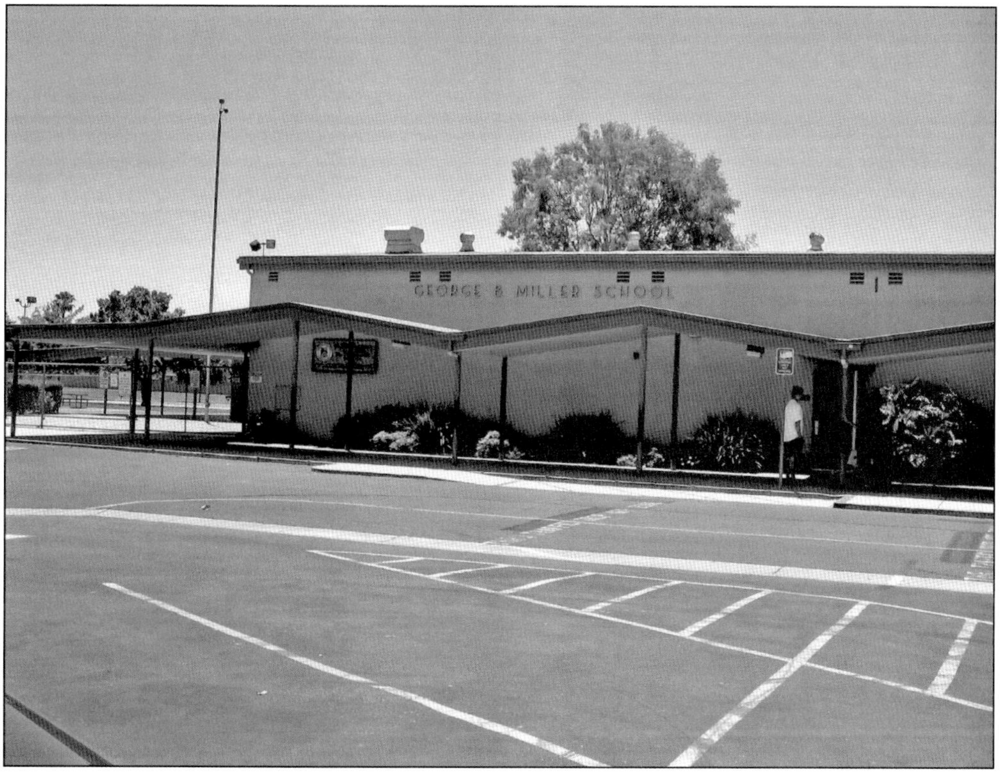

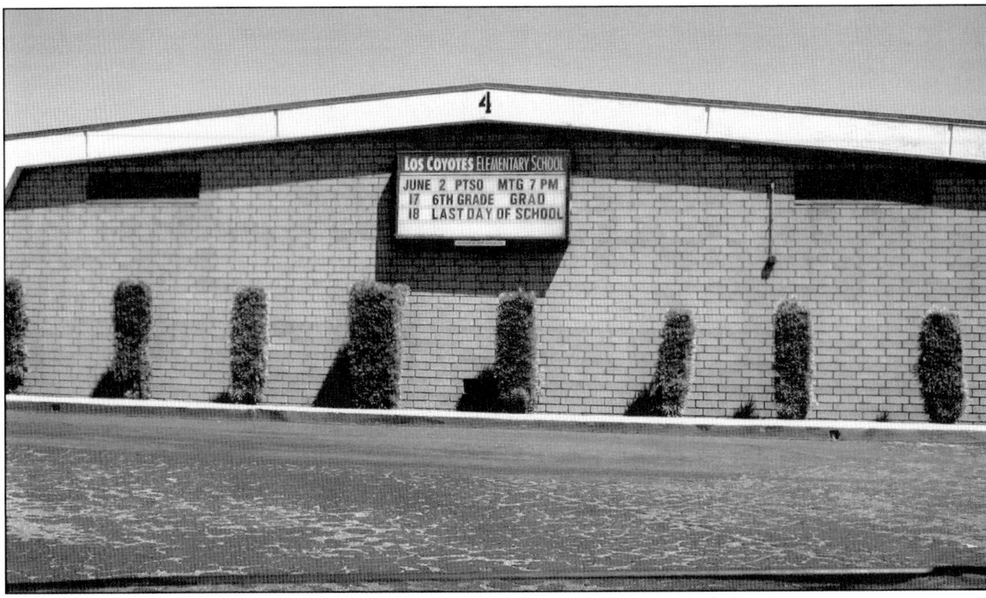

Los Coyotes Elementary School was named for the largest of the six subdivided land grants, which began as the Nieto land grant in 1784. The school was dedicated on February 7, 1970. Below, from left to right, are the first principal of Los Coyotes School, Dr. Joseph Fairbanks; grand master mason Chester R. MacPhee; La Palma mayor Jake Westra; and the superintendent of Centralia School District, Dr. Paul Doss. (Both, courtesy of Ron and Elfriede Mac Iver.)

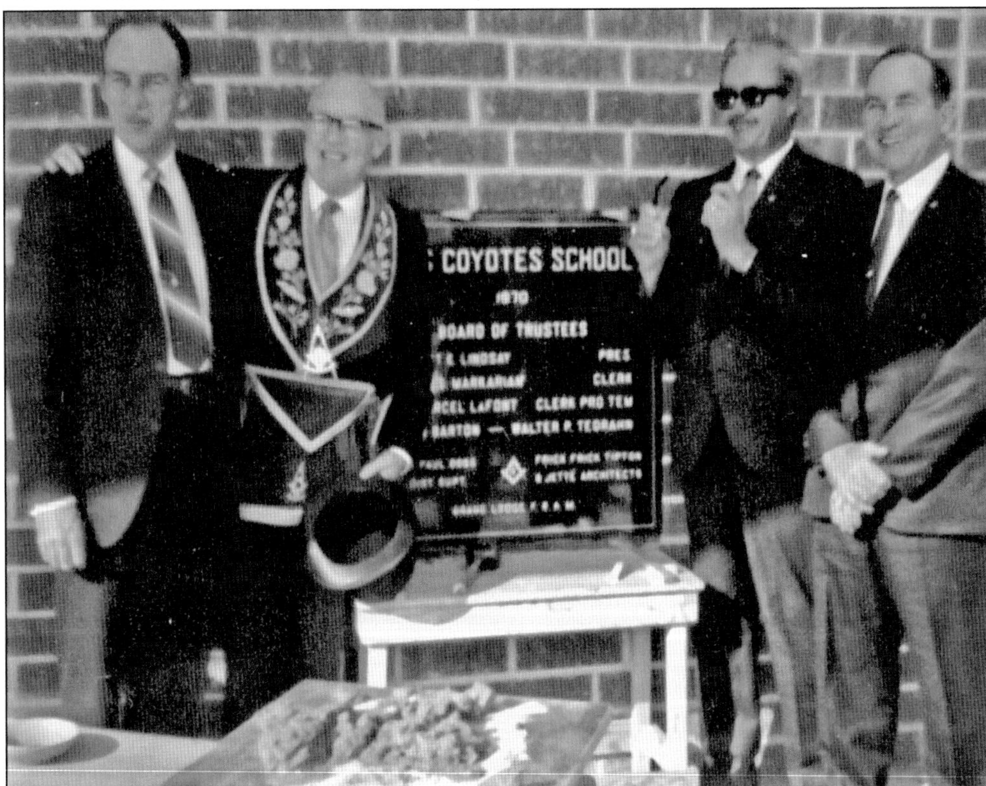

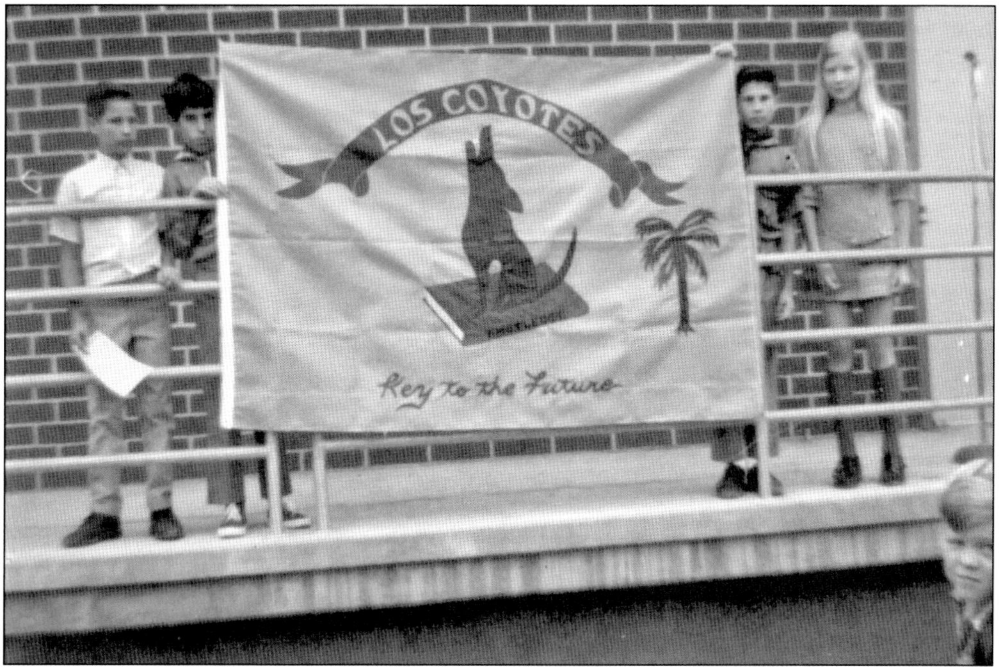

The first Los Coyotes School flag was designed by Peter Mac Iver, Alex Mac Iver, and Dawn Heiss. Showing the flag to the assembled student body are, from left to right, Peter Mac Iver, Kenneth Felig, Alex Mac Iver, and Dawn Heiss. (Courtesy of Ron and Elfriede Mac Iver.)

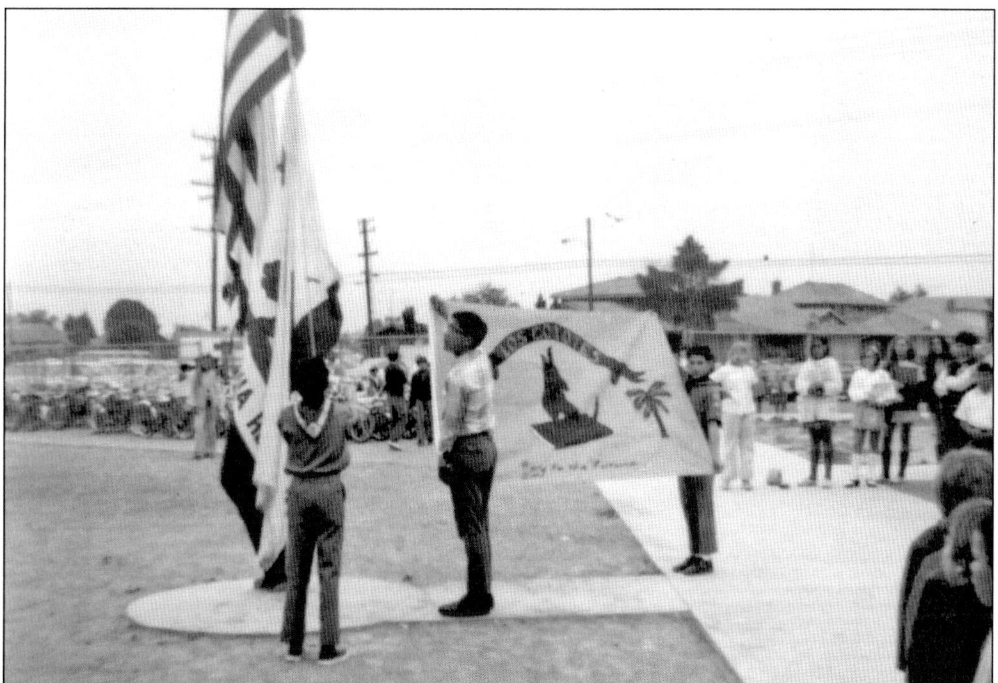

Raising the Los Coyotes flag for the first time are, from left to right, Boy Scout Troop No. 161 members Ken Felig, Ernie Santos, and Alex Mac Iver, with student body assembled to watch the ceremony. (Courtesy of Ron and Elfriede Mac Iver.)

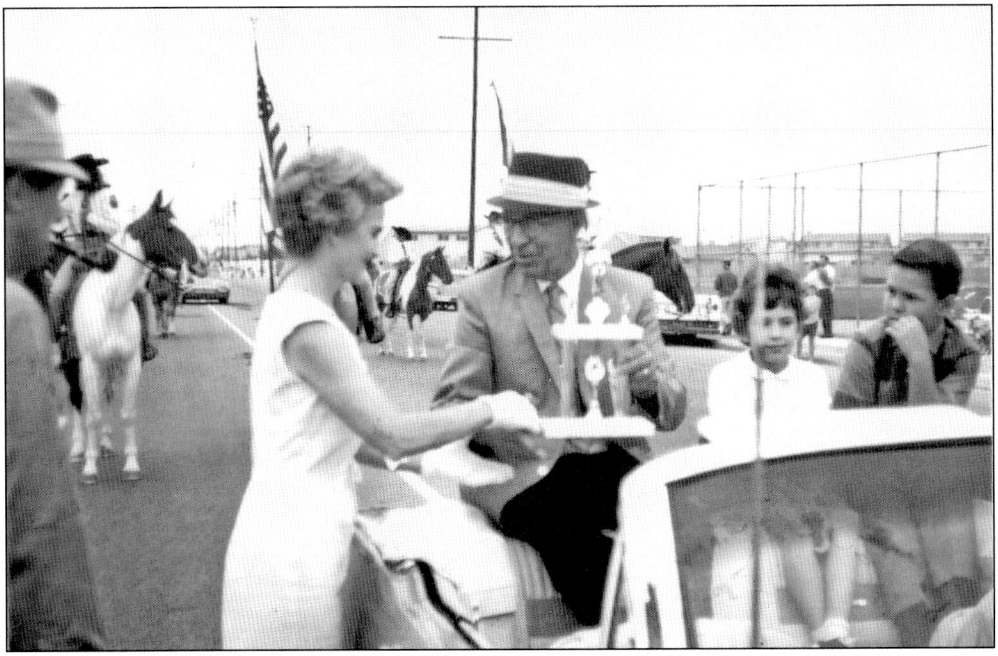

The first City of Vision Day started as a fun day at Cypress Park (now Cypress/Arnold) on July 4, 1966. In 1967, a parade and free fireworks show, encouraged by Mayor Pete Bouma, were added. The Fourth of July City of Vision Day parades lasted through 1978. Here Bea Sorrells presents the grand marshal's trophy to Mayor Pete Bouma, with unnamed bystanders in the background. The picture below is of an equestrian unit following the mayor's car. Mayor Bouma is riding with his granddaughter on Crescent Avenue, passing Kennedy High School, where the parade ends and festivities in the park begin. (Both, courtesy of City of La Palma Archives.)

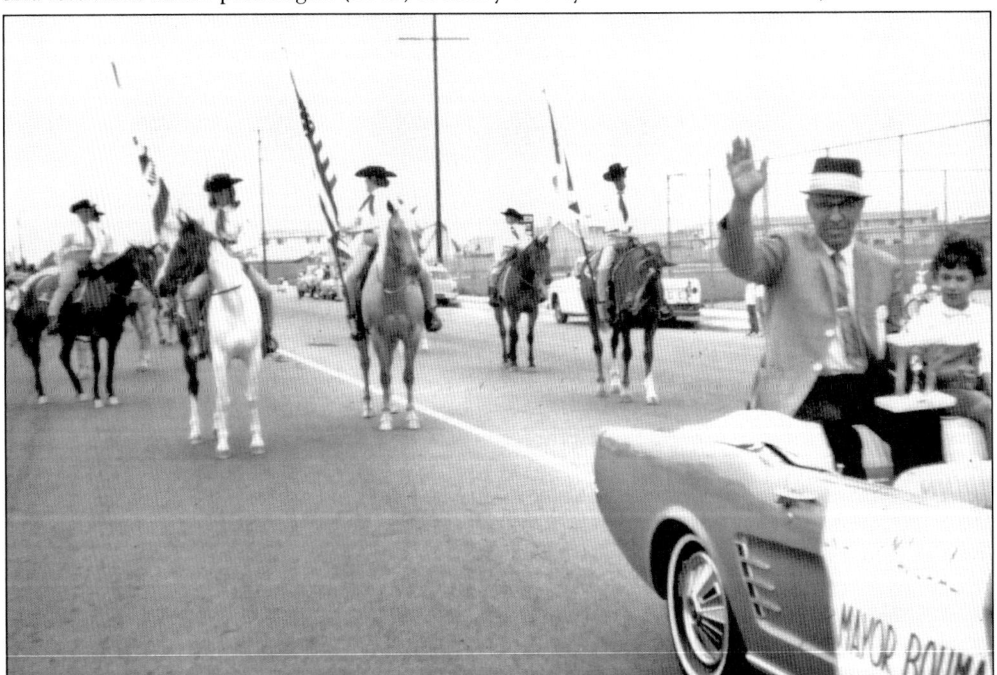

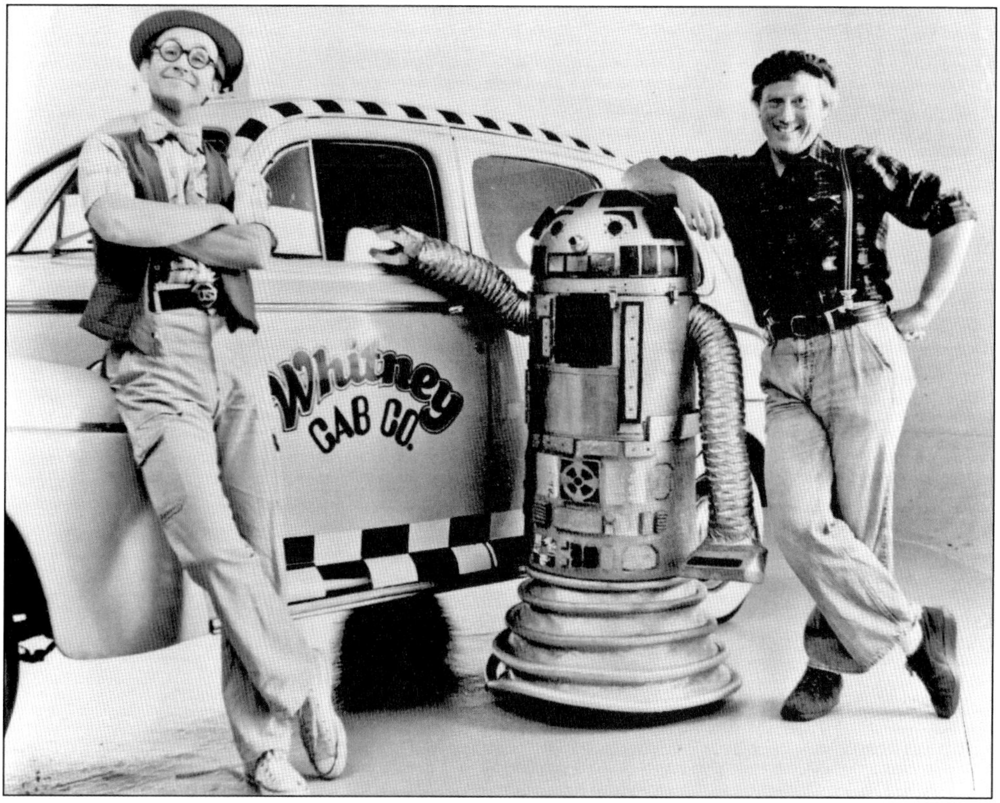

Many celebrities have participated in La Palma parades and main-stage entertainment in the park. In 1979, the Emmy Award–winning team from *Whitney and the Robot* appeared. Above are, from left to right, Whitney Rydbeck, Buddy Douglas (the robot), and Robert V. Greene (Corky). In 1972, the military services were represented. Participants are unidentified. (Both, courtesy of City of La Palma Archives.)

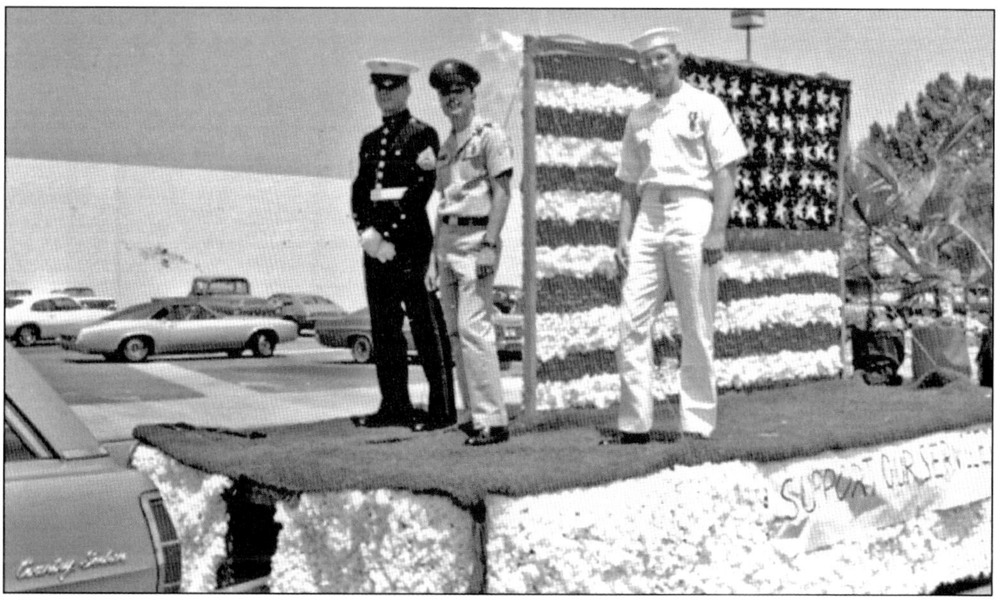

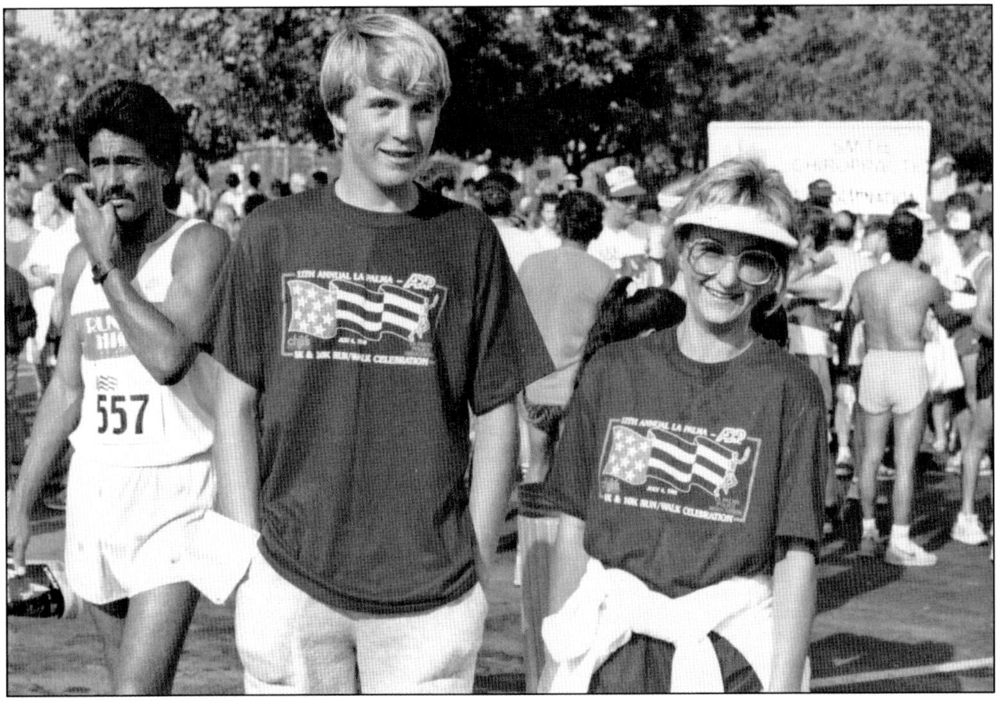

The first La Palma Fitness Run for Fun started on July 4, 1979. Unidentified volunteers are posted along the route to make sure that the runners and walkers have water available. The Kiwanis Club serves a pancake breakfast, and neighbors enjoy another opportunity to sit and chat. The picture below shows Mayor Ed Byrne (left) congratulating two of the 1984 participants, Alison Snow and Walt Hoges. (Both, courtesy of La Palma Recreation and Community Services.)

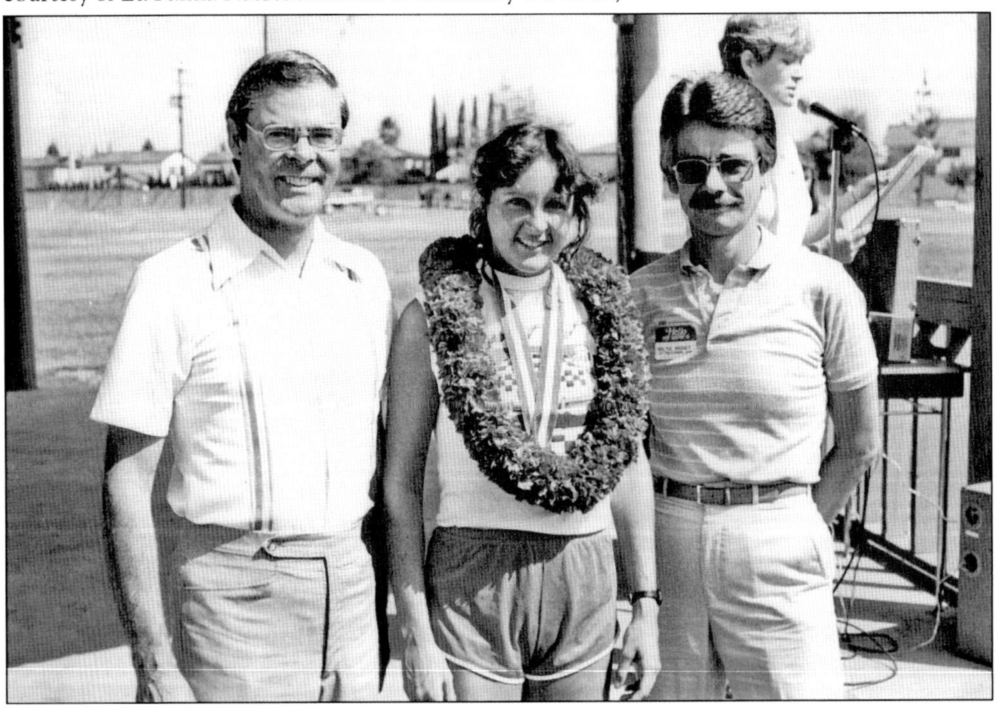

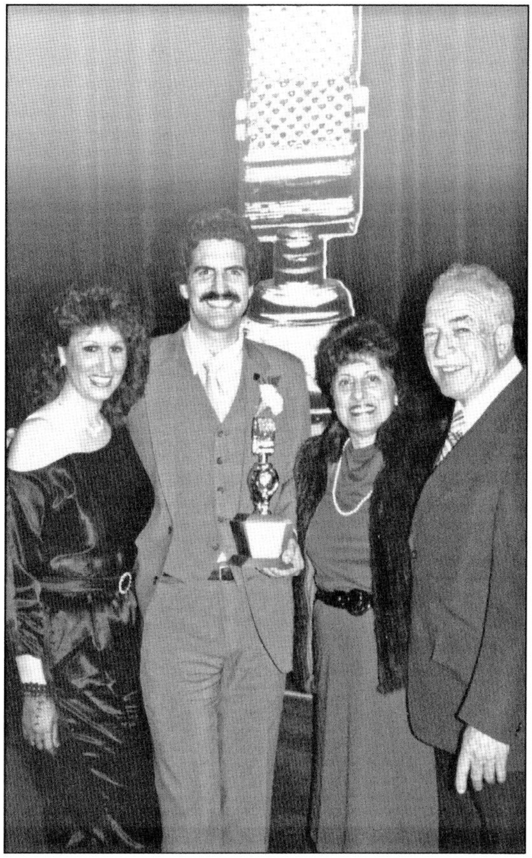

Pictured at left are, from left to right, unidentified, John Palminteri, Ana Palminteri, and Frank Palminteri. John was awarded the Radio and Television Association of Southern California award for Best Live Coverage, Division B, in 1992. Frank Palminteri served on a number of committees on behalf of La Palma and received a retirement plaque from the City of Los Angeles as "Nighttime Mayor" for his career as director of Public Works. Ana's story first appeared in the *La Palma Police Community Newsletter* (June 2005, Issue 4) as a tribute because she has been a participant in the La Palma Fitness Run for Fun events since 1988. She came in first place in 1988 and 1989. She continued to participate until 1998 when she placed third at the age of 80. Over the years, the La Palma Fitness Run for Fun has welcomed participants of all abilities. The participants pictured below are unidentified but coucilman Larry Herman, at far right, is timing them as they set off. (Both, courtesy of La Palma Recreation and Community Services.)

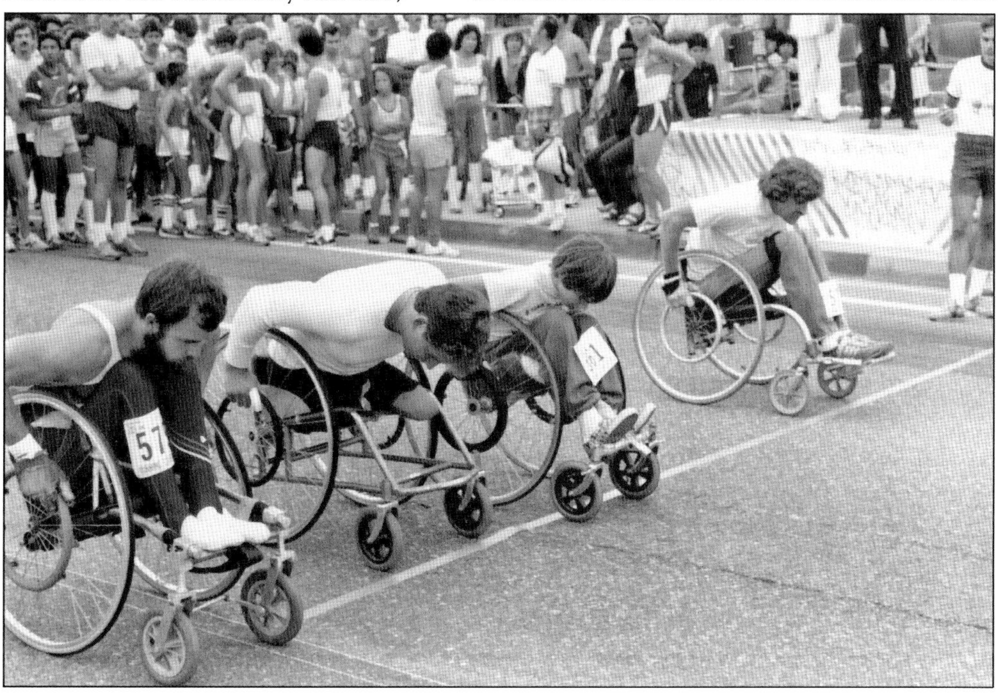

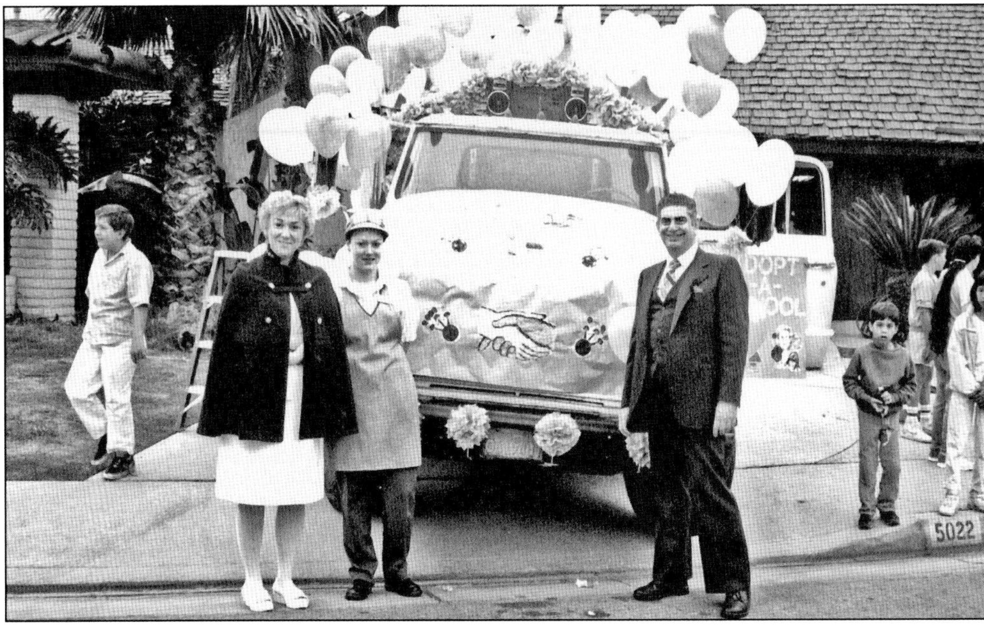

The Los Coyotes School float for International Days is prepared in Barbara Kahn's driveway in 1987. The open door of the truck is marked "Adopt a School." Jay Goldberg is one of the parents dressed as an attorney. He is with the "school nurse" and "cafeteria lady." They are parents who will ride on the float with Jay. The others in the picture are unidentified neighbors. (Courtesy of La Palma Recreation and Community Services.)

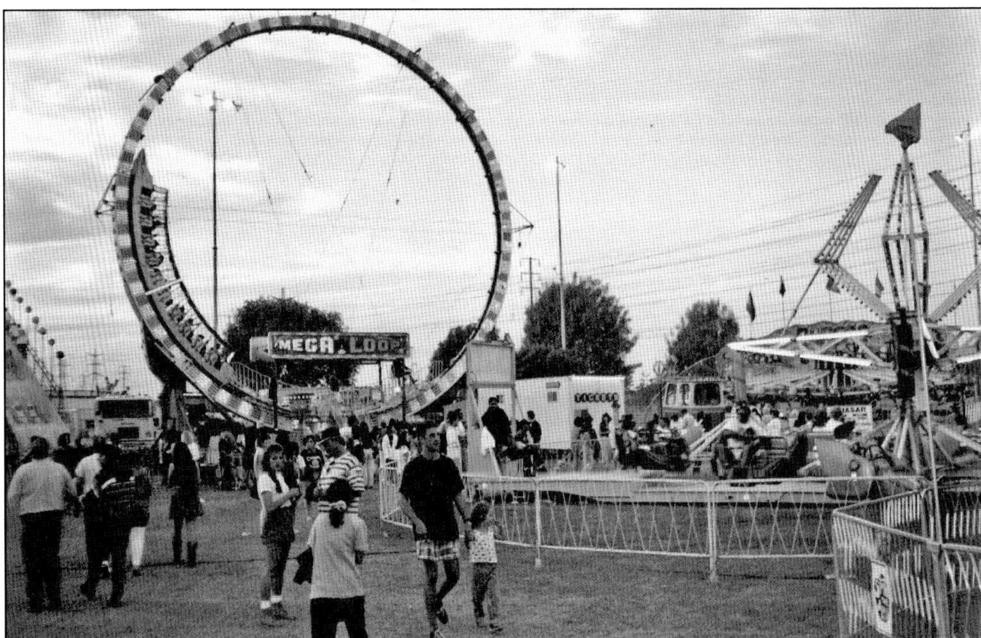

International Days had its beginning in October 1985 and was replaced in November 1989 by La Palma Days, which was celebrated on Veteran's Day weekend. The picture shows the celebration in Central Park in 1987. Circus Vargas first appeared in 1986 and came to La Palma for the last time in February 1990. (Courtesy of La Palma Recreation and Community Services.)

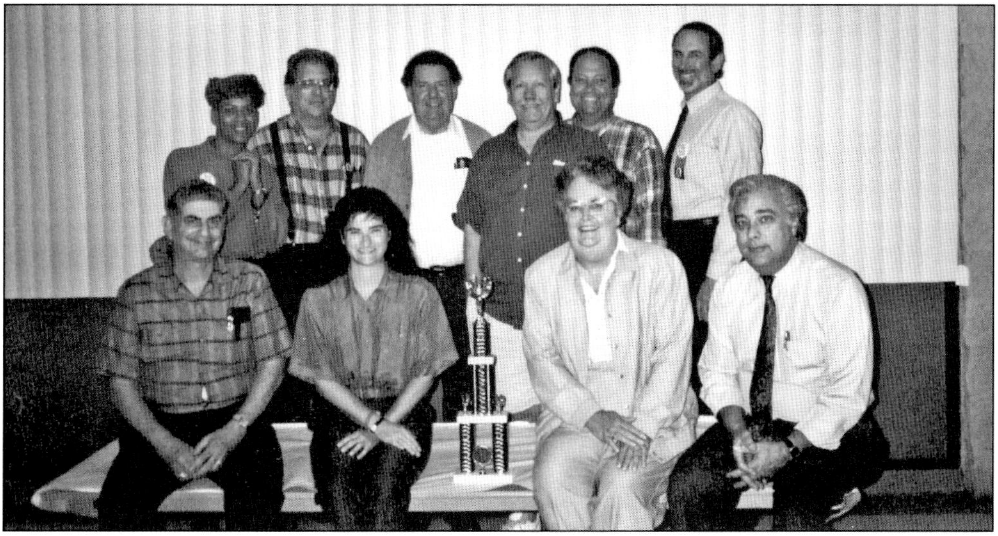

Events in La Palma depend upon organization, planning, community dedication, and involvement for success. La Palma's continued volunteer participation is nurtured by the regular acknowledgement of its volunteers. The picture of the parade and awards committee shows a large group of volunteers, who put in their time and effort for many years. From left to right are (first row) Jay Goldberg, Laura Smilkstein, Kay Pease, and Richard Polis; (second row) Angie Thompson, Carl Ericksen, Howard Pease, Keith Nelson, Dale Oates, and Ron Kenney. (Courtesy of La Palma Recreation and Community Services.)

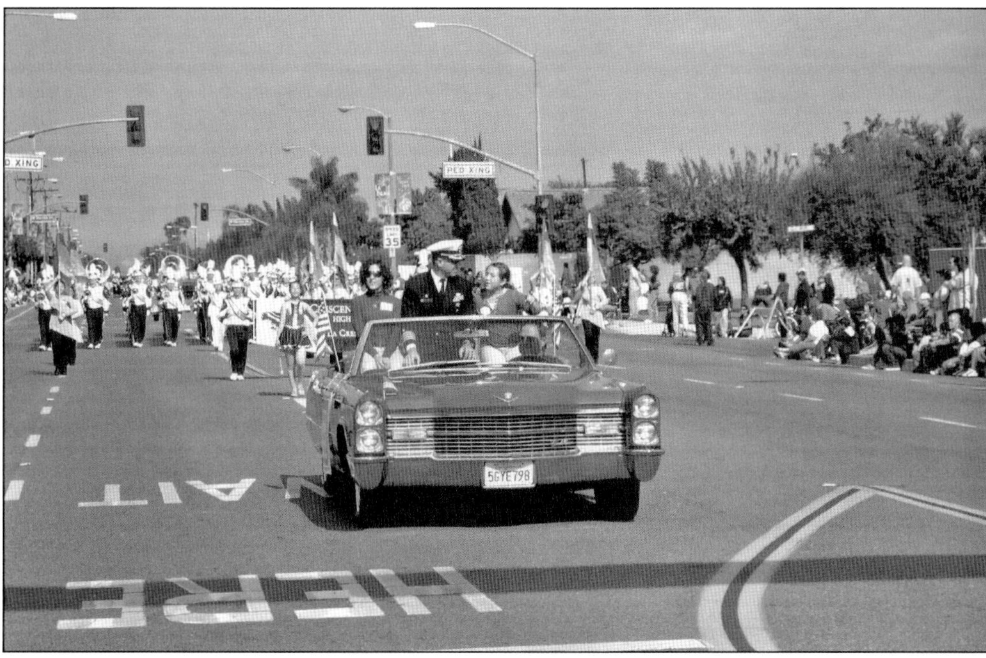

This is the final stretch of a typical parade coming down Walker Street. Changing La Palma Days to November made it possible for school bands to participate. Uniforms were unavailable in July because schools were closed for summer vacation. La Palma has also been given the distinction of holding the official Veteran's Day parade by proclamation of the Orange County Board of Supervisors. (Courtesy of City of La Palma Archives.)

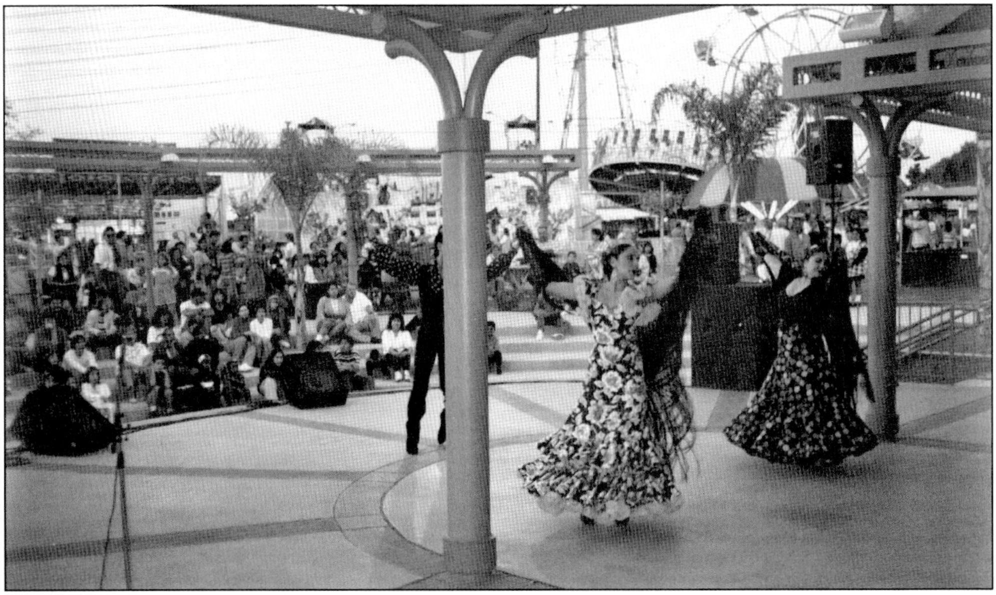

Central Park is the hub of family community involvement. Large audiences gather to watch the dancers performing on the main stage for International Days in 1987. Children are entertained by the rides shown in the background. Community groups, such as the Kiwanis Club, provide food, hobbyist show their crafts, and the chamber of commerce and cultural/ historical committees set up booths to entertain and inform guests about what the city offers. The picture below shows La Palma Days in 2005 and another diverse group of entertainers taking center stage. This community event has grown more successful each year. (Above, courtesy of La Palma Recreation and Community Services; below, courtesy of Mike Yasuda, photographer.)

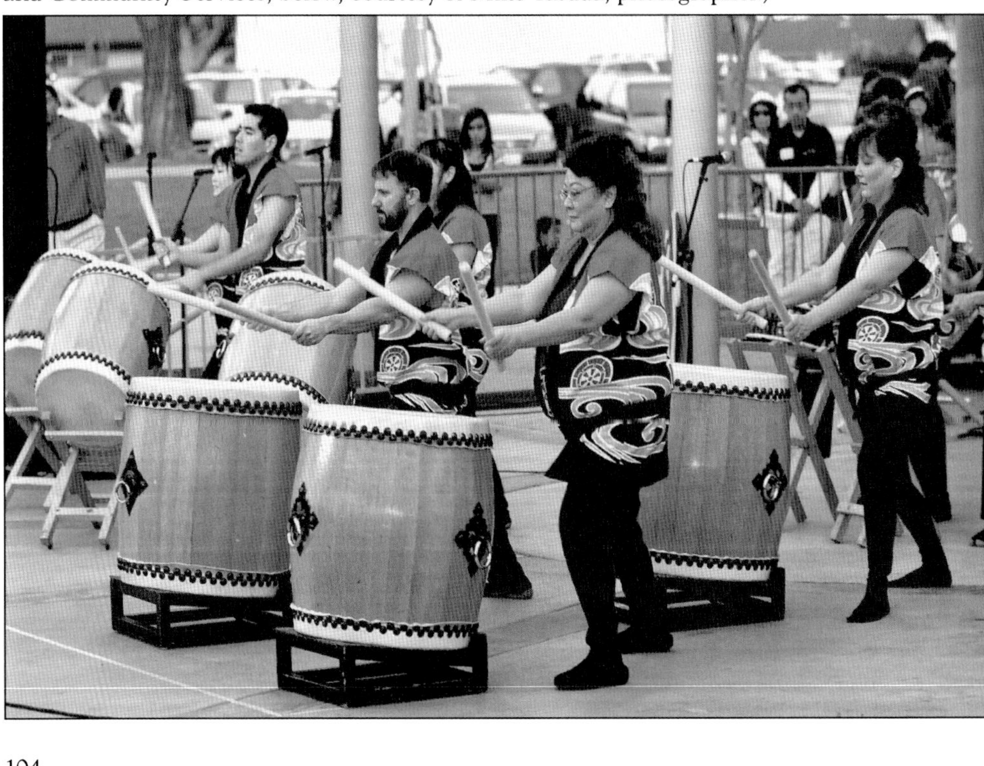

La Palma, for the official Veteran's Day parade, had planned to honor retired M.Sgt. Alfredo Lagmay Sr., once again. Master Sergeant Lagmay was a La Palma resident for 36 years and the oldest World War II veteran in Southern California. Unfortunately, he died at age 91, just three days before the parade in November 2003. His daughter Bella Lagmay-Funk and grandson Diamond Preston Lagmay rode in the parade in his honor, holding his picture. (Courtesy of Loreen Berlin.)

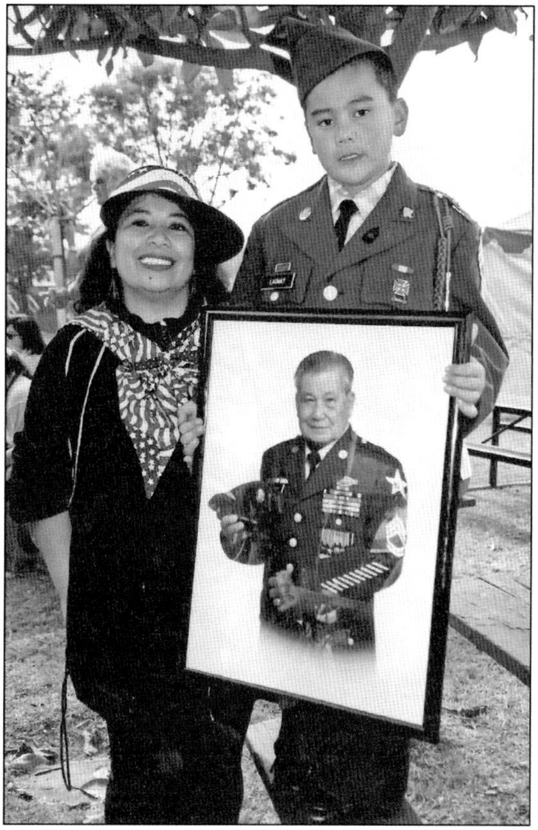

Knott's Berry Farm participated in the 2005 City of Vision Day parade with Snoopy riding in a stagecoach (below), to the delight of the audience. (Courtesy of Mike Yasuda, photographer.)

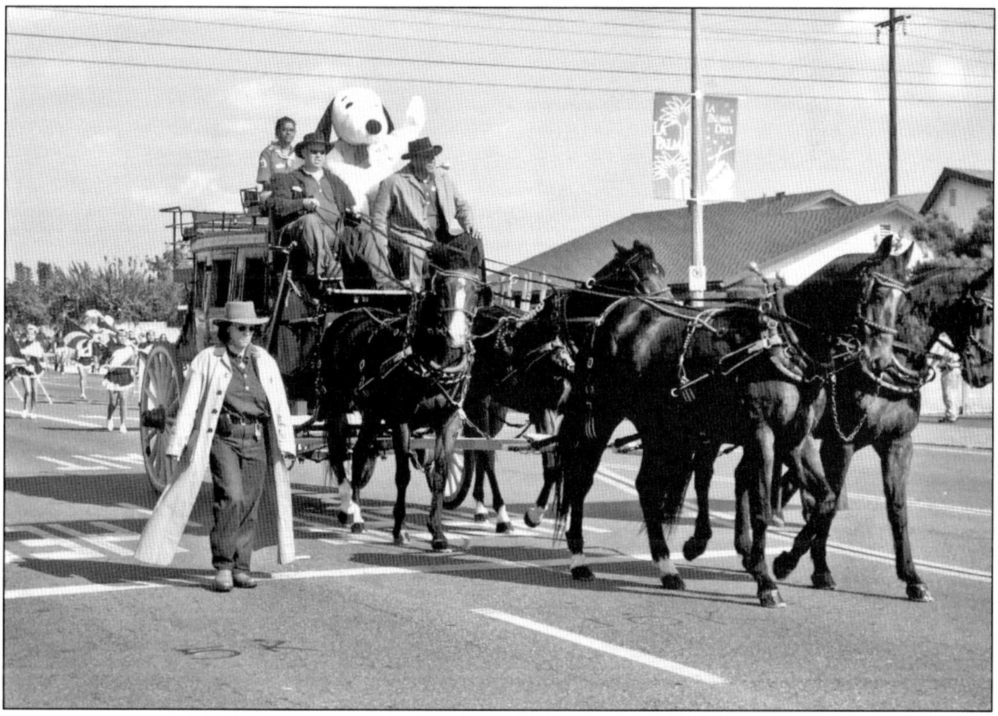

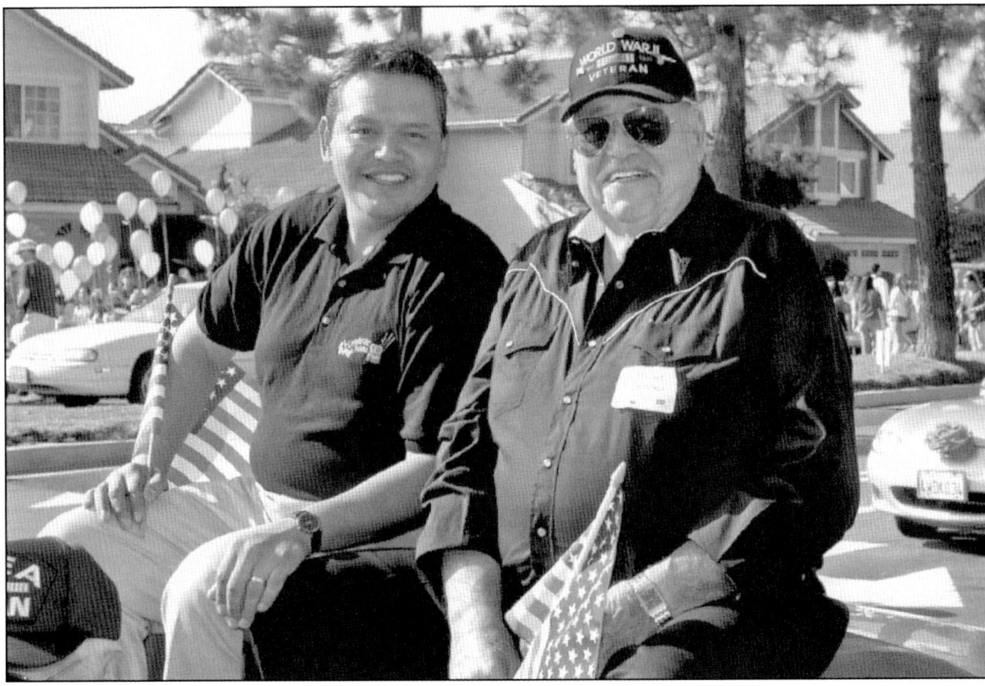

Councilman Ralph Rodriguez rides in the La Palma Days 2005 Parade with his dad, Manuel M. Rodriguez, a World War II veteran. Manuel Rodriguez fought in five major European battles, including the Invasion of Normandy (D-day). He is also the recipient of a Purple Heart and a Bronze Star. (Courtesy of Mike Yasuda, photographer.)

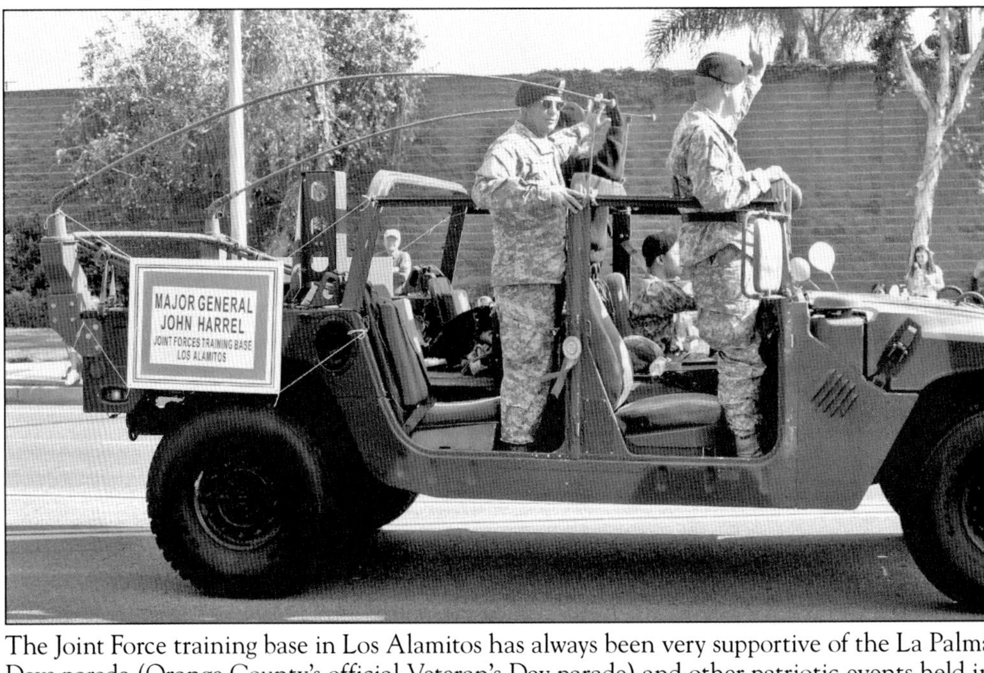

The Joint Force training base in Los Alamitos has always been very supportive of the La Palma Days parade (Orange County's official Veteran's Day parade) and other patriotic events held in La Palma throughout the year, such as the Memorial Day ceremonies. (Courtesy of City of La Palma Archives.)

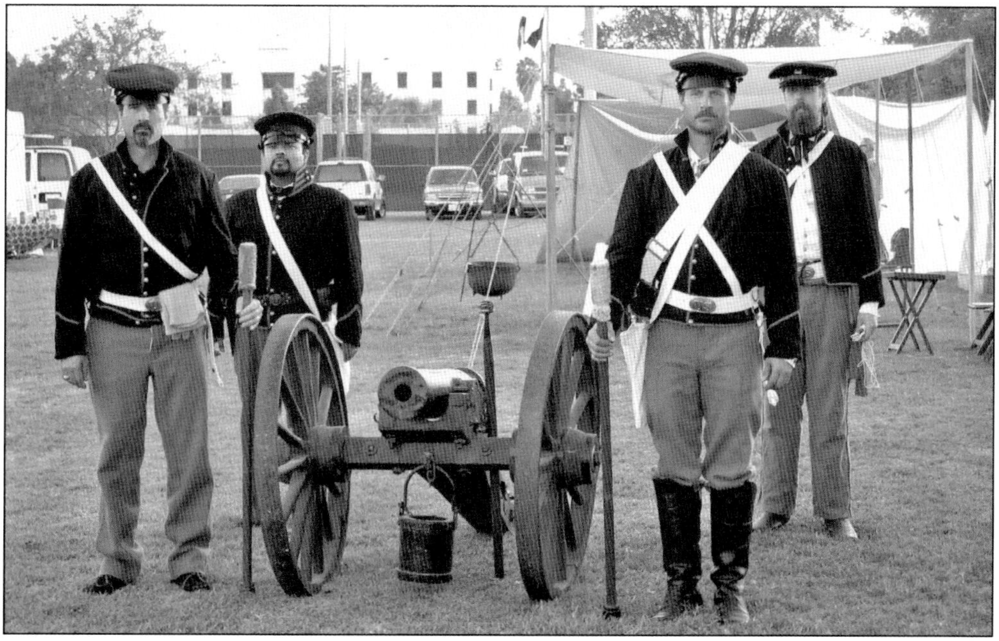

The "Army of the West, Corps of Topographical Engineers" served in California. These reenactors have appeared during La Palma Days for several years, with a campsite, uniforms, and artifacts of the period, as authentic as possible. They are happy to explain and demonstrate, when possible, the uses of each item to the public. From left to right are Alex Mac Iver, Alfredo Torres, Michael Mac Iver, and Mark Carlisle. (Courtesy of La Palma Recreation and Community Services.)

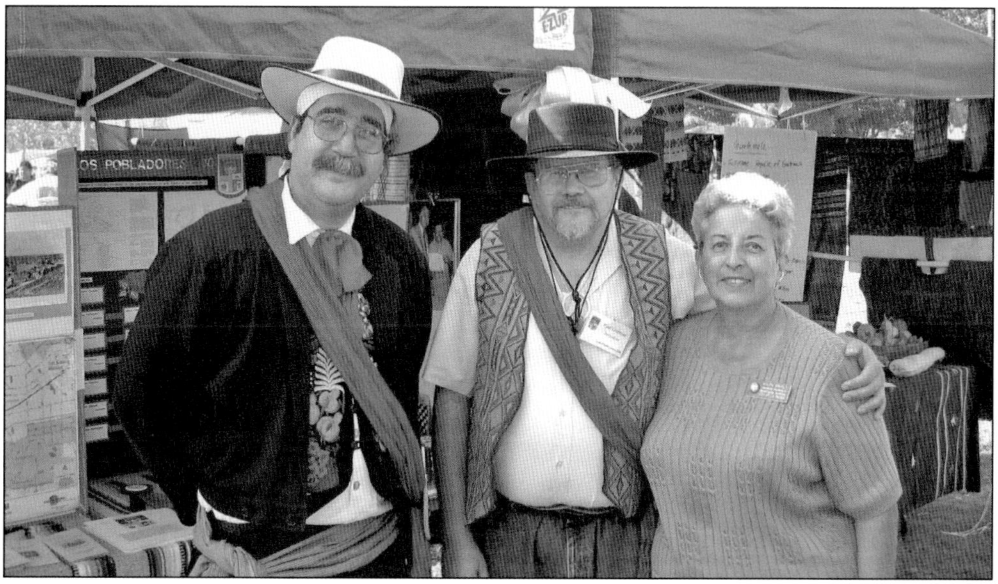

Los pobladores (settlers) are the descendants of the original 11 families to establish the city of Los Angeles in 1781. They came to La Palma Days in 2004 and shared many interesting stories and artifacts with the visitors in their booth. From left to right are Ed Moch, also known as "Al Cota;" Paul Guzman; and Hilda Braly, a member of the community activities and beautification committee (CAB) and active in various other volunteer organizations in La Palma. (Courtesy of Ron and Elfriede Mac Iver.)

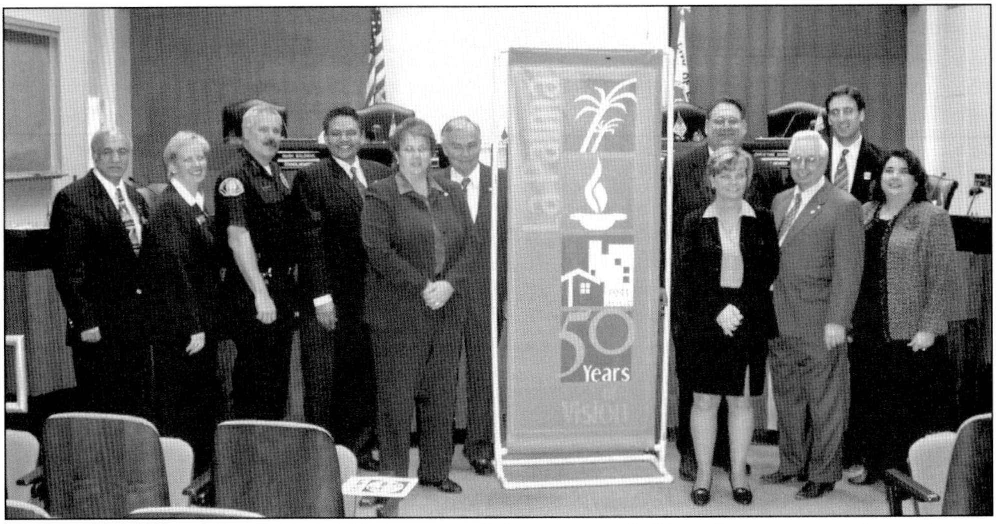

The kickoff for La Palma's 50th anniversary celebration was held at the city council meeting on January 4, 2005. The logo banner for the year was unveiled and everyone posed for a group picture to mark the happy occasion. From left to right are director of public works Ismile Noorbaksh; city manager Catherine Standiford; police chief Ed Ethell; city councilman Ralph Rodriguez; director of recreation and community services Jan Hobson; Mayor Pro Tem Larry Herman; director of finance Robbeyn Bird; Mayor Ken Blake; and council member Christine Barnes; (second row, to the right of the banner) city councilman Mark Waldman and director of community development Dominic Lazzaretto. (Courtesy of City of La Palma Archives.)

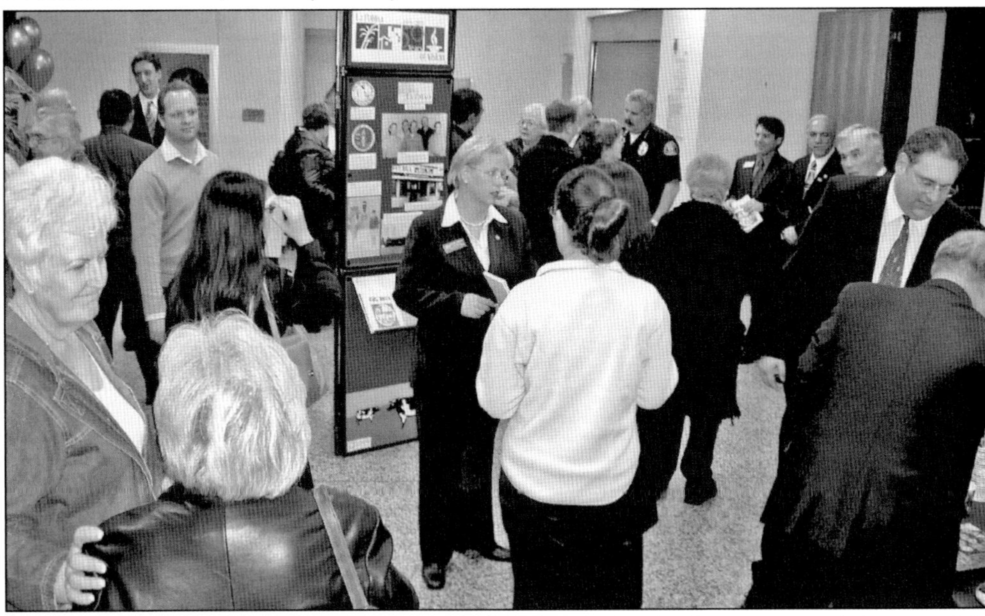

The traveling kiosk was created as a portable history exhibit for the coming celebration of La Palma Days in November. It included anniversary history pamphlets for distribution to the local schools and businesses with a sign-up schedule so everyone who had an interest could view it. Each side contained a different display of the city's history. City manager Catherine Standiford is in front of the kiosk chatting with the group, which included city departments, the council, police, and interested members of the public. (Courtesy of City of La Palma Archives.)

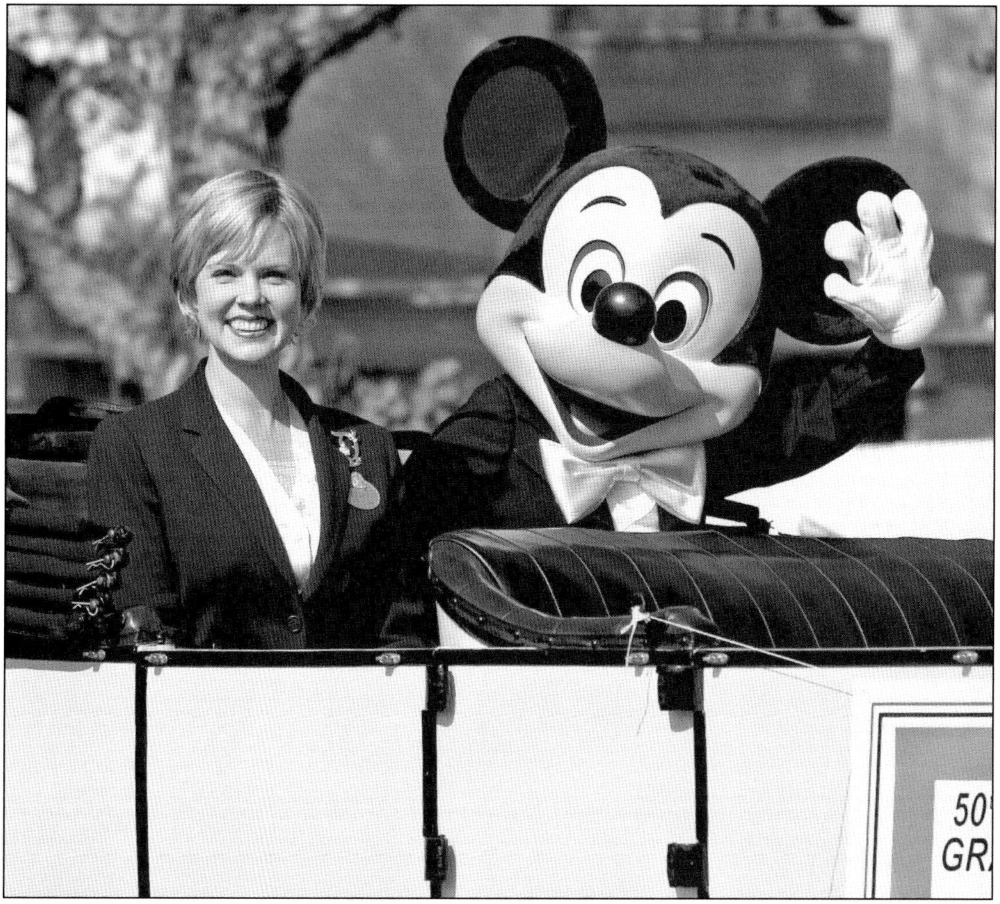

Disneyland and La Palma shared a 50th anniversary. Mickey Mouse became the grand marshal and rode in the La Palma Days Parade in November 2005. (Courtesy of Mike Yasuda, photographer.)

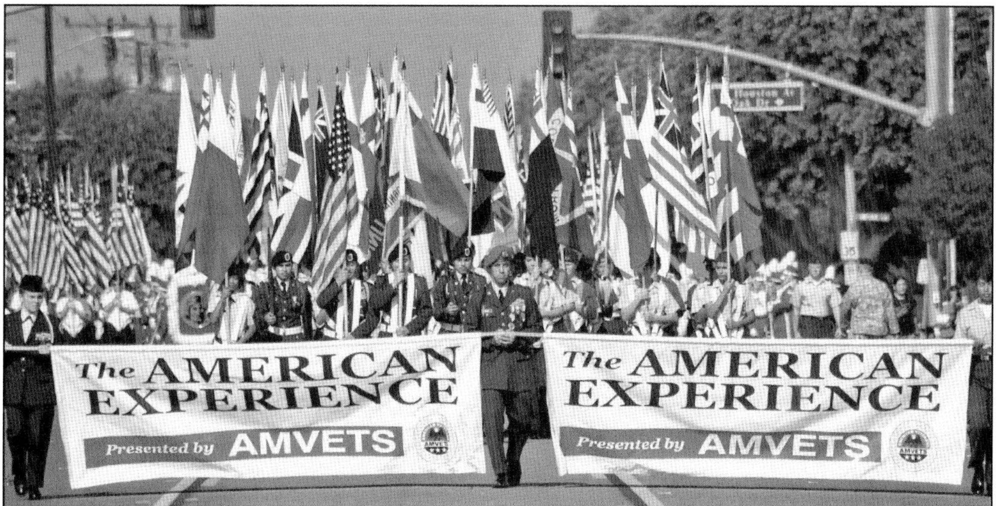

AMVETS marched in the La Palma Days Parade with an impressive, massed display of flags. (Courtesy of Mike Yasuda, photographer.)

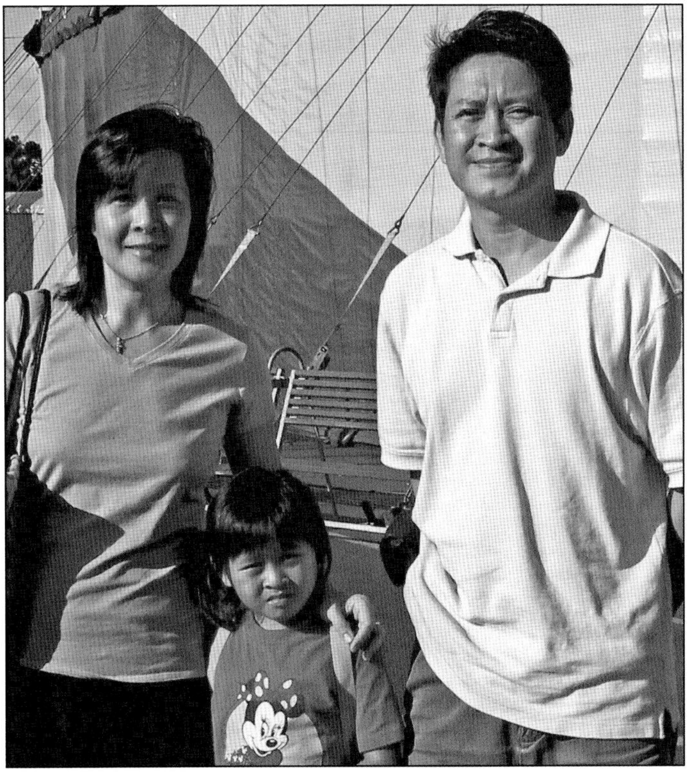

Joely and Ken Ng of Minuteman Press enjoy a few moments of relaxation with their daughter at La Palma Days. They are active members of the chamber of commerce and are kept busy at all the special events when everyone needs a rush job. They somehow manage to meet these deadlines and remain calm. (Courtesy of Ron and Elfriede Mac Iver.)

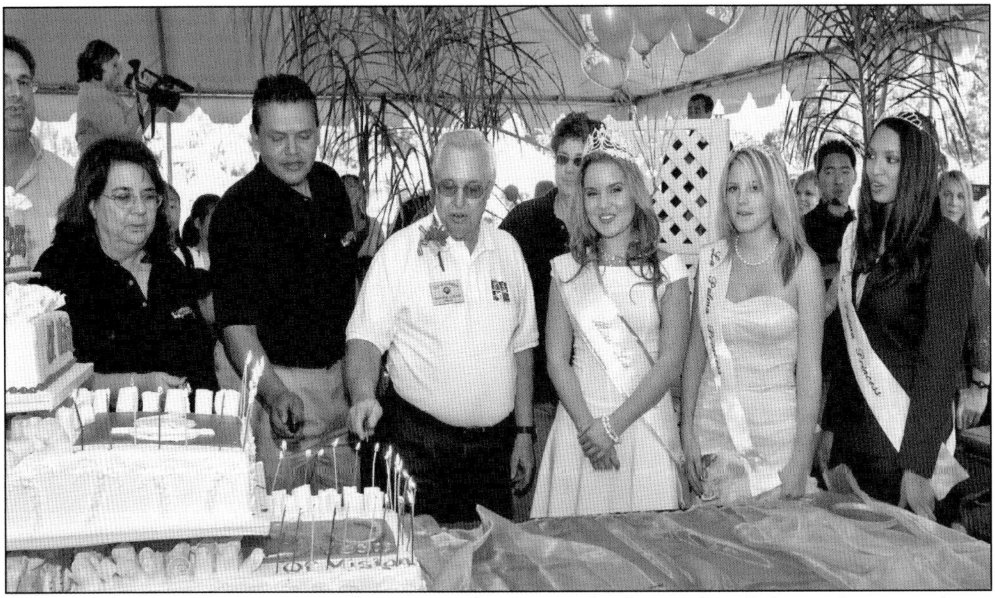

Lighting the 50th anniversary candles on La Palma's special cake are, from left to right, councilman Mark Waldman, council member Christine Barnes, councilman Ralph Rodriguez, Mayor Ken Blake, Miss La Palma 2005–2006 Nicole O'Leary, Jenna Rose Keahey, and Breanna Mayland; (second row) director of recreation and community services Jan Hobson (behind Miss La Palma), recreation specialist Anthony Kim, and staff Lisa Nestoff. Others in picture are unidentified. (Courtesy of Mike Yasuda, photographer.)

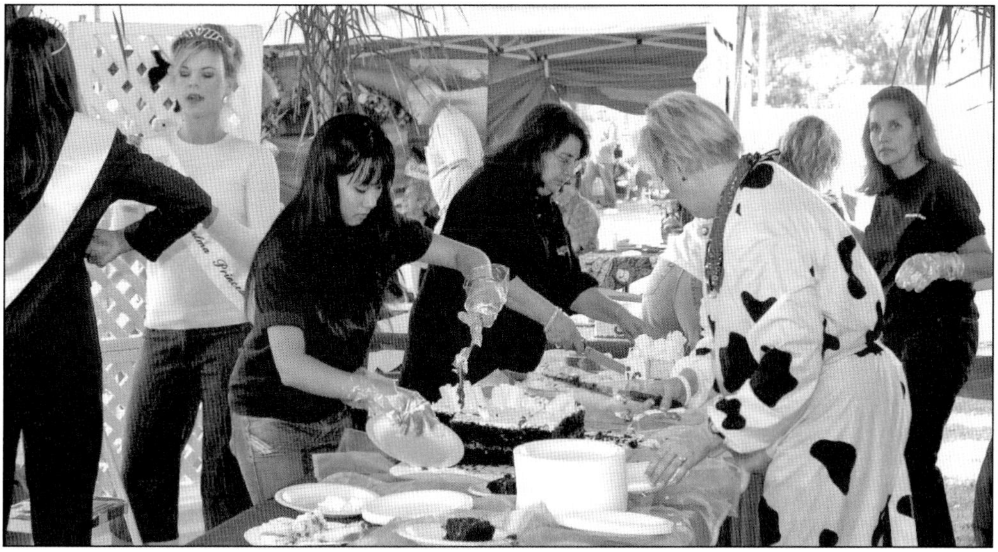

After candles were lit and ceremoniously blown out, the team cut a piece of cake for everyone in attendance, not forgetting those who had to remain in their booths. Park staff delivered to everyone. From left to right are princesses Breanna Mayland and Kelli Wallace, recreation staff member Maureen Guinoo, council member Christine Barnes, and unidentified. City manager Catherine Standiford, who graciously spent the day in a cow costume to honor the occasion, is on the right with senior office staff member Jill Olivier. (Courtesy of Mike Yasuda, photographer.)

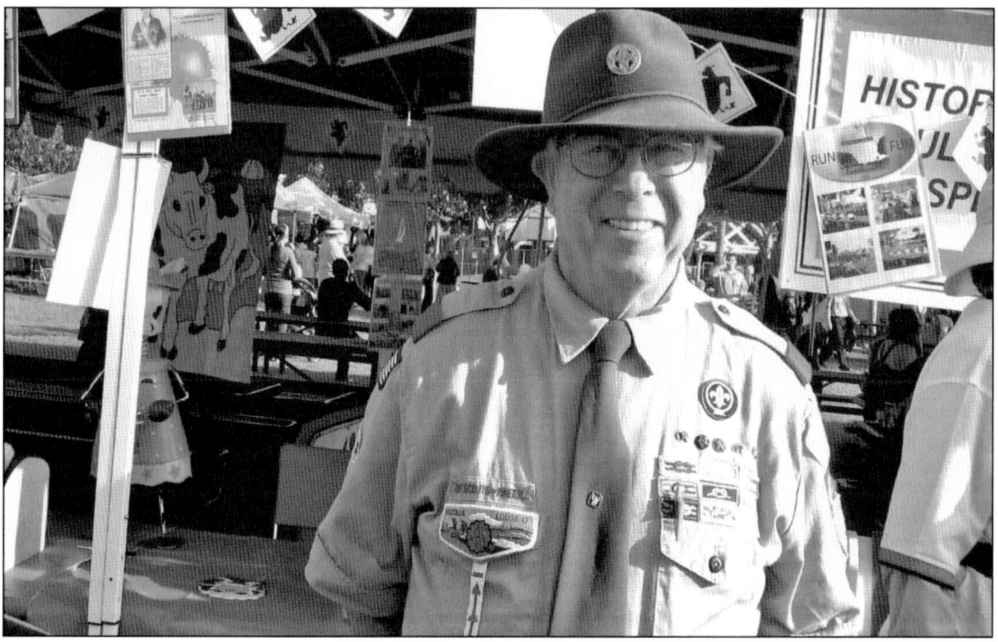

The parade is the highlight of the morning. When it is over, people converge on the park exhibits, food, and entertainment. George Mast is the scoutmaster of Troop No. 650. He posed for this picture in front of the combined chamber of commerce and history booth in 2007. George, like other La Palmans, wears several volunteer hats. He worked in the Kiwanis booth last year. La Palma's first Eagle Scout is pictured on a placard hanging on the left. (Courtesy of Ron and Elfriede Mac Iver.)

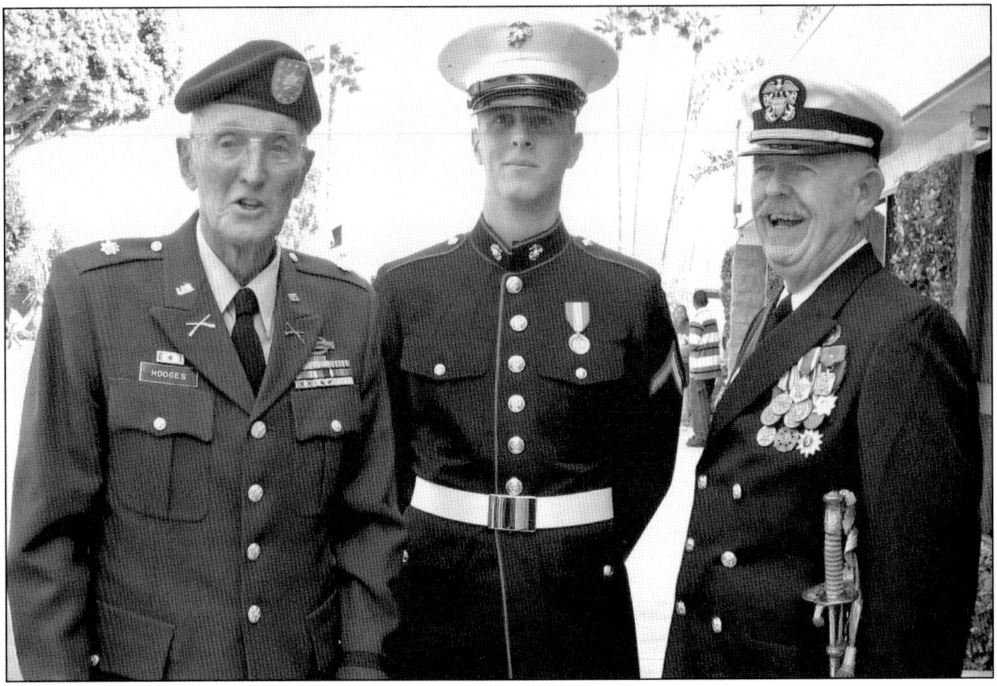

La Palma Days is a tribute to local veterans and their families. This picture has captured two generations of servicemen. From left to right are retired Lt. Col. William A. Hodges; his grandson Pfc. Michael Hoffert, USMC; and retired Lt. Comdr. David M. Bradley, U.S. Navy. La Palma has been fortunate to have Lieutenant Colonel Hodges and Lieutenant Commander Bradley on the parade-reviewing stand for the last several years. (Courtesy of Ron and Elfriede Mac Iver.)

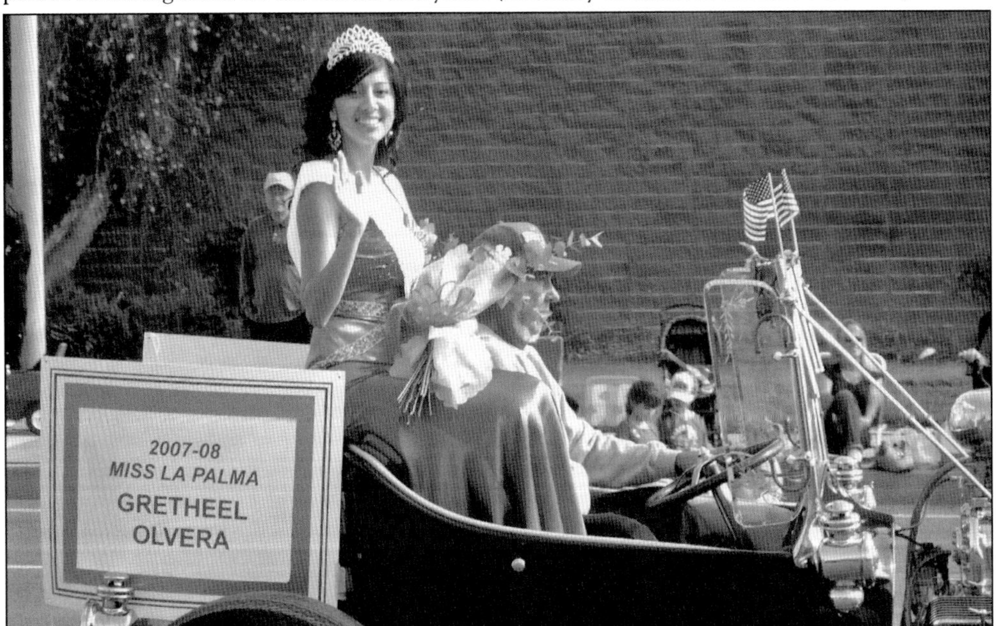

Miss La Palma, Gretheel Olvera, begins her reign, on a float in the La Palma Days Parade. (Courtesy of La Palma Recreation and Community Services.)

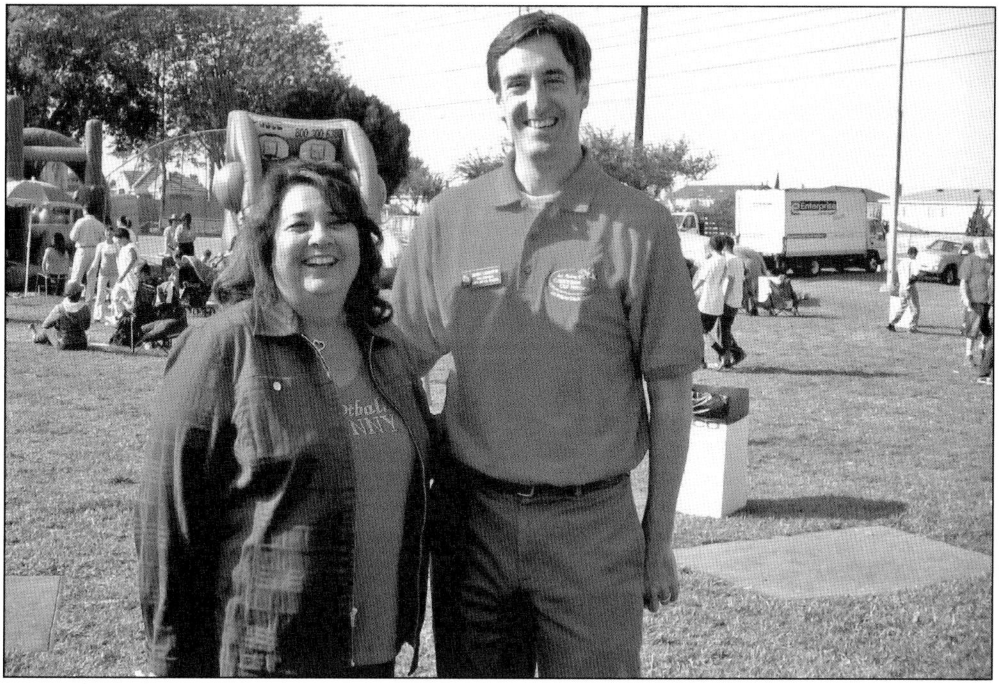

Council member Christine Barnes and city manager Dominic Lazzaretto enjoy the opportunity to chat with residents and guests as they stroll around the park. (Courtesy of Ron and Elfriede Mac Iver.)

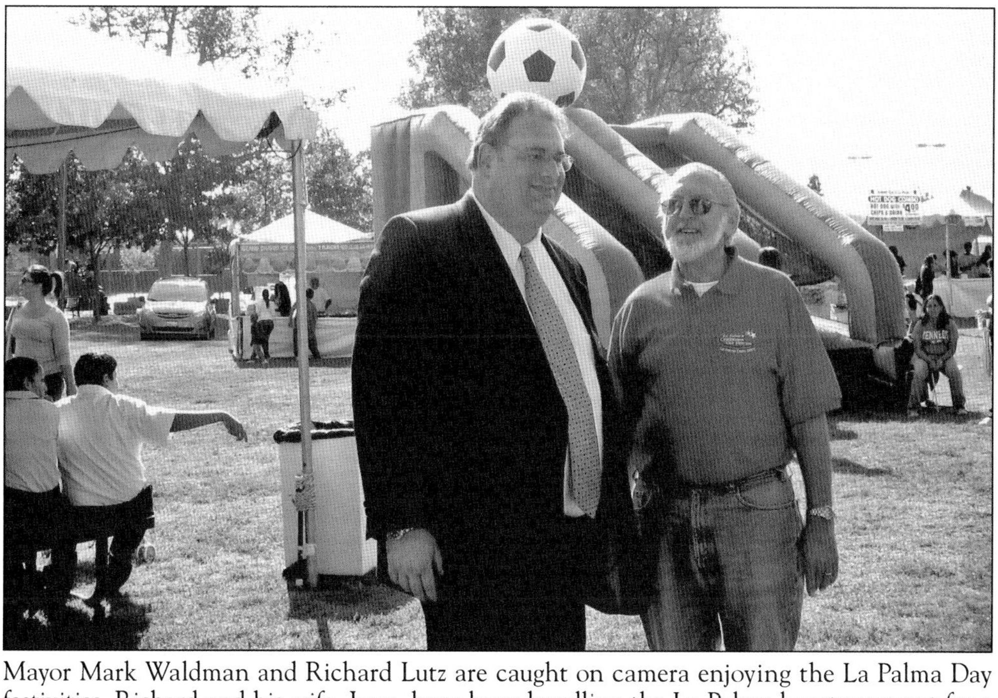

Mayor Mark Waldman and Richard Lutz are caught on camera enjoying the La Palma Day festivities. Richard and his wife, Joan, have been handling the La Palma beauty pageant for a number of years. Their daughter Amy Lynne Lutz was Miss La Palma 1993–1994. (Courtesy of Ron and Elfriede Mac Iver.)

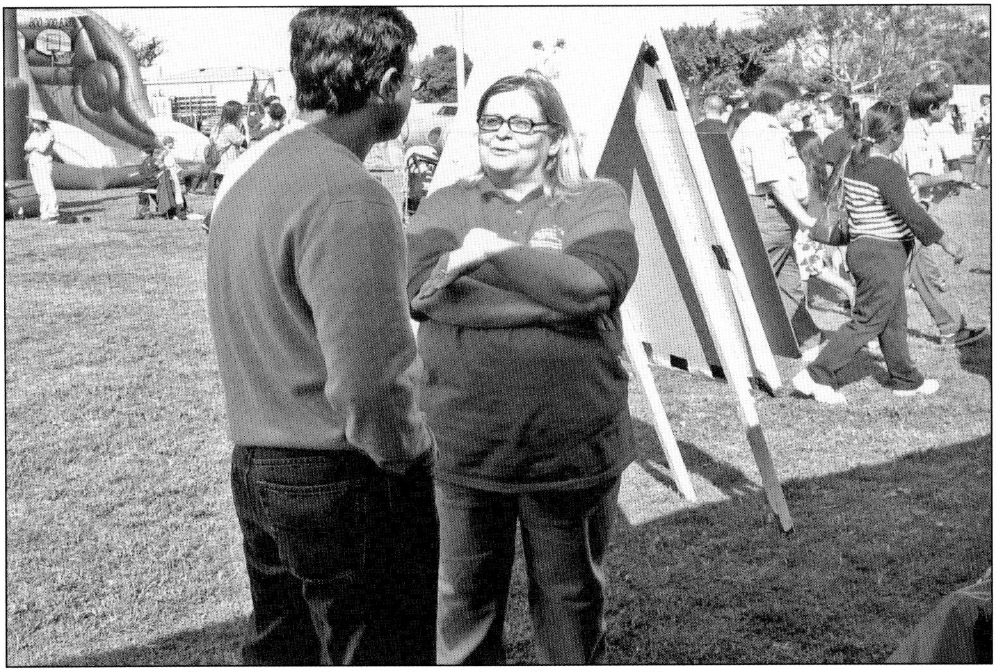

Linda Houston talks with a park guest during La Palma Days. The community enjoys this event, and the volunteers, who begin meetings in mid-May, come back year after year. (Courtesy of Ron and Elfriede Mac Iver.)

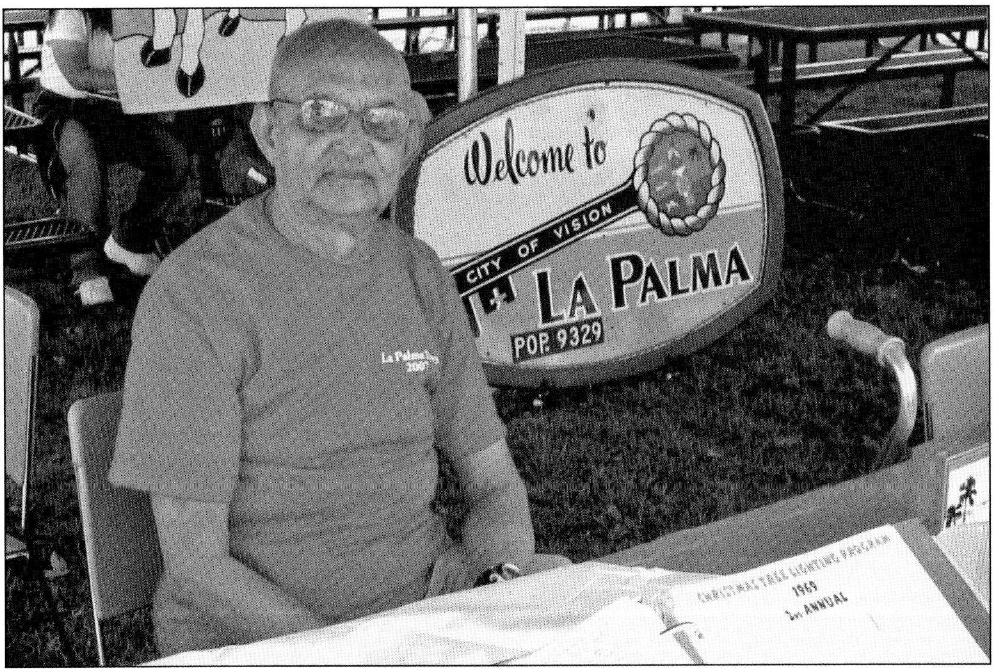

Arvind Patel is an amazing volunteer. He walks everywhere in the city and accepts few rides. Arvind is always available to help in whatever job is needed. Here he is "manning the history booth." He answers questions for the public and keeps the last remaining city sign safe. (Courtesy of Ron and Elfriede Mac Iver.)

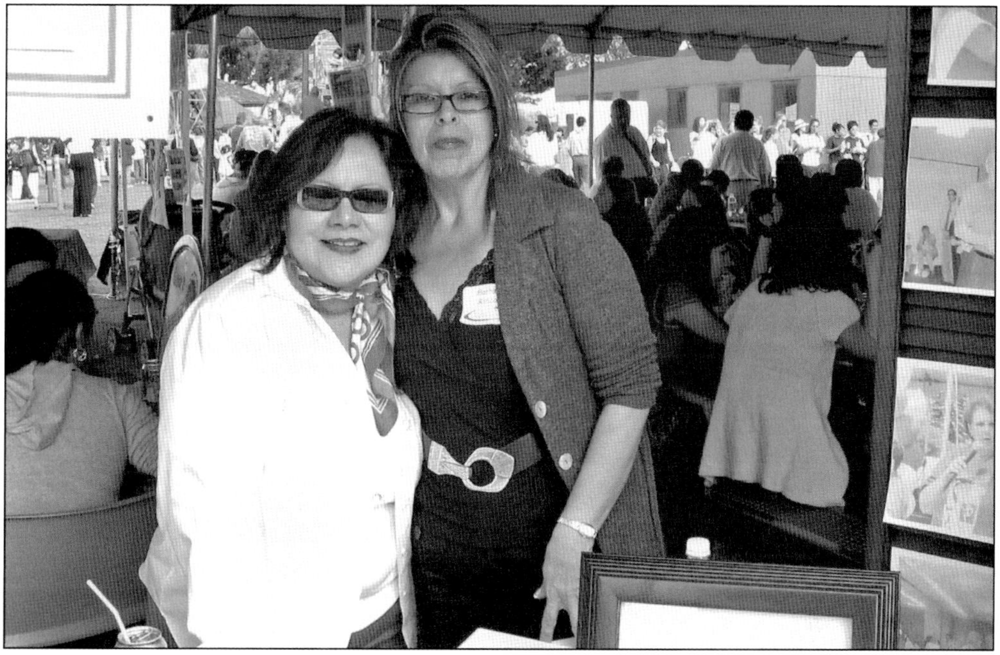

La Palma Chamber of Commerce shared a booth with the cultural and historical committee. The chamber gave away cookbooks with international recipes and souvenirs to guests. In the background on the right, guests could also pick their own design for henna hand painting. From left to right are executive director Esther De Leon Hernandez and president Barbara Rincon. (Courtesy of Ron and Elfriede Mac Iver.)

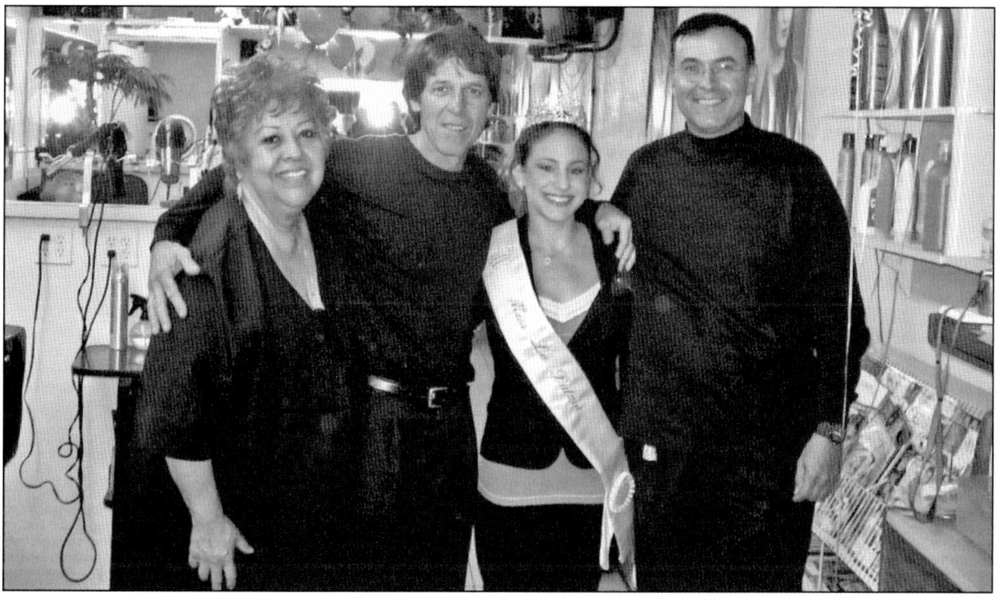

The Shear Artisan celebrated its 25th anniversary on November 2, 2007, with a party for chamber of commerce members and guests. This shop has been in business since the time the city was called Dairyland. Its first barber was John Reinhart, whose customers went to "John the Barber" for a haircut. From left to right are Fran Betancur, John Gonzalez, Miss La Palma Gina Bartoli, and owner and stylist Tim George. (Courtesy of Ron and Elfriede Mac Iver.)

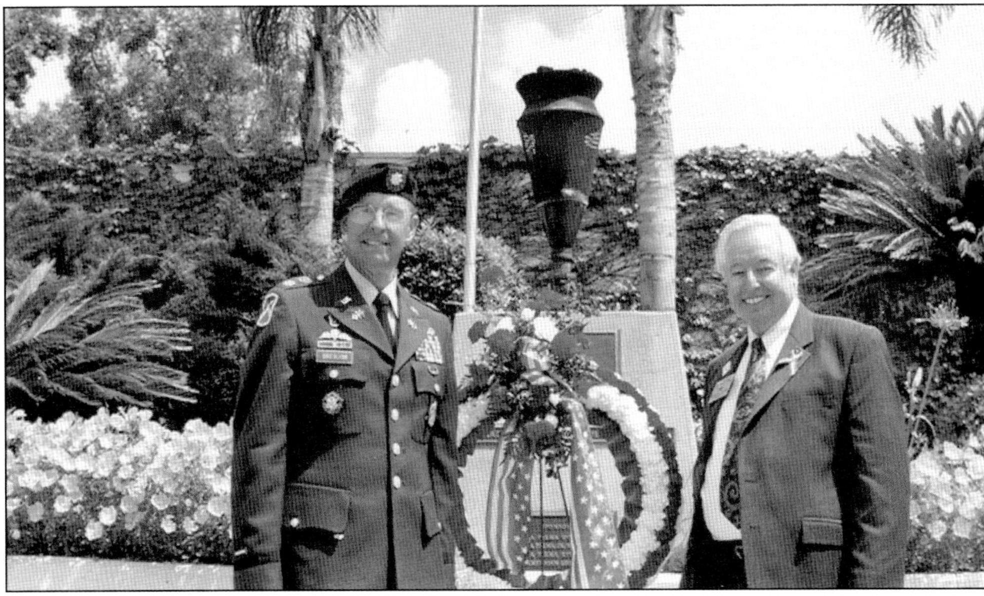

La Palma has held its Memorial Day services at the Eternal Flame since 1972. Walker Junior High School and the Kennedy bands merge for the ceremony. Veterans are recognized and thanked for their service to the country. From left to right are Lieutenant Colonel Breslow and Mayor Blake laying the wreath. The Kennedy JROTC presents and retires the colors. (Courtesy of La Palma Recreation and Community Services.)

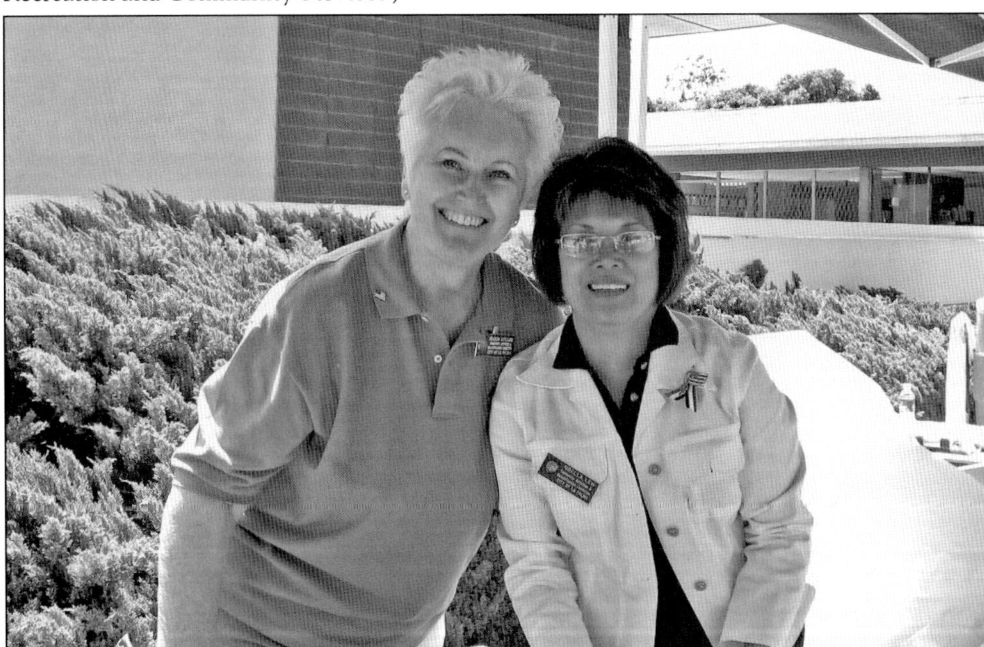

At the close of the solemn Memorial Day ceremonies, the JROTC invites guests to see their military equipment in a special tent area. The two ladies from left to right, Sharon Gutjahr and Noel Lew, are part of a team accepting donations and asking the public to sign cards for the young men currently in the service. This is also done at Christmastime. (Courtesy of La Palma Recreation and Community Services.)

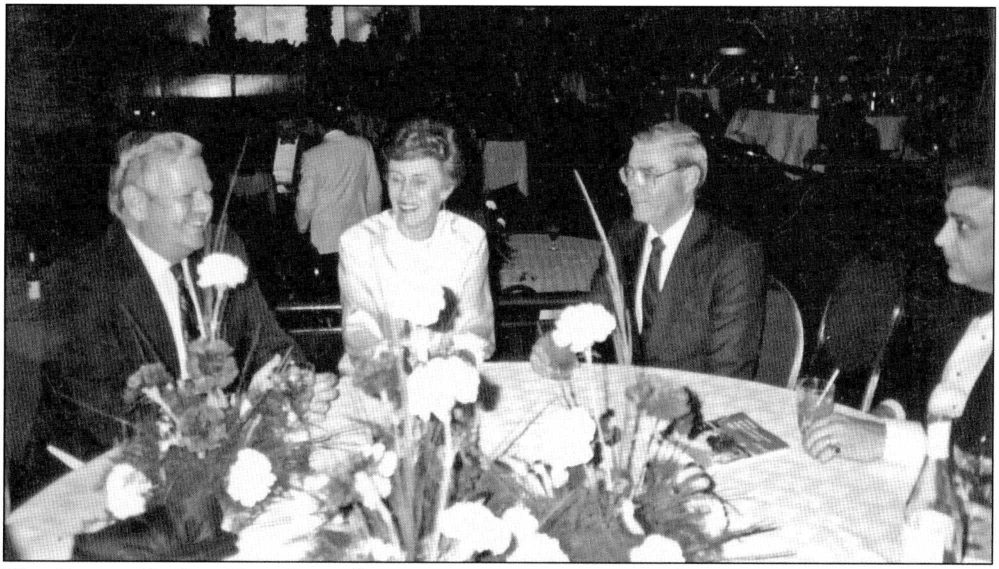

The Cypress College Foundation began recognizing an outstanding person from eight cities—Anaheim, Buena Park, Cypress, Garden Grove, La Palma, Los Alamitos, Seal Beach, and Stanton—with a special Americana award. The very first recipient, from La Palma, pictured here, was Tom Wright, left, with Marilyn and Ed Byrne, and Richard Polis. Linnea Wright, Tom's wife, is not shown. (Courtesy of City of La Palma Archives.)

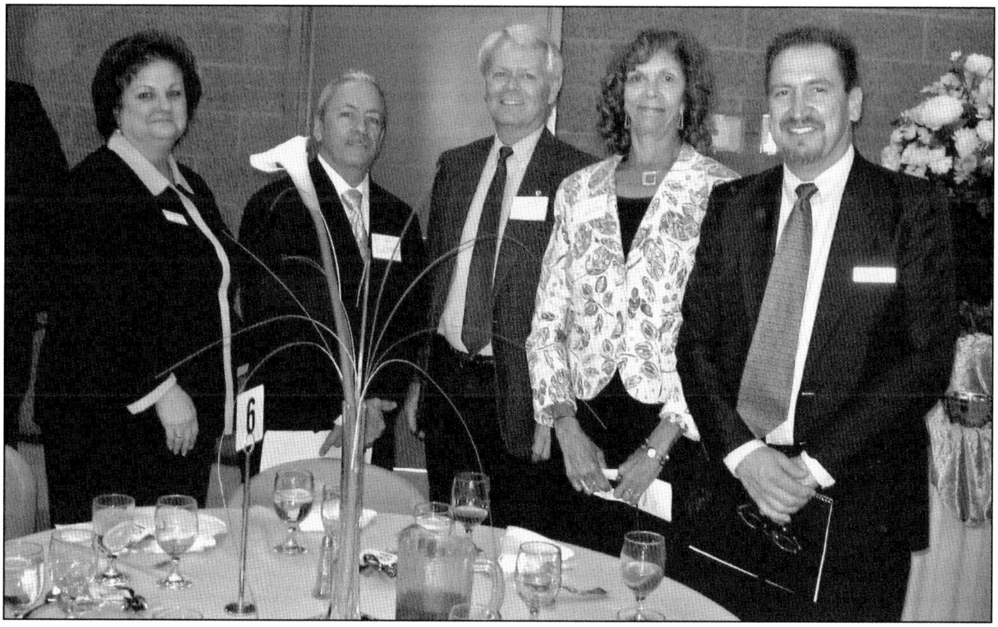

The State of the City luncheon is a yearly event hosted by the chamber of commerce. Dignitaries from neighboring cities, members of the city council, various city departments, police and fire departments, local government, and interested citizens attend. Mayor Henry Charoen was the keynote speaker in 2008. Pictured from left to right are Marlene Pritchard from the Bank of America, Anaheim Union High School superintendent Dr. Joseph Farley, AUHS board members Brian O'Neal and Anna L. Piercy, and Cypress College Foundation executive director Raul Alvarez. (Courtesy of City of La Palma Archives.)

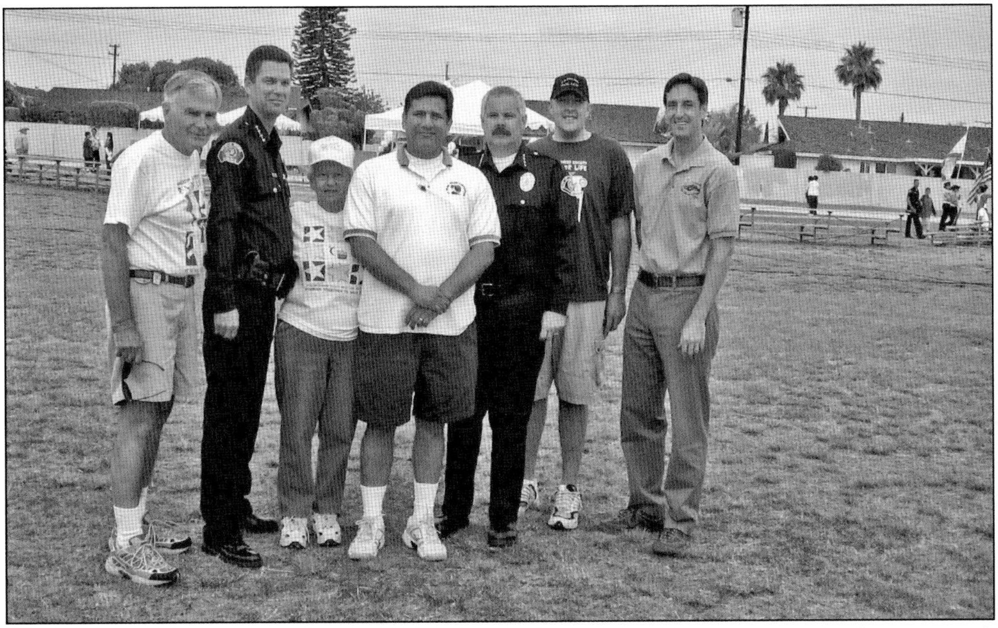

Relay for Life is another annual event cosponsored by the cities of La Palma and Buena Park and held at Buena Park Junior High School. An impressive number of cancer survivors and members of the public attend to support each other. From left to right, in 2007, are councilman Larry Herman, Buena Park police chief Tom Munson, volunteer Rosemary Scichilone, officer Raul Morales, La Palma police chief Ed Ethell, officer Nick Johnson, and La Palma city manager Dominic Lazzaretto. (Courtesy of Ron and Elfriede Mac Iver.)

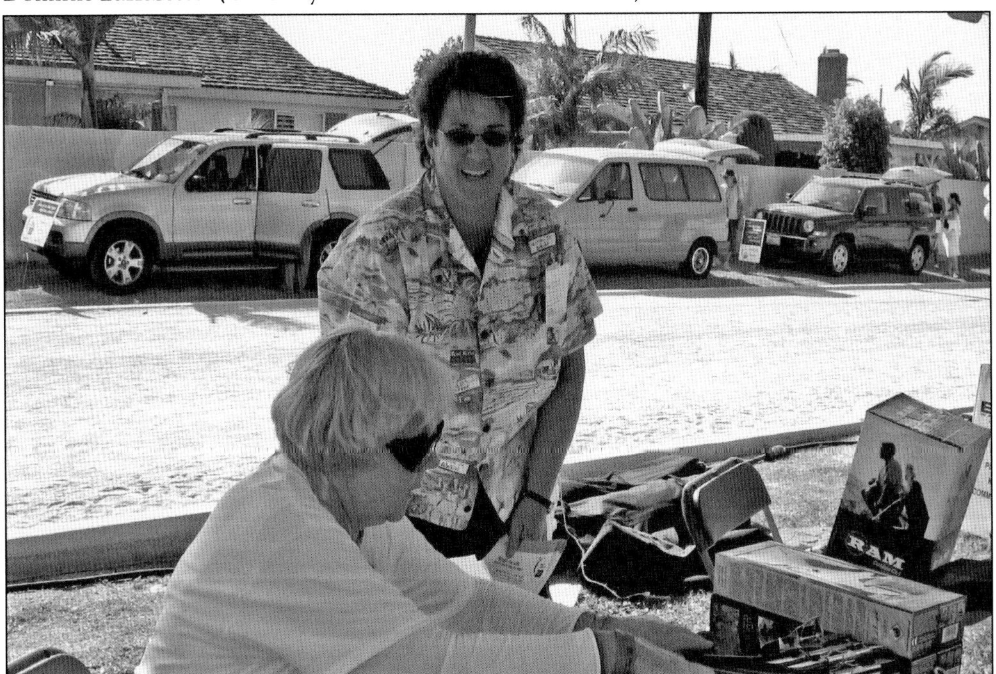

Ulla Herman and Jan Hobson catalog silent auction items during the Relay for Life. (Courtesy of Ron and Elfriede Mac Iver.)

Councilman Ralph Rodriguez and Ric Maurice take a moment away from cooking on behalf of the Kiwanis Club. (Courtesy of Ron and Elfriede Mac Iver.)

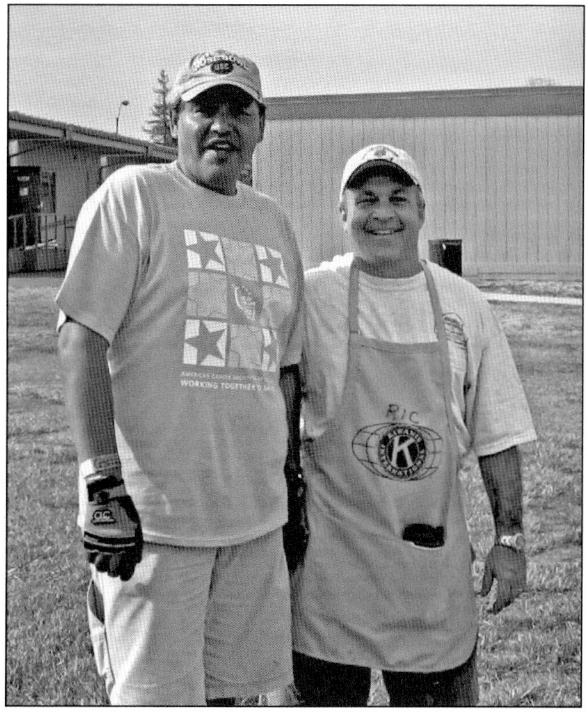

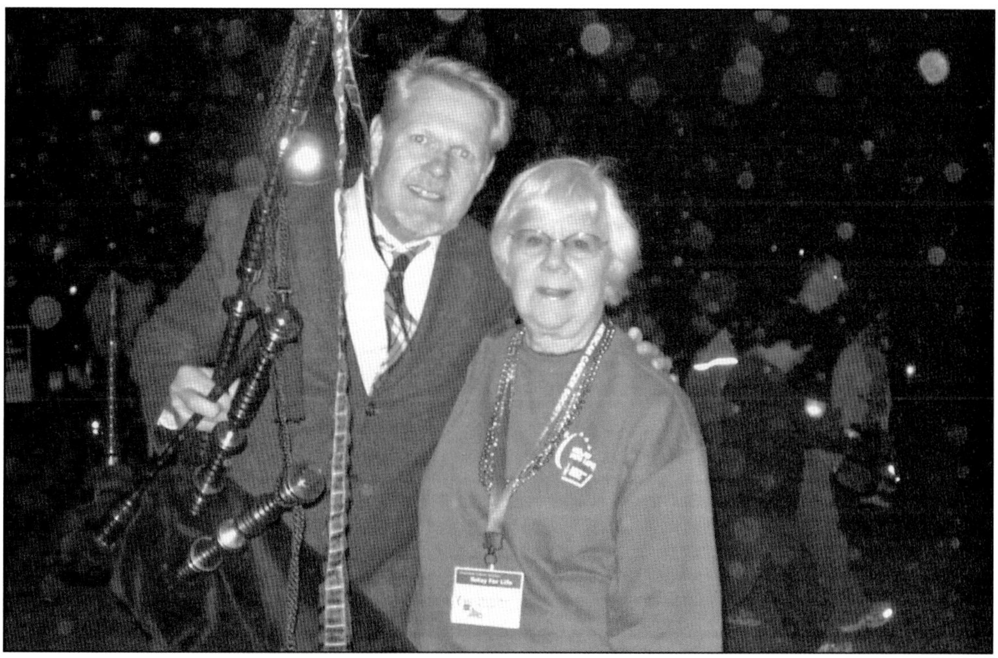

The luminaria ceremonial walk is an impressive walk around the track after dark. The people (cancer survivors and others who honor those they have lost) follow the mournful music of the piper, carrying lighted candles with the glowing luminarias illuminating their path. John Miller, who works for the Orange County Vector Control District, is the volunteer piper, in full kilt, pictured here with Ulla Herman, a cancer survivor and a tireless worker for the cause who inspires many by her indomitable spirit to join her. (Courtesy of Ron and Elfriede Mac Iver.)

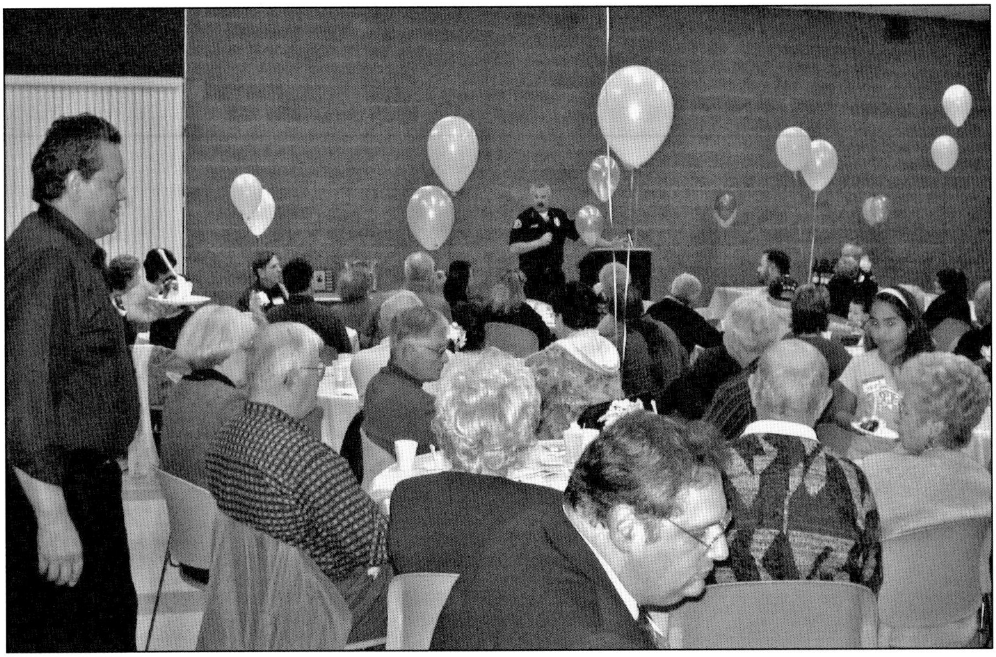

The yearly Block Watch dinner recognizes the efforts of the Block Watch captains and volunteers. This picture captures only a small part of the audience. Police chief Ed Ethell is speaking to the audience after dinner. A good dinner, awards, excellent prizes, and an evening of camaraderie between the city government and the citizens encourages continued interest and participation in the well-being of the city. (Courtesy of Ron and Elfriede Mac Iver.)

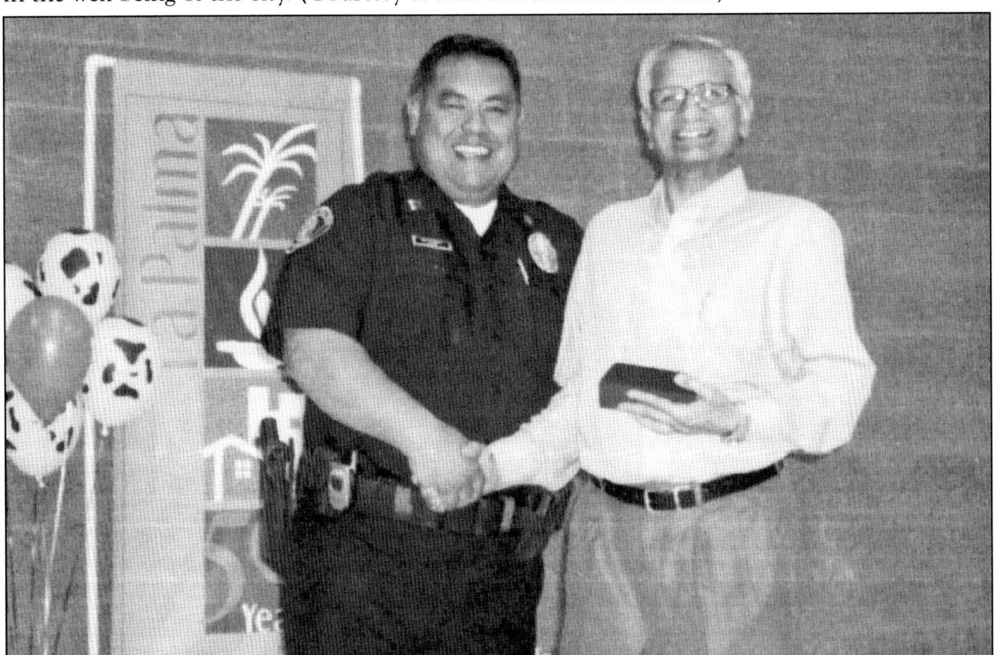

Capt. Eric Nunez presents the Volunteer in Policing (VIP) Volunteer of the Year award to Abe Waheed. (Courtesy of La Palma Recreation and Community Services.)

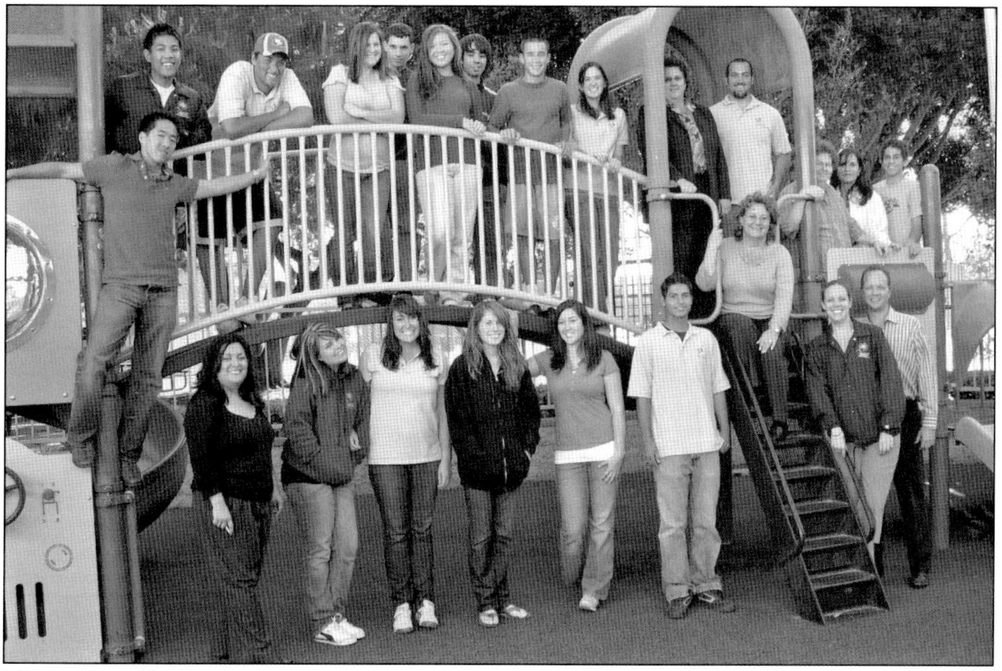

The park staff takes their jobs seriously, but not themselves! From left to right are (first row) Anthony Kim (hanging on railing), Sylvia Hinojosa, Tamara York, Allison Riach, Sarah Schrader, Kristen Hara, Victor Amezquita, Janet Cates, Cindy Robinson, Mike Belknap; (second row) Richard Huerto, Dustin Brown, Meghan Maher, Austin Greene, Tarra Van Meter, Jesse Matsukawa, Marshal Salley, Erin Peters, Jan Hobson, Joe Cooper, Nancy Brewer, Jill Olivier, and O. J. Albarian. (Courtesy of La Palma Recreation and Community Services.)

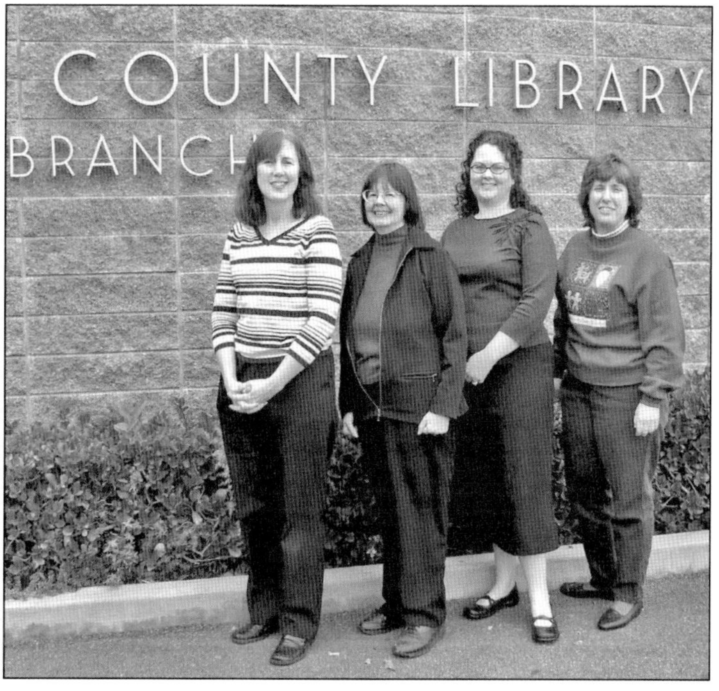

The La Palma library is a friendly place for the preschool set with its colorful picture books. Older students and grown-ups gather to do homework or research with a modern bank of computers, a great selection of books in several languages, and access to any books available in the library system. From left to right are branch manager Julia Reardon, former branch manager Susan Sassone, library assistant Amy Pierce, and senior clerk Antonette Ferguson. (Courtesy of La Palma Library Archives.)

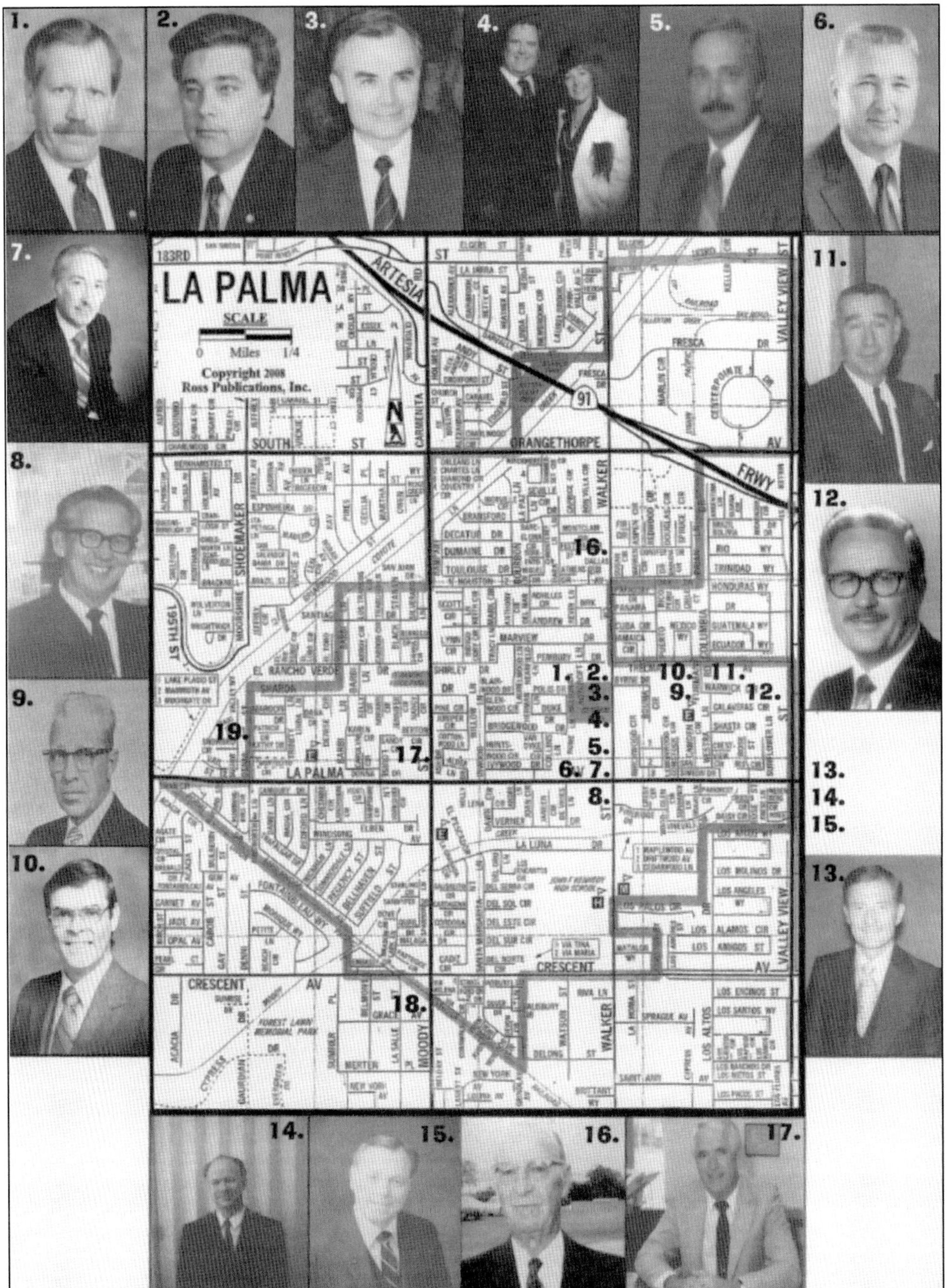

Many streets have been named for former mayors and three city managers. The 17 represented here are numbered to correspond with the location of their street on the map: 1) Keith Nelson, 2) Richard Polis, 3) Larry Herman, 4) Orbrey and Alta Duke (both served terms as mayor), 5) Richard Rowe, 6) Dan Collins, 7) Anthony Van Dyke, 8) Jack de Vries, 9) Peter G. Bouma, 10) Edward Byrne, 11) Paul Furman, 12) Jack Westra, 13) Henry Frese, 14) Burton Wesenberg, 15) Alan Priest, 16) Ron Dallas, 17) John Berton, 18) Joseph Moody (see page 14), and 19) Jobe Denni (see page 18). (Courtesy of Ron and Elfriede Mac Iver.)

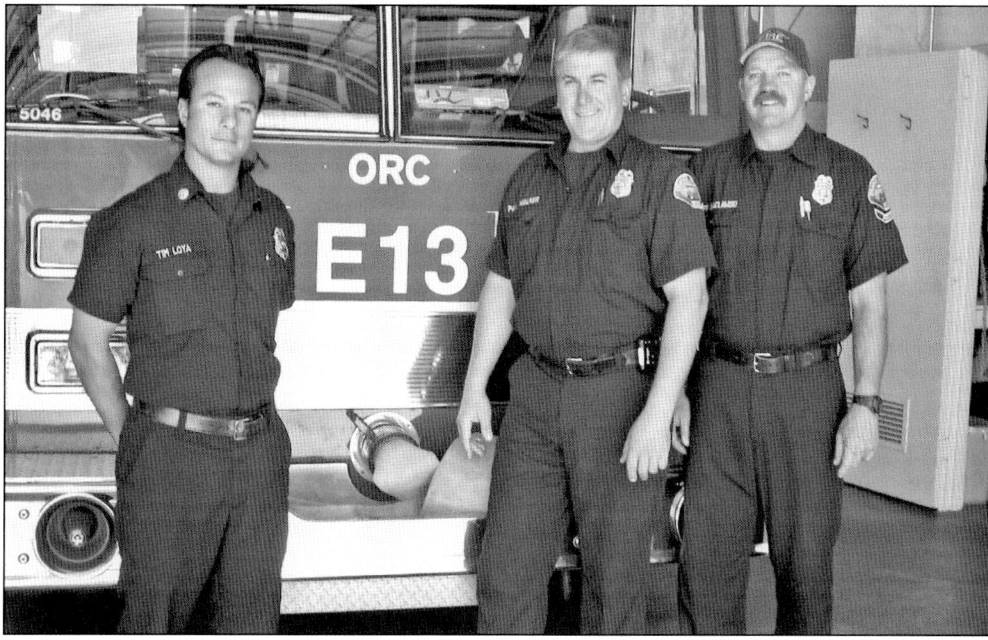

The fire department is officially part of the Orange County Fire Authority, Station No. 13. That title gives our small city access to better fire protection in case of an emergency. The response time and trained personnel answering a call within the city is outstanding and reassuring. Standing in front of their fire truck are, from left to right Capt. Tim Loya; engineer Paul Walker, who also served as mayor of La Palma in 2001; and fireman and paramedic Jeff Baclawski. (Courtesy of Ron and Elfriede Mac Iver.)

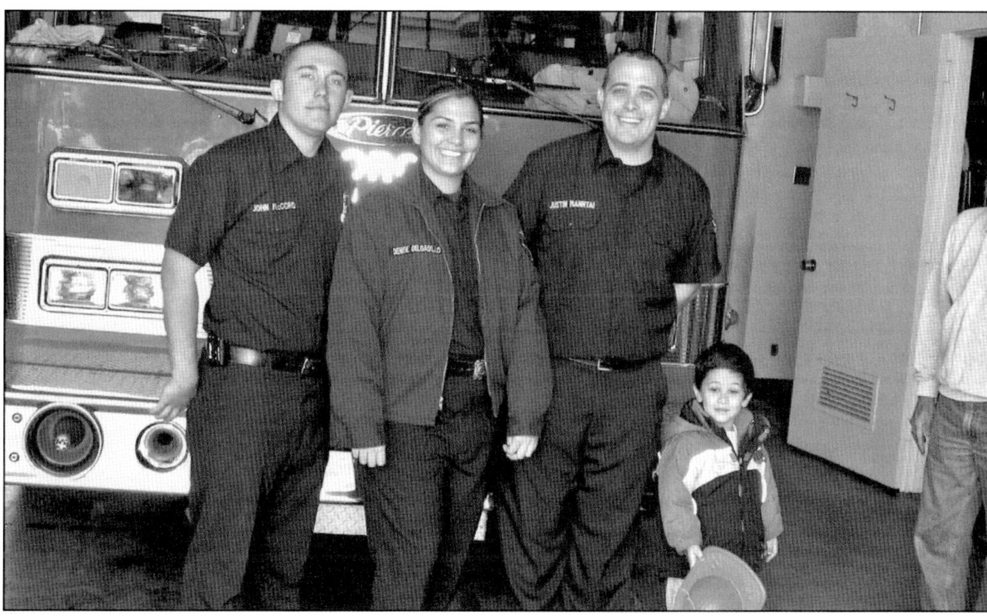

The La Palma Fire Station held an open house on October 13, 2007. This annual event is always well attended and great fun for the younger members of the community, who enjoy meeting the firefighters and checking out the awesome fire trucks. From left to right are John McCord, Denise Delgado, and Justin Manntai with a small guest. (Courtesy of Ron and Elfriede Mac Iver.)

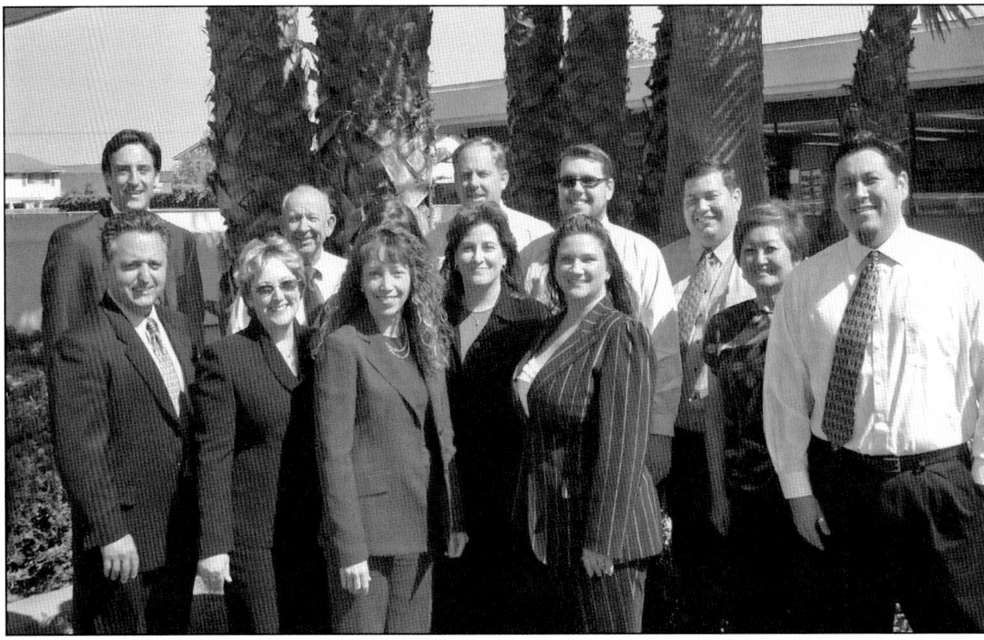

City administration staff are pictured, from left to right, (first row) John Di Mario, Laurie Murray, Kimberly Kenney, Lori Rake, Crystal Wilkerson, and David Morgan; (second row) Dominic Lazzaretto, Paul Pitts, Keith Neves, Scott Hutter, Chet Corbin, and Susan Baker. (Courtesy of City of La Palma Archives.)

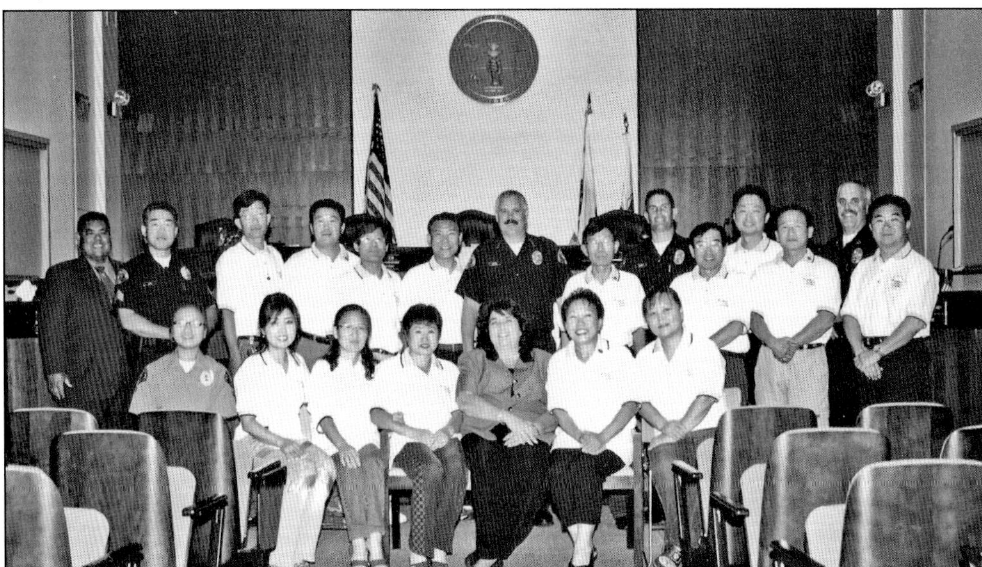

The Korean Citizens Police Academy group picture includes Sergeant. J. Woo (first row, far left), council member Christine Barnes (first row, center), Capt. Eric Nunez (second row, far left), Sergeant Kim (second row, second from left), chief Ed Ethell (second row, center), Sergeant Wilkerson (second row, sixth from right), and Captain Enright (second row, second from left). Members of the academy are seated with them. The following, listed in no particular order, are some of the academy members: Tae Young Seo, Timothy Lim, Sang Hun Park, Young A. Yoon, Kevin C. Kong, Hearyung Yu, and Dae K. Chang. (Courtesy of La Palma Police Department.)

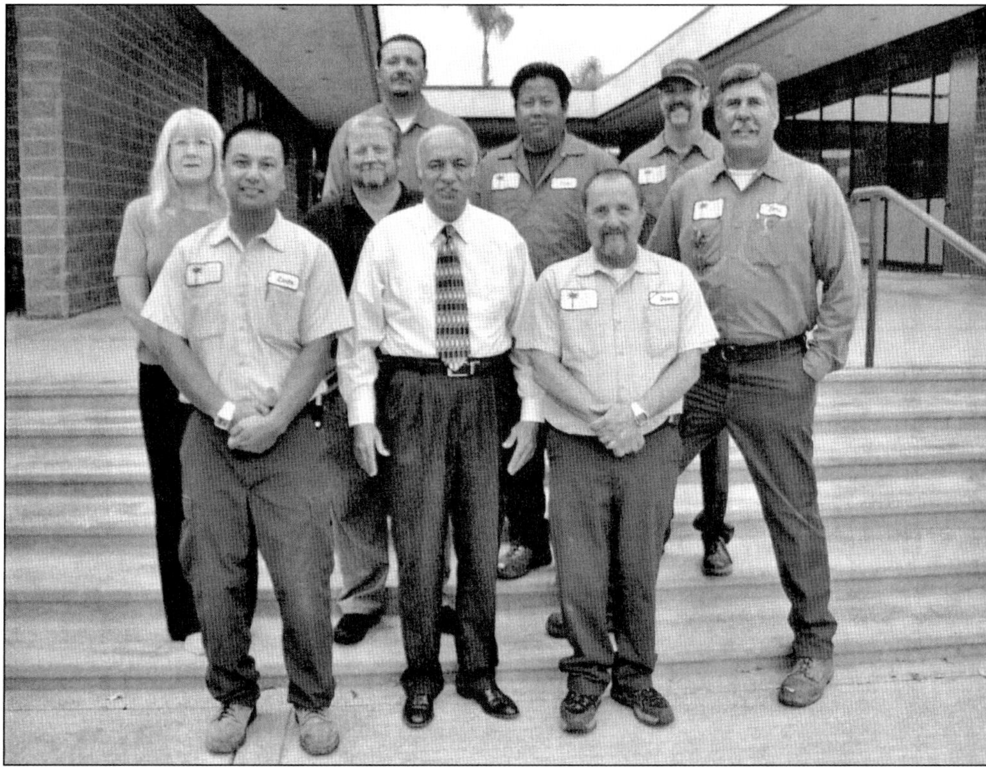

The Public Works Department staff includes, from left to right, (first row) Carlo Nafaratti, Ismile Noorbaksh, Dave Gaudio, and James Hambleton; (second row) Michelle Rusu, Larry Baldwin, James Tsumura, and David Fleming; (third row) Mark Diaz. (Courtesy of Public Works Department.)

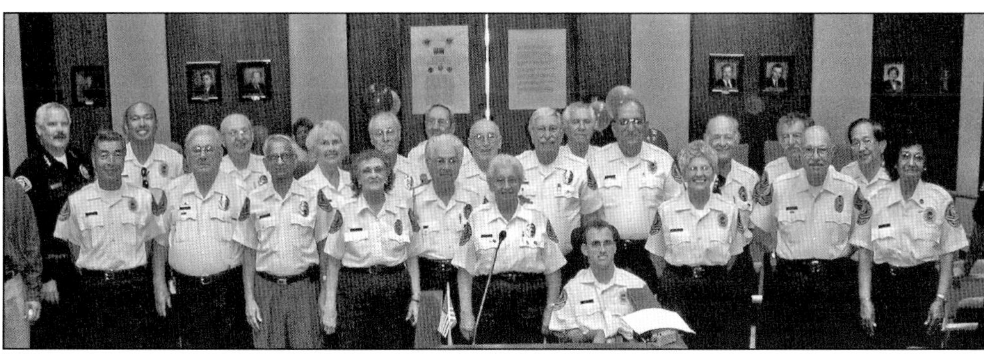

Volunteers in Policing (VIP) are, from left to right, (first row) Mits Kosaka, Ray Drake, Abe Waheed, Virginia Hartzell, Guillermo Lopez, Rosemary Scichilone, Robert Hall (seated), Maria Anderson, Bob Jordan, and Jean Guppy; (second row) La Palma police chief Ed Ethell, Jeff Genvino, Tony Burkart, Elfie Pangburn, Ted Allen, Ed Monti, Duane Schuster, Ted Reina, Bill Meil, Atma Kanda, Frank St. Germain, Bert Poan, and Teodoro Luna. (Courtesy of La Palma Police Department.)

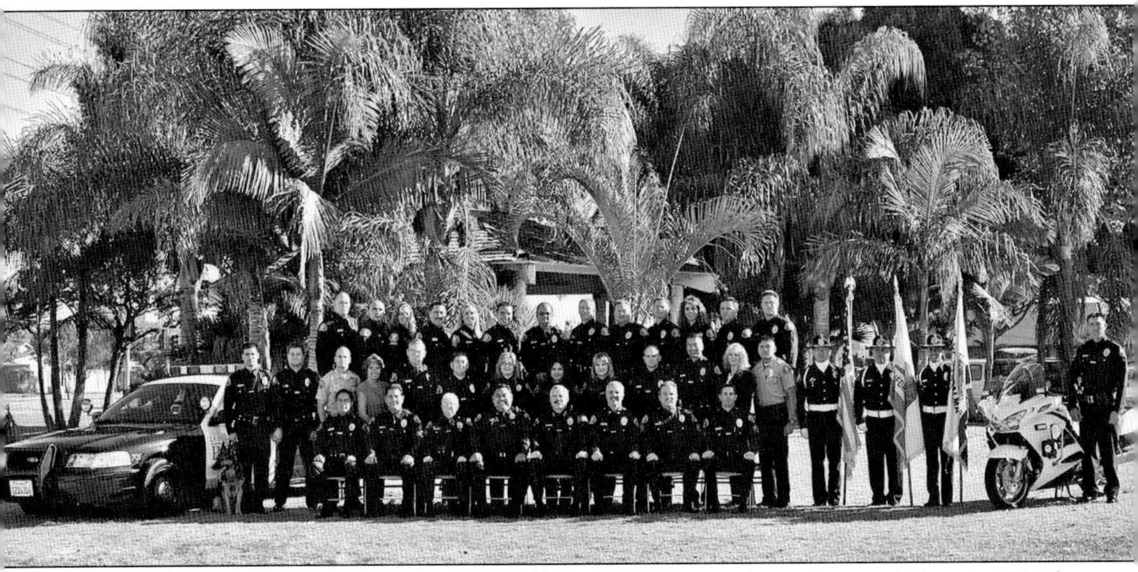

The La Palma Police Department, pictured here from left to right, is (first row) Sgt. Art Wright, Sgt. Raul Morales, Sgt. Maggie Faust, Capt. Eric R. Nunez, Chief Edward O. Ethell, Capt. Jim Enright, detective sergeant Jim Engen, and Sgt. Ron Wilkerson; (second row) K-9 officer Tom Lomeli (and Ajax), officer Eric Kent, parking control officer Chad McGowan, civilian investigator Josta McDowell, reserve officer Paul Edholm, officer Jesse Amend, dispatcher Charlotte Deardorff, dispatcher Vanessa Zuniga, dispatcher Pat Valentino, officer Andy Pinvidic, officer Julian Gonzalez, chief executive assistant Ginger Molar, police service aid Ruben Portillo, Sgt. Terry Kim, detective Les Parsons, officer Joe Guerrero, and motorcycle officer Ed Pastor; (third row) officer Nick Johnson, reserve officer Lorenzo Hernandez, dispatcher Tracy Nolan, reserve officer Glen Miyoshi, records clerk Nicole Distefano, officer Jeff Beatty, reserve officer Alan Moore, reserve officer Bob Griffith, officer Brian Rapp, detective Brad Miller, dispatcher Rita Ramirez, officer Paul Braccidieta, and officer Adam Foster. (Courtesy of La Palma Police Department.)

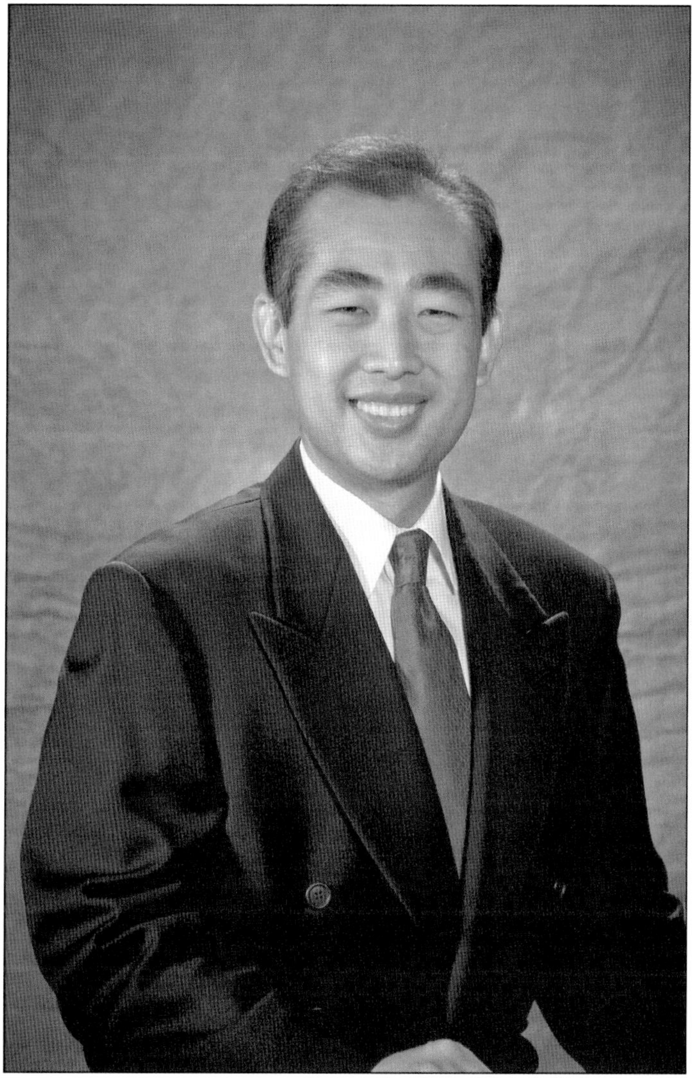

The annual State of the City luncheon, hosted by the La Palma Chamber of Commerce, featured Mayor Henry Charoen as guest speaker. *Money* magazine chose La Palma as the "16th best small city in the entire country and the 2nd best small city to live in California." The mayor reviewed La Palma's accomplishments in 2007. The recreation department earned two awards for collecting "A Little Bit of Home" items for troops at the annual Memorial Day ceremony, and an award for creating the motto and logo "Creating Unity in Community." The finance department won their eighth-consecutive-year award for financial reporting documents and three further awards from the joint powers insurance authority. The public works department received recognition for their community outreach program. The city council provided funds for all third-, fourth-, and fifth-grade students to attend performances at the Cerritos Performing Arts Center. Two new teen events were introduced this year. The mayor spoke to the financial health, a 100-percent reserve because of controlled expenditures. The infrastructure of the city upgrades. The renovation of the community center is almost finished. Translation capabilities in Spanish, Korean, Chinese, Japanese, and Tagalog will be available. Concerts in the park will add multicultural performances. La Palma's business community will receive even greater attention in the coming year, a very positive outlook for the City of Vision.

ACROSS AMERICA, PEOPLE ARE DISCOVERING SOMETHING WONDERFUL. *THEIR HERITAGE.*

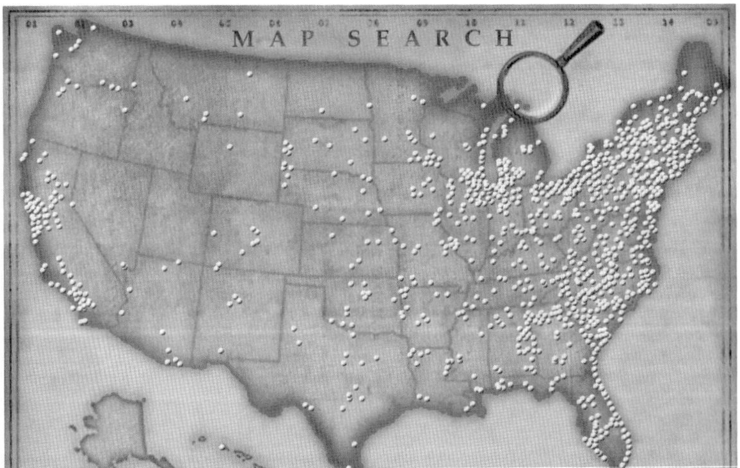